What is Existential Anthropology?

What is Existential Anthropology?

Edited by
Michael Jackson and Albert Piette

NEW YORK · OXFORD
www.berghahnbooks.com

First edition published in 2015 by

Berghahn Books

www.berghahnbooks.com

© 2015, 2017 Michael Jackson and Albert Piette
First paperback edition published in 2017

All rights reserved. Except for the quotation of short passages for the purposes of criticism and review, no part of this book may be reproduced in any form or by any means, electronic or mechanical, including photocopying, recording, or any information storage and retrieval system now known or to be invented, without written permission of the publisher.

Library of Congress Cataloging-in-Publication Data
What is existential anthropology / edited by Michael Jackson and Albert Piette.
   pages cm
Includes bibliographical references and index.
   ISBN 978-1-78238-636-0 (hardback) — ISBN: 978-1-78533-743-7 (paperback) — ISBN 978-1-78238-637-7 (ebook)
   1. Anthropology—Philosophy.   I. Jackson, Michael, 1940–.   II. Piette, Albert, 1960–
   GN33.J26 2015
   301.01—dc23

2014033553

British Library Cataloguing in Publication Data

A catalogue record for this book is available from the British Library

ISBN: 978-1-78238-636-0 (hardback)
ISBN: 978-1-78533-743-7 (paperback)
ISBN: 978-1-78238-637-7 (ebook)

Contents

Introduction
Anthropology and the Existential Turn   1
Michael Jackson and Albert Piette

Chapter 1
Conversion and Convertibility in Northern Mozambique   30
Devaka Premawardhana

Chapter 2
Both/And   58
Michael Lambek

Chapter 3
Reading Bruno Latour in Bahia:
Or, How to Approach The "Great, Blooming, Buzzing
Confusion" of Life and Being Without Going Mad   84
Mattijs van de Port

Chapter 4
The Station Hustle:
Ghanaian Migration Brokerage in a Disjointed World   104
Hans Lucht

Chapter 5
Mobility and Immobility in the Life of an Amputee   125
Sónia Silva

Chapter 6
Existential Aporias and the Precariousness of Being   155
Michael Jackson

Chapter 7
Existence, Minimality, and Believing   178
Albert Piette

Chapter 8
Considering Human Existence:
An Existential Reading of Michael Jackson and Albert Piette   214
Laurent Denizeau

Notes on Contributors   237

Index   243

Introduction

Anthropology and the Existential Turn

Michael Jackson and Albert Piette

Although Michael Jackson's *Existential Anthropology* and Albert Piette's *Anthropologie Existentiale* were published in 2005 and 2009 respectively, the two authors were unaware of each other's work at the time—evidence, perhaps, of the communications gap between American, British, and Continental traditions of anthropological thought, and the radically different ways in which anthropologists engage with philosophy.[1] Something of a communications gap also applied to the coeditors of this volume. While we shared an interest in the themes of existence and coexistence, we had carried out fieldwork in very different societies and pursued somewhat divergent projects in existential anthropology. While Michael Jackson had engaged with philosophy, particularly the work of Merleau-Ponty, Sartre, Adorno, Arendt, James, and Dewey, Albert Piette had developed his project in opposition to social anthropology and sociology. There were stylistic differences too. Michael Jackson's ethnography was grounded in inductive method, making use of narrativity and reflexivity to convey a radically empirical understanding of lived events and experiences. By contrast, Albert Piette's focus was the phenomenographical observation and description of human beings in their individual singularity and ever-changing situations; as such, existential anthropology sought to analyze what Heidegger called "existentiality," and its aim was discovering the general characteristics of the human way of existing, in time, through space, and with others (Heidegger 1996: 10).

Notes for this chapter begin on page 25.

Despite these differences in orientation and style, we decided, after an exchange of emails in early 2013, to explore the possibility of dialogue and collaboration. Indeed, our experience of cowriting this introduction came to exemplify a central tenet of existential anthropology, for in as much as we came to feel comfortable with writing "we" despite the fact that we were two separate "I"s, we found ourselves inadvertently demonstrating in our "collective" work the paradox that the presence of the singular "I" is never completely eclipsed in any collective activity, and the collective has no reality apart from the persons who comprise it. Sartre refers to this as the paradox of the "singular universal," since every individual is at once universalized by his or her location in a historical moment, yet "singular by the universalizing singularity of his [or her] projects" (1981: 7–8). Thus, human beings everywhere oscillate spontaneously and situationally between egocentric and sociocentric modes of being without necessarily experiencing these as mutually antithetical.[2] Yet, ironically, two different disciplines have evolved—psychology and anthropology—as if our humanity were itself fundamentally divided into *anthropos* and *ethnos*, the singular and the shared, or even the cultural and the biological.

Our hope is that the concept "existence" will help overcome these antinomies and build bridges between anthropology and the humanities, as well as between Continental and Anglo-American schools of anthropological thought—recognizing divergences yet finding common ground.

In this spirit, we invited several anthropologists on both sides of the Atlantic whose published work had engaged with existential anthropology to join us in addressing the question of how their approaches to the human condition could be brought together both at the level of method and theory. Specifically, we asked contributors to address the same set of questions: What is existential anthropology for you, and how would you define it? What has been gained by using existential perspectives in your fieldwork and writing? What contribution do these perspectives make to the art and craft of anthropology? Contributors were also urged to write from empirical situations and direct experience in a style that was accessible and unencumbered by jargon.

Existence and Existents

It must be said at the outset that our aim is not to present a philosophical or genealogical account of the theme of existence, but to describe how various refractions of this intellectual tradition find expression in the work of several contemporary anthropologists. Thus, Kierkegaard's claim that "truth is subjectivity,"[3] Binswanger's famous definition of existentialism as a project for overcoming the subject-object split,[4] Sartre's adage that existence precedes essence,[5] Viktor Frankl's (1973) emphasis on meaning (logos) as an existential imperative, or popular conflations of existentialism with postwar Left Bank preoccupations with alienation (not being-at-home-in-the-world), absurdity, angst, and irrationalism all figure to various degrees in our research and writing without any of these leitmotifs defining the project of existential anthropology. It is even possible to define existential anthropology, and locate it within the human sciences, without reference to philosophy.

We begin with the assertion that, while individual acting, thinking, and feeling are always situated historically, socially, and environmentally, every person's existence is characterized by projects, intentions, desires, and outcomes that outstrip and in some sense transform these prior conditions. This perspective of existential mobility is central to many of the essays in this volume, including Devaka Premawardhana's analysis of religious conversion in Northern Mozambique, Hans Lucht's account of Ghanaian migrants en route to Europe, Sónia Silva's essay on refugees and displacement, Michael Jackson's exploration of continuities and discontinuities in a Sierra Leonean family over several generations, Laurent Denizeau's reflections on the passage from life to death, and Albert Piette's project of tracing an individual through time and space in order to appreciate the nuanced changes and instantaneous transformations he or she undergoes.

Given the impermanence of any state of body or of mind, the question arises as to whether human beings exercise choice or determine their own fates. But human beings typically act *as if* they choose, even while freely admitting that there are things they cannot choose, and in choosing themselves in the first-person singular, "a first-person *plural*, a 'we,' is simultaneously constituted."[6] There is, however, always an unresolved tension between personal dispositions and external circumstances. Accordingly, no individual is wholly reducible to his or her ascribed identity, and every existence calls the collective into question. Our concern, therefore, is not only with how we locate and theorize the human subject and human subjectivity within society and history, but with how we recognize the *presence* of the human subject in academic research and writing. A recurring concern in the essays that make up this volume is how one may broach the question of the human through direct engagements with the lived experiences of *particular* human beings. This implies calling into question the category thinking that prevents us from continually refreshing our sense of the nuanced complexities of life as lived. Perhaps this is the strongest point of agreement between Michael Jackson and Albert Piette—a refusal to reduce lived reality to culturally or socially constructed representations, and a determination to explore the variability, mutability, and indeterminacy of that lived reality as it makes its appearance in real time, in specific moments, in actual situations, and in the interstices between interpretations, constructions, and rationalizations, continually shifting from certainty to uncertainty, fixity to fluidity, closure to openness, passivity to activity, body to mind, integration to fragmentation, feeling to thought, belief to doubt. If, as Horkheimer and Adorno wrote, reification is a form of forgetting (2002: 230), then existential anthropology may be construed as a project to remind us of what is occluded and ignored in the process of constructing any worldview, whether academic or otherwise, and of recognizing that we ourselves, with our personal biases and backgrounds, are always implicated in the processes of constructing and deconstructing views of the world.

We are disconcerted that one can move from one academic treatise to another without encountering a living soul. Individuals are cited, to be sure, but they are usually other academics. The voices of those who live outside the academic pale and on the margins of the Euro-American world are heard only occasionally, or in snatches, to make a point or confirm a hypothesis. These individuals are seldom described in depth or detail. Their presence is never deeply felt, and their own words are eclipsed by the specialist jargons of the academy. They are like the ghosts that haunt a desolated landscape where some nameless catastrophe has rendered human existence superfluous. Over these depopulated fields of knowledge, however, one figure looms large—the figure of the academic authority. This figure casts a long shadow, obscuring our view of the many others who share his world, and whose worldviews have as much claim to be taken seriously as his. But, like God, this figure is omniscient, and speaks as though reason were its sole possession. Inheriting the mantle of the hierophant, he purports to see into the hearts and minds of mere mortals, even as he casts doubt on the views they swear and live by.

The irony is that contemporary anthropology—the study of humankind—is often proven guilty of this glaring omission. There is a tendency to shift vitality, power, consciousness, and will from persons to the transpersonal realms of abstract ideas, global forces, historical processes, genetic patterns, social structures, and discursive formations. The determinants of meaning in human life are found in the structures of the unconscious mind, or in political and economic infrastructures, both local and global. In our view it is precisely those forms of human life—transitive, ambiguous, idiosyncratic, elusive, irreducible, and resistant to what John Dewey called "cognitive certification"—that are existentially most imperative for humanity, and are at stake in the critical moments that define human lives. But, as Mattijs van de Port asks, what language do we have for these marginal realms? We gesture toward phenomena that lie outside of logos with terms like "spirituality," "mystery," "intuition," "soul," "the more," "the uncanny," "the numinous," or "the love that passes all understanding"—as if it were possible to close the gap between ourselves and that which cannot be completely covered or contained by language, or brought under control by the scientific technologies at our disposal. We are equally aware that the human struggle for love, recognition, respect, dignity, and well-being is never *entirely* dependent on a person's circumstances—her social class or ethnicity, his location in a social hierarchy, an economic field, or a state—despite the power of such "givens" to determine the general direction of any life course. This is why we resist constructing "a universal and anonymous subject," like Hobbes' State, which possesses "all the functions and predicates that were previously scattered and assigned to many different *real subjects*—groups, associations, or individuals" (de Certeau 1984: 94). Yet, by shifting our focus from macrocosm to microcosm, or from focal to fringe, we do not mean to deny that impersonal powers, presences, or processes, at once transcendent and concealed, govern our lives; rather we wish to restore to the anthropological worldview a sense of the small and tangible things that make life viable and negotiable despite the forces that elude our comprehension and control. As David Graeber puts it, "If we really want to understand the moral grounds of economic life, and by extension, human life, we must start . . . with the very small things: the everyday details of social existence, the way we treat our friends, enemies, and children—often with gestures so tiny (passing the salt, bumming a cigarette) that we ordinarily never stop to think about them at all" (2011: 89).

Most of Albert Piette's work has been devoted to this kind of detailed observation of particular details of human presences and of life "in the minor mode"—details that photography can sometimes capture better than ethnography.[7] This is how we construe the term "existence" (from the root *ex-sistere*, "to stand out," "to emerge"). In as much as every human life involves gaps or aporias between expectations and outcomes, acting in the world and being acted upon by the world, being alone and being with others, finding and losing one's way, rising and falling,[8] no life is ever completely assimilated to *or* alienated from the world. Nor can a person's frame of mind be directly inferred from his or her behavior. As George Devereux notes (1978: 125), citing a Latin adage, *Si bis faciunt idem, non est idem*, if two people do the same thing, it is not necessarily the same. This may be taken as a summons to do justice to how an individual directly experiences his or her world, regardless of how that experience is preconceived by science.[9]

Life and Concept

Wilhelm Dilthey insisted that the analysis of "the life-unit, i.e. the psychophysical individual," be made fundamental to the human sciences, and that "abstract entities such as art, science, state, society, and religion" are all too often "like fog banks that obstruct our view of reality" (1989: 80, 93). But this emphasis on lived reality—on human lives as they unfold and are transformed in everyday situations, events, and interactions—immediately broaches the question of the relationship between life and concept, being and thought. While life is dynamic, mutable, and many-faceted, concepts are by contrast relatively static. Comparing the alternating rhythms of existence to the life of a bird, William James (1950: 243) asked how it is possible to describe a phenomenon that is sometimes moving in flight and sometimes perched or nesting? How is it discursively possible to accommodate, let alone integrate, the transitive and intransitive, or write in the spirit of a radical empiricism that does justice to both ontology (the logic implicit in our ways of being present in the world) and epistemology (the logic explicit in our ways of knowing the world)?

In charting the "divided and dialectical character" of French philosophy through the twentieth century, Alain Badiou draws a contrast between Henri Bergson's "philosophy of vital interiority" and Léon Brunschvicg's mathematically based "conceptual formalism" (Badiou 2012: liii). Both philosophers published seminal works in 1911 and 1912 respectively, initiating radically different intellectual orientations and genealogies—the first focused on life, the second focused on the concept. As Badiou notes, though both orientations "coincide" in the human subject, who is simultaneously a living organism and a creator of concepts, the quarrel between the "existential vitalism" of thinkers like Bergson, Sartre, Merleau-Ponty, Bachelard, and Deleuze and the "conceptual formalism" of thinkers like Brunschvicg, Lévi-Strauss, Althusser, and Lacan has never been resolved. The illusion persists "that the concept can transcend the concept" and "thus reach the nonconceptual"—and this remains "one of philosophy's inalienable features and part of the naïveté that ails it" (Adorno 1973: 9). Similar dilemmas and divisions have pervaded late twentieth-century cultural anthropology, for while some anthropologists argue that human emotions, thoughts, sensibilities, motivations, and interests are largely shaped by cultural and historical forces, others emphasize the surprising malleability and multiplicity of the human subject, whose potential to adapt to different situations and respond to other human subjects renders it irreducible to the conceptual forms and essences with which it is customarily identified.

In arguing for the complementarity of these perspectives, Michael Jackson has often invoked Sartre's "progressive-regressive method" whose focus is the dynamic *relationship* between the preexisting conditions that circumscribe an individual's possibilities and the purposeful actions whereby that individual projects himself or herself into the world, making something of what he or she was made (Sartre 1968: 150–151; Jackson 1998: 27–28). According to this view, concepts are like tools and techniques that lie ready-to-hand; whatever meaning they may have acquired in the minds or at the hands of others, one takes them up and deploys them on one's own terms, in relation to one's particular situation or project. Rather than separate concept and existence, we therefore seek "to demonstrate that the concept is a living thing, a creation, a process, an event, and, as such, not divorced from existence" (Badiou 2012: lxi).[10] At the same time, however, it is important to acknowledge the limitations of any tool—material or conceptual—in securing the ends to which it is applied, be this interpreting the world, changing the world, or renegotiating our relationship with the world. In stressing the nonidentity of words and worlds, thought and being, Adorno's negative dialectics reminds us that concepts never fully cover or contain our life experiences (1973: 5, 8). Life cannot be wholly "tamed and symbolized by language," which is why all theorizing leaves an immense remainder, and it is "the memory of this remainder" that haunts us" (de Certeau 1984: 61). No matter how sophisticated our concepts become, they fail to do justice to what William James called the "plenum of existence"—the full range of human experience, intransitive and transitive, fixed and fluid, rational and emotional, coherent and wild, real and symbolic. For Albert Piette, these constitute "the minor modes of reality." For Michael Jackson, they suggest "an ethics of small things"—sovereign expression of life (2013: 213–220). For Mattijs van de Port, they make up "the-rest-of-what-is"—what lies outside socially constructed reality and cannot be put into words (2011: 26–30)—and he advocates risking oneself on the kinds of openness to others and to otherness that will engage our emotions, senses, and bodies, and not simply our intellects.

Though concepts may be limited, they remain existentially necessary, for like other discursive and practical techniques they enable us to process experiences that threaten to overwhelm us, and give us consolation that life is intelligible, comprehensible, and controllable. Jackson stresses the significance of ontological metaphors as mediators between life and concept, and uses the image of the penumbral to capture this ambiguity of our experience as it oscillates between what we can and cannot grasp (2009: xii). The penumbral bears comparison with what Karl Jaspers (1997) calls "the Encompassing" (*das Umgreifende*), and refers to as "border situations" (*grenzsituationen*)—situations in which we come up against the limits of language, the limits of our strength, the limits of our knowledge, yet are sometimes thrown open to new ways of understanding our being-in-the-world, new ways of connecting with others. Whether such border situations are quintessentially "religious," "spiritual," "historical," "social," or "biographical" may be beside the point, for though such terms help us describe the conditions of the possibility of our experience or help us retrospectively explain our experience to ourselves and to others, the meaning of all human experience remains ambiguous, containing within it both the seeds of its own comprehensibility *and* nuances and shadings that go beyond what can be comprehensively thought or said.[11]

Appearance and Reality

From its Pre-Socratic beginnings, Western philosophy has split the world into the world of appearances and the world of the real. While the world of appearances includes what we see, touch, hear, taste, and smell, it has been considered a façade beyond which lies unconscious meanings, invisible processes, implicit rules, hidden hands, and divine motives that can only be brought to light by revelation or reason. In his great work, *The Discovery of the Unconscious* (1970), Henri Ellenberger calls this the unmasking trend, in which hidden or invisible forces, often associated with a prior period in time—a cause, a prime mover—set something in motion that shapes all subsequent moments in time, or in which something happened in our personal life that evaded our consciousness, laid beyond our control, and shaped our destiny thereafter.[12] Though we may remain blissfully or tragically ignorant of these hidden forces, factors and fates, hierophants, academics, diviners, seers, and scientists presume to identify them and help us understand them, even control them. A hierarchy is thus established between ordinary people who are at the mercy of their circumstances, their instincts, their history, their class, their ethnicity, and an elite whose expertise enables it to transcend its particular circumstances and see things as they "really" are. Whether we are speaking of a sociologist, a Freudian analyst, a neurosurgeon, or a physicist, the same assumption holds true—that reality is seldom what it seems. The sun appears to rise and set each day, as though it were circling the earth, but science shows us that the earth goes round the sun. Looking toward any horizon, the world seems flat, though science has long ago shown it to be a globe. Though we speak of the heart as the seat of the emotions, science shows that it is the limbic brain. We think we remember exactly what we were doing on the day of a national disaster, but—as psychologists have shown—most recollections, even a few years after a critical event, prove to be inaccurate, and several years later, when witnesses are asked to answer a set of questions as to where they were and what they were doing on the fateful day, significant discrepancies emerge between the original and subsequent recollections, although everyone is convinced his or her memories were entirely accurate. Clearly, then, there is an evidential gap or rupture between the lifeworld in which we exist and the views of the world we carry in our head—whether these are informed by a belief in higher powers, the celebration of scientific method, or skepticism. The world of thought, memory, dream, and imagination is, moreover, so rich and dynamic that it far outstrips the mundane world we actually inhabit. Is it any wonder, then, that this second world, the world of thought and language, comes to be regarded as much more real than the physical world, and that we come to regard science and divine revelation as offering us a greater reality than the immediate, tangible, perceptible world around us? The trouble is, once we have drawn this conclusion, we tend to devalue the world at hand as less interesting and even more illusory than the ultimate reality that has been glimpsed behind the scenes.

But what if we bracketed out this distinction between real and the illusory and considered both as appearances—but appearances that arise from different circumstances, serve different interests, and have different effects?

In a dialogue with Theaetetus, Socrates refers to Protagoras's view that "man is the measure of all things," and the corollary—that "things are to you as they appear to you, and are to me such as they appear to me" since we are both men. In support of this phenomenological emphasis on the appearance of things, Socrates goes on to observe that "the same wind is blowing, and yet one of us may be cold and the other not, or one may be slightly and the other very cold" (Plato 1908: 352). One might call this a foundational moment for existential anthropology, since the quest for certain knowledge of the nature of things should not, in Socrates's view, *necessarily* preclude, or regard as essentially mistaken, any understanding that informs a particular person's experience of being-in-the-world.

Existential anthropology is less a repudiation of any one way of explaining human behavior—scientific, religious, humanist, animist—than a reminder that life is irreducible to the terms with which we seek to grasp it. Truth and understanding, like well-being, is never securely possessed, and human existence always implies a vexed, imperfectly realized relationship between what is given and what is aspired to, what is within and outside our reach, what can be comprehended and what cannot. We live not in stable states, with fixed identities, but experimentally—*en passage* between different narratives and worldviews, as well as different modes of being—participants and observers, in relation to others and yet alone, physically grounded yet lost in thought, filled with life yet bound to die, looking back and looking forward.

The importance of "recovering the human being" from the philosophical, theological, psychological, and anthropological constructs with which existence has been theorized (Piette 2009b: 21–22) is also underlined by the tragic consequences of pathologizing, demonizing, or otherwise writing off certain populations as having lost or forfeited their humanity, or having become "inhuman." Whether we are speaking of murderers, psychotics, witches, religious zealots, or simply those who do not share our own core values, we tend to operate in one-dimensional terms, as if the humanity of the other were reducible to a single "negative" trait or aberrant moment. Speaking of her father, who died of liver cancer in prison, while serving time for a white-collar crime, a young American woman made this point compellingly: "A person is more than the worst thing he did in his life." Consider, too, Oliver Sacks's refusal to reduce his clients to their "conditions." Describing a 49-year-old patient called Jimmy who was suffering from Korsakov's Syndrome—a profound and permanent, but "pure," devastation of memory caused by alcoholic destruction of the mammillary bodies—Sacks writes that Jimmy was seen as a spiritual casualty, a "lost soul." "Do you think he has a soul?" Sacks asked the sisters who cared for him. "They were outraged by my question, but could see why I asked it. "Watch Jimmie in chapel," they said, "and judge for yourself." Sacks did so and was profoundly moved, for Jimmy clearly partook of the Sacrament in the "fullness and totality of Communion . . . wholly held, absorbed . . . in an act, an act of his whole being." And Sacks recalled the words of the great Russian neuropsychologist, A. R. Luria, "A man does not consist of memory alone" (Sacks 1986: 36).

In approaching this question of the irreducibility and multisidedness of the person, Albert Piette has made human singularity and the empirical individual foundational to his work (2012: 65–80), while Michael Jackson has emphasized the relational, the intersubjective (1998: 1–8). But what at first sight might appear to be an insurmountable difference is quickly resolved if we bracket out the question as to what mode of being is prior or foundational, and see them as potentialities—extremes between which we oscillate, and modes of being we apprehend to different degrees, depending on context and circumstance. Rather than define entire human societies in terms of individuality or relationality, we seek to explore the conditions under which these modes of being make their appearance in consciousness, or become articulated as epistemologies or ideologies. This implies not only a *methodological* suspension of theoretical concepts in order to engage with life as lived, but an integration of historiography, ethnography, and biography in our explorations of the human condition.

What characterizes the existential-phenomenological perspective is not only a refusal to reduce human experience to a priori categories such as the social, the cultural, the biological, or the historical, but a determination to open our minds to domains of human experience that fall outside of or defy the rubrics with which intellectuals typically seek to contain or cover what William James called "the undifferentiated plenum" of lived experience or Virginia Woolf spoke of as "moments of being." In *Phenomenology of Perception*, Merleau-Ponty notes that "red and green are not sensations, they are sensed (*sensibles*)," and that it is *analysis* that discovers the meaning of redness or greenness in the phenomena we subsequently come to *know* in these terms (1962: 4–5). As I walk along the snow-covered path to my house, the words, "walk," "snow," or "path" do not come to mind, and as I climb the stone steps, the words, "climb," "stone," and "steps" do not occur to me. It is not simply because this path is familiar and my actions habitual that I do not give them a second thought, for language is often equally absent when I am out of my comfort zone, doing new things, exploring new worlds. It is not that my experience is cognitively unstructured or "preconceptual," since it is deeply informed by learned habits of bodily movement, bodily skills, and spatial judgment, as well as prior knowledge of stone and snow. What *is* absent from my immediate consciousness are the higher-order abstractions we call worldviews, ideologies, beliefs, or explanatory theories. Certainly, these abstract substantives are brought to mind when I reflect on my presence-in-the-world, and render retrospective accounts of my experience, but most of the time there is a gap or hiatus between my direct encounters with the world and the ways in which I make it retrospectively intelligible—between the stream of sensations and the islands of ideas. This is what Merleau-Ponty meant when he wrote of "that world which precedes knowledge, of which knowledge always *speaks*, and in relation to which every scientific schematization is an abstract and derivative sign language, as is geography in relation to the countryside *in which we have learnt beforehand what a forest, a prairie or a river is*" (1962: ix). Unlike Husserl and Merleau-Ponty, however, we resist defining phenomenology simply as a return to "things themselves," and prefer to think of it as a method for exploring the tension and dialectic between immediate and mediated experience, reducing reality neither to some purely sensible mode of being nor to the theoretical language with which we render existence comprehensible.[13] Another way of making this argument is to point out that "things themselves" or "things as they are" have no stable or essential "isness" or "selfhood," but appear and emerge quite differently for us depending on our situation, interest, and perspective.

Existential Anthropology and the Study of Religion

Our interest in how human beings reconcile their own limited personal existence with the limitless world that precedes, surrounds, and outlasts them leads us to consider the implication of an existential perspective for the anthropological study of religion.

Negotiating the uncertain relationship between mundane and extramundane realms is, arguably, the *fons et origo* of what is called "religion," though cross-cultural comparison is only possible if we find a vocabulary that speaks to what is existentially *there* before we invoke words like religion, ritual, or belief to define it.

In this vein, Paul Ricoeur avows that he is not concerned with Spinoza's "theology." Spinoza's alleged pantheism or atheism is irrelevant; only the notion of *conatus* matters. In this sense, "God is Life" (Ricoeur 1992: 315).[14] But life is more than the impulse to passively "persevere in being"; it consists in the search for "adequate ideas" that enable us to *actively* sustain our sense of presence and purpose (Ricoeur 1992: 316). God is but one of such ideas, and its adequacy consists in its ability to help us realize our capacity for speaking, acting, praying, and even narrating our story. To submit to a higher power is not, therefore, to forfeit one's own agency but to recover it through a relationship with something beyond oneself, be this a supportive friend, a divinity, a diviner, or a material object. Here, the divine and the utopian coalesce as alternative symbols of what William James calls "the more." For we are all susceptible to the uneasy sense "that there is *something wrong about us* as we naturally stand," and what we call religion is a set of ideas and practices for getting in touch with an "elsewhere," an "otherness," or a "wider self" that lies beyond the horizons of one's immediate lifeworld, especially at times when our "lower being has gone to pieces in the wreck" (James 1958: 383–384). This process of othering, that places one's own agency in abeyance, is a precondition for clearing one's head of confusing subjective preoccupations and returning to oneself as someone capable of taking a hand in determining his or her own fate.

Lambek's, Premawardhana's, and Piette's contributions to the anthropology of religion in this volume share the emphasis of several contemporary scholars of religion on a polythetic rather than monothetic approach to religiosity. Monothetic approaches are anchored in the classical Aristotelian system of classification, whereby all members of a given class share one or more defining features or discrete characteristics, and each characteristic is held by every member. This monothetic approach means that we accept the reified categories of Christianity, Judaism, Buddhism, and Islam, and frame our research in these terms from the outset, assuming that everyone who identifies with one of these labels shares or subscribes to a fairly similar and stable worldview. If they don't, they do not belong, or they are heretics. The polythetic approach switches our focus to what Wittgenstein called "family resemblances," what Jonathan Z. Smith called "maps of characteristics," and Albert Piette calls "minor modes of reality"—approaches that recognize the variability with which certain beliefs are held, the fact that not everyone shares identical characteristics either of feeling or faith, and that one can be in two minds at the same time without necessarily feeling a contradiction, doubting *and* believing, or experiencing "negative capability" (Jackson 2009; Lambek, this volume; Luhrmann 2012; Piette 2005).

Rather than defining religion in terms of belief or ritual, Piette (2005) emphasizes what Dan Sperber calls the quasi-propositional dimensions of religious experience in a "minor" rather than institutional mode. This approach echoes recent explorations of everyday religious experience (Orsi 2009; Shielke and Debevec 2012) as well as attempts to identify what Ann Taves (2009) calls the "building blocks of religious experience," and Jonathan Z. Smith (1982) calls "the bare facts of ritual." In these endeavors, an *ascriptive* rather than sui generis model of religious experience is required.

In an ascriptive approach, "religion" covers those experiences we import into a box we have predesignated in this way, much as what we call "art" or "music" is defined by whatever the art or music world accepts under this rubric (think of the urinal Marcel Duchamp placed in an art gallery and called "Fountain," or John Cage's provocative question, "Which is more musical, a truck passing by a factory or a truck passing by a music school? Are the people inside the school musical and the ones outside unmusical?"). Alternatively, one might follow Wilfrid Cantwell Smith's preference for the study of "religious persons" over "religious systems" (1962) or Samuli Shielke and Liza Debevec's emphasis on "ordinary lives" rather than "grand schemes" (2012). The general thrust of all these approaches is to get behind the scenes of what we conventionally demarcate as religious life, religious belief, or ritual, and identify what Williams James called the varieties of religious experience. In other words, we suspend or set aside the terms whereby we conventionally categorize and classify institutional religion under such rubrics as Islam, Christianity, and Buddhism in order to explore the experiences that become cognitively certified, colonized, or collectivized in these ways.

Existence as Anthropology's Blind Spot

To further elucidate the project of existential anthropology, let us review some of the defining moments in the history of the social sciences.

Many "classics" in this field have tended to focus on what can be securely grasped—on problems rather than mysteries, social norms rather than human quandaries, thoughts rather than feelings, collective characteristics rather than individual particularities. This bias toward phenomena that are intransitive and rule-governed, or data that can be systematically analyzed, quantified, or conceptually organized, has left vast reaches of human experience unexplored. Consider the way in which Durkheim specified the aims of sociology: "We must establish the prime bases of the sciences on a solid foundation and not on shifting sand," and "leave outside science for the time being the concrete data of collective life" (1982: 83). But how is one to describe the fluidity of social life if one assumes that social phenomena "must be studied from the outside, as external things" (70)? Durkheim insisted that, as a methodological rule of sociology, social facts were to be treated as realities that were irreducible to individual data. "In order for a social fact to exist, several individuals at the very least must have interacted together and the resulting combination must have given rise to some new production" (45). Social facts are constituted, according to Durkheim, by "the beliefs, tendencies and practices of the group taken collectively" and "some of these ways of acting or thinking acquire, by dint of repetition, a sort of consistency which, so to speak, separates them out, isolating them from the particular events which reflect them" (54). Collective phenomena "possess a reality existing outside individuals, who, at every moment, conform to them" (45). It is "vastly distinct from the individual facts which manifest that reality" (54).

In an effort to break with all forms of psychologism, Durkheim presented society as a moral author beyond the individual, or as a collective consciousness imposing rules and taboos on persons and guaranteeing their welfare through integration into a group. The individual is nothing more than a passive vehicle for the expression and affirmation of collective norms and values. This valorization of a collective consciousness that Durkheim defined as a "community of beliefs and sentiments" is directly associated with a "communitarian conception" of society that leaves hardly any possibility for an interval or interruption between the singular and the shared. "By aggregating together, by interpenetrating, by fusing together, individuals give birth to a being, psychical if you like, but one which constitutes a psychical individuality of a new kind" (1982: 129).

Even the being of God is reduced to the social. "God is only a figurative expression of . . . society" (Durkheim 1965: 258).[15]

The tenets of Durkheimian sociology are therefore threefold: on the theoretical level, the primacy of the social over the individual; on the methodological level, a reification of social reality and a focus on collective representations and dispositions; on the thematic level, a valorization of the community as a whole. By implication, there is no individual existence.

It is difficult not to see Bourdieu's work as a continuation of this holistic vision of society, even if the structuralist temptation, on the basis of which society is conceived of as a system of relations transcending individuals, is counterbalanced by the integration of some phenomenological principles. Habitus is defined as a set of dispositions inculcated by, and in accordance with, the social context. Produced by objective social conditions, the habitus does not, however, imply a mechanical reproduction of these conditions. In fact, Bourdieu insists on the strategies available to individuals—their socially acquired capacities for invention and play that produce "the 'fuzzy,' flexible, partial logic of [a] partially integrated system" (1990a: 267 and ff). In some ways, the individual eliminated by structuralism is reintroduced by Bourdieu, not as a subject but as an "acting agent" (1990b).

Social strategies that are not, however, those of an automaton obeying a rule, result from the practical logic acquired by social experience and by sustained exposure to a set of social conditions. Practical logic is incorporated into, and at the same time exteriorized by, the individual without any conscious aim or rational calculation. If practical logic does not impose the strict regularity of a law but contains an element of indetermination and uncertainty, the transgression it permits, in playing with the rules while remaining within them, would seem to depend on a principle such as excellence and virtuosity, though this principle is always already incorporated. Paradoxically, even a strategic capacity appears to be an adaptability determined by the habitus and therefore by the social context.

According to Bourdieu, practical sense concerns the immediate and blind comprehension that characterizes one's participation in the world. It is a lived experience of a world that is taken for granted and not viewed from afar. On numerous occasions, Bourdieu insists on the unconscious, unreflective, and implicit aspect of practical logic: "Caught up in 'the matter in hand,' totally present in the present and in the practical functions that it finds there in the form of objective potentialities, practice excludes attention to itself (i.e. to the past). It is unaware of the principles that govern it and the possibilities they contain; it can only discover them by enacting them, unfolding them in time" (1990a: 92). In short, total identification and conformity appear in Bourdieu as the necessary corollaries of incorporated practical logic: "One does not embark on the game by a conscious act, one is born into the game, with the game; and the relation of investment, *illusio*, investment, is made more total and unconditional by the fact that it is unaware of what it is" (1990a: 67). We cannot agree with this characterization of human existence.

A twofold lesson can be drawn from Bourdieu's theories. First, like Durkheim or Lévi-Strauss, Bourdieu seeks to construct his social object through a rupture with a person's immediate experience of being-in-the-world. By contrast, Piette's phenomenography and Jackson's radical empiricism work toward an anthropology that does not mutilate and reify, and whose concepts possess a mediatory force or metaphorical character that brings relationships into play and discloses lived reality to maximum effect. Second, while Bourdieu's practical logic is incorporated, unconscious, and connected to the individual's unreflective conformity to implicit rules, existence involves a perennial and partial dissociation from a person's social situation and social role. It testifies to a play with the possibility of nonconformity that is, however, never fully consummated. The person is both assimilated to the social and at the same a singular being that stands out from it. The state of the body, as Bourdieu observes, is always filled with wandering thoughts.

Whereas rigid sociological theories of social constraint leave no room for the individual's reflective capacity, ethnomethodology, on the contrary, argues against any representation of the individual as a "judgmental dope" (Garfinkel 1967),[16] and assumes that social actions are not invariably the product of interiorized norms. Instead, this theory stresses the continual activity of individuals using their "know-how," employing various procedures, and making their actions intelligible and "accountable" to themselves and others.

What place, then, does ethnomethodology assign to existences?

In ethnomethodology, "practical logic" (which for Bourdieu is nothing but a product of external norms) involves a reflexive dimension. Although the procedures followed by social actors are essentially practical, and employed in a "seen but unremarked way" (without the explicit reflection that would prevent an activity occurring), the practice of any particular behavior constitutes a nonverbal way of expressing and constructing the cultural code. At the same time that it is tacitly self-produced, this code structures the situation. Social action certainly does not necessarily involve any awareness that the actor is rationally constructing a social order. Yet prediscursive reflexivity does not exclude the explicit (and also reflexive) formulation of "accounts" of what has taken place, formulating a sense, a reason, and a motive, particularly when it is a question of remedying a local problem or making good a lack of understanding of a particular situation.

Whether it involves interpretative procedures or practical reasoning, there is a set of instructions that gives group members a sense of the significance of the social order through continual reflexive feedback. If this interpretation is pushed to the extreme, the activities of individuals do not seem to contain interests other than ensuring the system's functioning (Rossi 1983: 233). Thus, it is interesting to note that ethnomethodology's individuals are analyzed as always working in order to assure social order and to create a coherent situation. Thus, in this view, there is no such thing as "time-out" for members of a social group. Perturbing and confusing situations always involve the effort to reestablish order and affirm subjacent rules. By contrast, the contributors to this volume insist on movements between moments of activity and passivity, and are dismissive of reifications that would create the illusion of certain societies as fatalistic (the individual submerged in the group) and others as agentive (the individual standing out and acting autonomously).[17]

In conclusion, whether one opts for (in sociology) the primacy of the social or not, there is often a theoretical difficulty in assigning an analytical status to the individual's diffuse reflexivity (which is very specific to human modes of presence). This is a crucial point. Practical logic, produced by social structures (in Bourdieu), or producing social situations (in Garfinkel), and nonreflexive on the one hand, reflexive on the other, fails to capture the individual's presence in a social situation.

Does Erving Goffman offer an important reference point for existential anthropology?

The concepts of the author of *The Presentation of Self in Everyday Life* are quite determinant, such as role distance, involvement and subordinate involvement, byplay, wings, backstage and others, many of which are drawn from Sartre.

Goffmanian analysis of social life is both relevant and limited. *Frame Analysis* is a study not only of the "fundamental frames" of social experience—i.e., the primary frames without which an activity would remain meaningless—but also and above all an analysis of their particular vulnerability, inducing incessant transformations of the primary frame. The Goffmanian frame underlies a veritable experience, stratified with different layers produced by the different types of transformation that a formal grammar of social experience has to decipher: keying, fabrication, out-of-frame activity, breaking frame, time-out, misframing. Between the individual's participation, fitted to a keyed frame, and the active transformations on the part of the individual himself, Goffman reintroduces the individual as an interpreter and user of frames. Individuals can speak with irony or indicate by their tone of voice or some other expressions that they mean just the opposite of the literal meaning of their remarks.

To this end, let us recall Goffman's marvelous text in *Encounters* concerning role distance, the levels of adhesion, and the deviations from an ideal role that are possible: the types of play engaged in by children of different ages and adults on a merry-go-round, the individual as player and synthesizer of numerous roles simultaneously, his adherence to the official definition of a situation and his irreducibility in relation to it as expressed by his simultaneous gestural activity. Goffman defines role distance in the following way: "Whether this skittish behavior is intentional or unintentional, sincere or affected, correctly appreciated by others present or not, it does constitute a wedge between the individual and his role, between doing and being. This 'effectively' expressed pointed separateness between the individual and his putative role I call *role distance*. A shorthand is involved here: the individual is actually denying not the role but the virtual self that is implied in the role for all accepting performers" (1972: 95). It is here then that the danger of Goffmanian analysis appears: it resides in the overly strict focusing on the concept of role, and, more specifically, on its sociological connotation, as if even these dispersals or the distance it allows also participated to some extent in some fixed role. "Role distance," writes Goffman, "is a part (but, of course, only one part) of typical role" (102). For Goffman, according to Murray Davis's commentary, "man is sociological almost . . . to the core, not just to the skin" (Davis 1975: 101). In this Goffmanian world, "each of us is reduced only to someone who is seen" (Craib 1978: 85). Rather than a study of activities in their concreteness, *Frame Analysis* proposes a formal grammar of social phenomena and their objective experiential possibilities. On the descriptive level, the consequences are inevitable and often result in an imperturbable and cold tone, betraying social life in its mirror mode by an overly analytic concept. By following Goffman too closely in his view that, in the presence of an individual, other people search for information about him or strive to bring into play information about him, one risks losing all the indetermination of life by focusing attention on a story of "espionage" and "counterespionage."

Goffman's concepts, heuristic and perhaps too rigid as they are, do not really encourage observation and description of miniscule facts. Goffman finally reduces everyday behaviors to normative conventions and sociostrategic goals, even those involving role-distance. This interpretation of Goffman's analysis should convince us of the need to work on two parallel fronts, using both descriptive and theoretical strategies.

Our purpose in this review has been to recall to the attention of anthropologists the *presence* of the individuals who make up any social field. Rather than gathering and synthesizing data on gestures and expressions that enable us to describe and understand collectivities, existential anthropology seeks to capture the human presence in its manifold and elusive modes of engagement in situations where individuals may agree with others on a collective issue, yet at the same time express idiosyncratic and socially "insignificant" comportments and attitudes that suggest fields of being that lie outside what is designated the social or the cultural.

Referring to this method of observation as "phenomenography" rather than ethnography is not to subvert or deny the sociocultural perspective. Phenomenography seeks to understand the collective dimensions of any situation, but it draws our attention toward data that are not deemed relevant, either by the actors or the observer, to this situation. All sociological theories tend to avoid addressing the *presence* of human beings, and it is precisely the objective of phenomenography to focus on this phenomenological field. That is to say, we strive to observe and describe what appears to be *there*—the human being in his or her presence, including all the subtle changes of expression and gesture that comprise a person's idiosyncratic being. Not only are human beings "there" in any given situation. They also come from somewhere and will move to somewhere else, always making and unmaking, modifying themselves, developing, from birth to death. Rather than focus on one activity or event, existential anthropology seeks to explore this continuity of existence, from situation to situation.

What discipline has been charged with this task? Psychology typically privileges experimentation in a laboratory. Philosophy prefers theoretical questioning to empirical observation. And social scientists prioritize the understanding of a group, a society, or forms of manifestly social action. It is the aim of the phenomenographer to undertake the observation-description of a human being's modes of presence. Phenomenography involves analyzing the act of existing, insofar as it goes beyond the social dimension of the person. It thus seeks to observe human beings in their modes of presence, as well as other beings who coexist with humans, such as animals, to better understand what is specifically human.[18]

The Question of Ontology

For several years now, the words "existents," "beings," and "existences" have become so current in social anthropology that one wonders whether

Terry Eagleton (2003: 1) is correct in seeing this "ontological turn" as a byproduct of "postmodernism's enduring love-affair with otherness," our desire to create "postmodern savages." Not only must we be wary of the overly homogeneous and apolitical image of Amerindian lives and minds that accompanies this paradigm (Ramos 2012), we must avoid resurrecting Lévy-Bruhl's view that it is possible to directly infer individual experience from collective representations, ideologies, mythologies, and cosmologies—i.e., that the relationship between thought and being is isomorphic. The mistake here is not simply one of reading the metaphorical too literally; it is the fallacy of what Adorno called "identity thinking"—the conflation of theories of knowledge with modes of consciousness.[19] As G. E. R. Lloyd observes in reference to Eduardo Vivieros de Castro's perspectivism, although many Amerindian societies assume that "the original common condition of both humans and animals is animality, not humanity," and all beings share a common "spirituality" despite their corporeal differences (Vivieros de Castro 2012: 83), it would be a serious reification to claim that this worldview shaped the consciousness of every individual to the same degree and in the same way, since "contexts change" and these are "all-important" (Lloyd 2011: 836). It would be equally remiss of us not to explicate the practical and social value such ontological assumptions about humans, spirits and animals might have in specific ritual or everyday situations (Lloyd 2011: 838). In other words, we cannot assume that ontology mirrors epistemology in any constant, unilateral, or direct manner; on the contrary, the relation between being and thought is context-dependent, mutable, and indeterminate. This is as true of societies as it is of persons. As Alfred Korzybski observed, we all too readily use the verb "to be" to signify a whole person when only referring to an aspect of him or her. Thus, to declare that someone *is* a fool is an unwarranted exaggeration if all we have observed is that the person in question has *done* something foolish. "The map is not the territory" (Korzybski 1941). William James makes the same point when he notes that every human being carries within herself or himself multiple self-states, any one of which has the potential to emerge in a given context or in a given relationship. "*A man has as many selves as there are individuals who recognize him* and carry an image of him in their mind," and a man's self "*is the sum total of all that he* CAN *call his*, not only his body and his psychic powers, but his clothes, and his house, his wife and children, his ancestors and friends, his reputation and works, his lands and horses, and yacht and bank account" (James 1950: 294). These observations help us explain why existential anthropology resists the ontological turn.

With regard to human presences, certain actions or gestures tend to be actualized in any given situation while others are not. This does not mean that certain possibilities are abandoned or do not exist in reality, for they may find expression in small and often unremarked details—an idiosyncratic figure of speech, a peculiar manner of sitting or standing, a sidelong look, a slight frown, an absent air (Piette 2011: 86–88). Rather than focus on conspicuous or dominant attitudes, gestures, and postures, and draw them together to create a synthetic description of a culture or a group, Piette seeks to capture the human presence in its various expressions of engagement in a situation, so that an individual may simultaneously be acting in concert or in agreement with others while simultaneously expressing dissent and difference—present and absent at the same time. Focusing on the variable and subtle ways in which a human being is simultaneously present and absent to others—rather than on manifest values and espoused beliefs, or latent structures and intrapsychic processes, Piette's focus is on the lived presence of human beings "in a minor mode," and as such constitutes a critique of both sociological theories and theories of mind that bypass the *presence* of human being. Our objective is to focus on this presence: that is to say, to observe, to note, to write what appears to be there, the human being in his or her living presence and as disclosed in and through his or her actions toward others. Clearly, such a project encompasses a phenomenological method of approaching the world as it appears to its inhabitants, as well as an existential focus on being-in-the-world. As Webb Keane notes, ethnographers "do not enter into ['dramatically different worlds of practice and thought'] primarily via the didactic virtuosity of indigenous metaphysical theorists. Those worlds are not inhabited first and foremost as talk" (2013: 188).

Although the ontological turn *alludes* to actual human beings, they tend to dissolve or disappear in metaphysical renderings of ontology itself, or to become obscured by a focus on relations between human and nonhuman beings, or on mythological and cosmological schema. Since so much weight is given to cosmology, culture, and worldview, one might ask whether the term "ontology" is not a misnomer, particularly when the analytical *focus* is not on human beings but on exclusively nonhuman beings (gods and animals) or the dead, and the empirical particulars of everyday practices are emphasized far less than collective representations.

In fact, in this "ontological turn," human beings do not exist. They are instantiations or effects of social or ideological structures that have been ontologized. Is this not an example of what A. N. Whitehead called "the fallacy of misplaced concreteness" in which persons are replaced by abstract ideas that are then treated as if they were living things? Ironically, this fallacy echoes the anthropomorphic thinking it seeks to understand, reducing the human subject to an object and endowing the extra-human world with the subjectivity it has removed from persons.

Philippe Descola fails to distinguish between anthropology as science of ontologies and anthropology as science of humans. In our view, however, it is vitally important to distinguish a science of ontologies (or local cosmologies), including naturalism—the relation of the scientist and the animal—and a science of the human that comprises comparative observations with other nonhuman beings. What are these beings like, how do they exist and subsist in—as well as apart from—their immediate relationships with human beings? In other words, there is a difference between a science of ontologies (that is, the properties attributed to beings) and ontology as a comparative science of beings—between a science of beings as categorized or associated and a science of beings as living, existing, continuing, subsisting, and present. The ontological turn runs the risk of losing contact with the reality of lived situations, while existential anthropology is searching for actual modes of being, not simply concepts.

The dialogue between Graham Harman and Bruno Latour (who also participates in the ontological turn) speaks both to this question and our comments (Harman 2010: 67–92; Latour, Harman, and Erdelyi 2011). At the same time that Harman presents Latour as a twenty-first-century metaphysician, thanks to his theoretical thinking about objects, Harman establishes a set of radical criticisms that we share.

Latour insists on a network, but gives little thought to individuals within that network (see also van de Port, this volume). The Latourian entity does not define itself except by its connections, and by actions whereby one thing changes another. The network is described not as a reservoir of potentialities, but as existing at every moment in its full deployment, as a field of dynamic interconnections among its entities. The slightest change in an object will mobilize a new actor: "every entity defines itself only by its relations. If the relations change, the definition changes in the same way." But according to Harman, the current use of an object cannot reveal the object in all its singularities. A relation distorts every entity involved. To sit down on a chair does not exhaust the chair. According to Harman, the object (especially if this is a human being, we would add) is more profound and complex than the relations in which it makes itself known. Harman presents the object, physical or otherwise, real or not, as "unified" and autonomous, and argues that its *qualities* are always more than its *functions* in a network. Harman is critical of the "demolition" and "burial" of objects. The first implies that the object is only a superficial effect and that it is necessary to look for basic elements or deeper realities.

The second supposes that the object is less important than the relations that it implies. Harman does not want to think of the object as exhausted in a presence for another object, or to reduce it to a series of relations. Objects, that are "deeper" than their relations, cannot be dissolved into them. It seems to us that Harman's argument even more urgently concerns human beings whose situated presence cannot be separated from their potentialities and reserves, including states of mind that are absent in actor network theory.

Latour asks, "But what about me, the ego? Am I not in the depth of my heart, in the circumvolutions of my brain, in the inner sanctum of my soul, in the vivacity of my spirit, an 'individual'? Of course I am, but only as long as I have been individualized, spiritualized, interiorized" (2007: 212). This is also an important question for existential anthropology. What am I when I am individualized and interiorized? Latour does not really provide an answer, and he returns to his conduits: "In doing away *both* with ungraspable subjectivity and with intractable structure, it might be possible to finally place at the forefront the flood of *other more* subtle conduits that allow us to *become* an individual and *to gain* some interiority" (2007: 214). Latour continues,

> What I am trying to do here is simply show how the boundaries between sociology and psychology may be reshuffled for good. For this, there is only one solution: make every single entity populating the former inside come from the outside not as a negative constraint 'limiting subjectivity,' but as a positive offer of subjectivation. As soon as we do this, the former actor, member, agent, person, individual—whatever its name—takes the same star-shaped aspect we have observed earlier when flattening the global and re-dispatching the local. It is made to be an individual/subject or it is made to be a generic nonentity by a swarm of other agencies. Every competence, deep down in the silence of your interiority, has first to come from the outside, to be slowly sunk in and deposited into some well-constructed cellar whose doors have then to be carefully sealed. (212)

How does any individual feel the evidence of existence at any given moment? What is the effect of existing here and now? We share the view of van de Port (this volume) that the anthropologist must *enter* much more profoundly into the life of the individual than is advocated by actor network theory. One must observe the details of individual presence, which is irreducible to the logic—indicated by Bruno Latour's italics—of the process, the network and its relations, and, for that matter, structure, since Lévi-Strauss's accents can be recognized in this reading of Latour. By criticizing Latourian lines of connection between points, Tim Ingold is certainly correct to emphasize the "real life lines" that characterize a human life course, as well as human actions and perceptions. "Life does not live on points but by following lines," he writes, in advocating an anthropology of life. "Anthropology, in my view, is a sustained and disciplined inquiry into the conditions and potentials of human life. Yet generations of theorists, throughout the history of the discipline, have been at pains to expunge life from their accounts, or to treat as merely consequential, the derivative and fragmentary output of patterns, codes, structures or systems variously defined as genetic or cultural, natural or social" (Ingold 2011: 3). We agree completely with this admirable program that would reintroduce "life as lived" in anthropology. The point, so to speak, is to recognize and observe the individual in situ as someone who is always continuing along, as well as crossing, lines—accumulating or modifying perceptions, skills, capacities, knowledge, know-how, and changing course even as he or she embodies at any one moment the entirety of all present and past relations. The person is a singular presence, existing beyond or below all relational logics. And our task of meticulous description must address the question, "In what consists my sense of being an 'I' now?"

Anthropology consists in observing and describing what really exists in a situation—in particular, what we must postulate as real entities in order for any situation to make sense. From this point of view, ontology would take a different meaning and would suggest, according to its etymology, a theoretical and empirical orientation that consists in observing, describing, and comparing beings, presences, individuals, and existences in and through their constantly changing, various and diverse situations (Piette 2011: 92; 2012: 9). "Ontos" or "onta" are forms of the present participle of the verb "to be" in classical Greek. Thus, etymologically, "ontology" invites us to focus on beings in situation, rather than on the speech and narratives beings produce. Therefore, we reiterate the point that ontology is not a sociological or anthropological *object*, but a modality of the anthropological gaze. Accordingly, ontology becomes a critical guarantee for not inferring inner states from outward behaviors, or assimilating singular beings to sociocultural wholes.

In this perspective, ontology cannot be extrapolated *directly* from the representations of a people; it must be inferred from what is happening and unfolding concretely in specific situations. Because language risks substituting itself for the world, it is all too easy for us to forget that people feel pain and joy, and think in ways that cannot be readily captured in words.

Following Heidegger, existential anthropology begins with the question as to what is existentially *there* before there is something we *know* as the social, the ethnic, the economic, the political, the religious, the moral, or the historical? With notable exceptions—such as Lévi-Strauss's structural anthropology—sociocultural anthropology has tended to privilege what Heidegger called "regional ontologies," and shy away from the issue of "fundamental ontology"—the question of Being itself, and of what is present and given before discursive colonization occurs—that sense that "there is always more than we can say" (van de Port 2011: 28). Paul Ricoeur captures this question in his compelling phrase "the enigma of anteriority"—that baffling sense that before we formulate any idea of an ethics, a politics, or personal identity, we possess a diffuse and inchoate sense of being human that these "regional" concepts only partially capture or describe (1998: 100).

From the standpoint of the ontological turn, social anthropology is, in Heideggerian terms, a regional ontology. It describes the social and cultural characteristics of humans in a particular linguistic or geographical region, or at a particular historical period. By contrast, existential anthropology does not reduce the human to a specific assemblage of social, cultural, psychological, historical, and biological characteristics. Its aim is to describe human beings as they exist, and this presumes a "fundamental ontology" whose focus is on what is there before the human is constructed in terms of a particular worldview, be this a local cosmology, theory of mind, or scientific model. This point of view urges us to think of anthropology not simply in terms of social, political, economic, or cultural anthropology but as an anthropology *tout court*, an anthropology that is as empirical as it is theoretical, but that resists reducing the human to the identities and designations that human beings deploy in order to know themselves, or to cope with and control the various situations they encounter in the worlds into which they are born.

Notes

1. Even within these regions, there are marked differences (for instance, Scandinavian anthropology has closer affinities with anthropology in the United Kingdom and United States than with anthropology in France). Furthermore, whatever disciplinary unity ethnography and anthropology originally possessed, it was lost as the discipline spread and took root in countries beyond Europe and the United States. Indeed, anthropology has come to resemble its fields of study, which are as multiplex as the interpretive methods anthropologists now draw upon in understanding them.

2. This theme is systematically elaborated and explored in Michael Jackson's *Between One and One Another* (2013) and, from a different perspective, in Albert Piette's *Fondements à une Anthropologie des Hommes* (2011).
3. Cited in Sartre 1973: 6.
4. Cited in May 1958: 11.
5. "What do we mean by saying that existence precedes essence? We mean that man first of all exists, encounters himself, surges up in the world—and defines himself afterward. If man as the existentialist sees him is not definable, it is because to begin with he is nothing. He will not be anything until later, and then he will be what he makes of himself. Thus, there is no human nature, because there is no God to have a conception of it. Man simply is" (Sartre 1973: 28).
6. "Existentialism," in *Stanford Encyclopedia of Philosophy*, 2010. Michael Jackson echoes Bernard Stiegler's observation (2009: 3) that individuation is a process whereby the self emerges in a context of other selves, and that "the *existential* dimension of all philosophy, without which philosophy would lose all *credit* and sink into scholastic chatter, must be analyzed through the question of the relation of the *I* and the *we*, in which consists this psychic and collective individuation."
7. See, for example, *Ethnographie de l'action* (Piette 1996), *Anthropologie existentiale* (Piette 2009), and *Propositions anthropologiques pour refonder la discipline* (Piette 2010).
8. Ludwig Binswanger's existential psychoanalysis plays close attention to these core ontological metaphors of rising and falling, as they find expression in individual experiences and dreams, and traditional mythologies (Binswanger 1963: 222–248).
9. It is important to remember that the vehement rejection of Sartre's existentialism by Marxists and communist intellectuals (especially Henri Lefebvre and Georg Lukacs) was based on the assumption that existentialism was an irrational, magical, intuitive, narcissistic philosophy that not only reflected a degenerate bourgeois worldview but eschewed the instrumental reason of science (see Poster 1975: 115–125). This Marxist critique was echoed by Lévi-Strauss's equally abusive dismissal of existentialism as a "sort of shop-girl metaphysics" that overindulges "the illusions of subjectivity" and cuts itself off from scientific knowledge "which it despises" (Lévi-Strauss 1973: 58; 1981: 640).
10. Adorno (1998: 12) makes an identical point when he writes that "dialectics means nothing other than insisting on the mediation of what appears to be immediate and on the reciprocity of immediacy and mediation as it unfolds at all levels."
11. Perhaps this explains why existentialists have often turned from philosophy to literature—Sartre's *Nausée*, Camus's *L'Étranger*, André Gorz's *Traître*. As the novelist John Updike put it, "Cosmically, I seem to be of two minds. The power of materialist science to explain everything—from the behavior of the galaxies to that of molecules, atoms and their sub-microscopic components—seems to be inarguable and the principal glory of the modern mind. On the other hand, the reality of subjective sensations, desires and—may we even say—illusions, composes the basic substance of our existence, and religion alone, in its many forms, attempts to address, organize and placate these. I believe, then, that religious faith will continue to be an essential part of being human, as it has been for me" (http://www.npr.org/templates/story/story.php?storyId=4600600).
12. Paul Ricoeur (1970: 32–35) speaks of this tradition as a "hermeneutics of suspicion."
13. By insisting on this dialectical relationship between what is there *in potentia* and what is actually brought forth or made present in any specific situation, we hope to avoid constructing what Robert Orsi (2012: 151) has called "the archetypal existential man of phenomenological anthropology, who appears to arrive always without a story or a past and without any relationship, making him an avatar of the modernist fantasy of the unencumbered and radically individualized self."

14. Cf. William James: "Does God really exist? How does he exist? What is He? are so many irrelevant questions. Not God, but life, more life, a larger, richer, more satisfying life is, in the last analysis, the end of religion" (1958: 382).
15. In contrast to Durkheim, Albert Piette (1999) has proposed a methodological theism whose goal is to describe divine modes of presence that it is anthropologically necessary to postulate in order that a situation—a cult, for example—be seen as coherent.
16. Garfinkel (1967) speaks of a judgmental dope (also "cultural dope"), in characterizing the Parsonian view of the person who produces the stable features of society—its roles, norms, or more generally social structures—by acting in compliance with preestablished and legitimating forms of action and thought.
17. The opportunistic switching between direct action and strategic inaction brings to mind Aristotle's distinction between "active" and "passive" agency (*Metaphysics* book V, chap. 12), the first referring to a subject's action on the world that changes it in some way, the second referring to a subject's being subject to the actions of others—suffering, receiving, being moved or transformed by external forces. Hannah Arendt (1958: 181–186) speaks of this contrast between being an actor and being acted upon as a difference between being a "who" and a "what."
18. Most of Albert Piette's work (in French) is devoted to the detailed observation and focus on human presences "in the minor mode." See, for example, Piette 1996; 2009a; 2010.
19. Webb Keane speaks of this as a "strong ontology" that implies that human beings inhabit different worlds rather than exhibit different worldviews. The problem with making a case for "strong ontology," Keane notes, is that it depends on an ethnographer possessing an unattainable, objective, god-like perspective (2013: 186–191).

References

Adorno, Theodor W. 1973. *Negative Dialectics* (trans. E. B. Ashton). New York: Continuum.
Arendt, Hannah. 1958. *The Human Condition*. Chicago: Chicago University Press.
Badiou, Alain. 2012. *The Adventure of French Philosophy* (trans. Bruno Bosteel). London: Verso.
Binswanger, Ludwig. 1963. *Being-in-the-World: Selected Papers of Ludwig Binswanger* (trans. Jacob Needleman). New York: Basic Books.
Bourdieu, Pierre. 1990a. *The Logic of Practice* (trans. Richard Nice). Stanford, CA: Stanford University Press.
———. 1990b. *In Other Words* (trans. Matthew Adamson). Stanford, CA: Stanford University Press.
Cantwell-Smith, Wilfrid. 1962. *The Meaning and End of Religion*. New York: Harper and Row.
Craib, Ian. 1978. "Review" of Erving Goffman's *Frame Analysis*, *Philosophy of Social Sciences* 8: 85.
Davis, Murray S. 1975. "Review" of *Frame Analysis*, *Contemporary Sociology* 4 (6): 601.
de Certeau, Michael. 1984. *The Practice of Everyday Life* (trans. Steven Rendall). Berkeley: University of California Press.
Devereux, George. 1978. *Ethnopsychoanalysis: Psychoanalysis and Anthropology as Complementary Frames of Reference*. Berkeley: University of California Press.
Dilthey, Wilhelm. 1989. *Introduction to the Human Sciences. Selected Works*, vol. 1, Rudolf A. Makkreel and Frithof Rodi (eds.). Princeton, NJ: Princeton University Press.
Durkheim, Emile. 1965. *The Elementary Forms of the Religious Life* (trans. Joseph Ward Swain). New York: The Free Press.

———. 1982. *The Rules of Sociological Method*. New York: The Free Press.
Eagleton, Terry. 2003. *Figures of Dissent*. London: Verso.
Ellenberger, Henri. 1970. *The Discovery of the Unconscious: The History and Evolution of Dynamic Psychiatry*. New York: Basic Books.
Frankl, Viktor. 1973. *Psychotherapy and Existentialism: Selected Papers on Logotherapy*. Harmondsworth: Penguin.
Garfinkel, Harold. 1967. *Studies in Ethnomethodology*. Englewood Cliffs, NJ: PrenticeHall.
Graeber, David. 2011. *Debt: The First 5,000 Years*. New York: Melville House.
Harman, Graham. 2010. *Towards Speculative Realism: Essays and Lectures*. Winchester, UK: Zero Books.
Horkheimer, Max, and Theodor W. Adorno. 2002. *Dialectic of Enlightenment: Philosophical Fragments* (trans. Edmund Jephcott). Stanford, CA: Stanford University Press.
Ingold, Tim. 2011. *Being Alive: Essays on Movement, Knowledge and Description*. New York: Routledge.
Jackson, Michael. 1998. *Minima Ethnographica: Intersubjectivity and the Anthropological Project*. Chicago: Chicago University Press.
———2009. *The Palm at the End of the Mind: Relatedness, Religiosity, and the Real*. Durham, NC: Duke University Press.
———. 2013a. *Between One and One Another*. Berkeley: University of California Press.
———. 2013b. *The Wherewithal of Life: Ethics, Migration, and the Question of Well-Being*. Berkeley: University of California Press.
James, William. 1950. *The Principles of Psychology*, vol. 1. New York: Dover.
———. 1958. *The Varieties of Religious Experience: A Study in Human Nature*. New York: Signet.
Jaspers, Karl. 1997. *Reason and Existenz*. Milwaukee: Marquette University Press.
Keane, Webb. 2013. "Ontologies, Anthropologists, and Ethical Life," *Hau: Journal of Ethnographic Theory* 3 (1): 186–191.
Korzybski, Alfred. 1941. *Science and Sanity: An Introduction to Non-Aristotelian Systems and General Semantics*. New York: The Science Press.
Latour, Bruno. 2007. *Reassembling the Social: An Introduction of Actor-Network-Theory*. Oxford: Oxford University Press.
Latour, Bruno, Graham Harman, and Peter Erdelyi. 2011. *The Prince and the Wolf, Latour and Harman at the LSE*. Winchester: Zero Books.
Lévi-Strauss, Claude. 1973. *Tristes Tropiques* (trans. J. and D. Weightman). London: Jonathan Cape.
———. 1981. *The Naked Man* (trans. J. and D. Weightman). London: Jonathan Cape.
Lloyd, G. E. R. 2011. "Humanity Between Gods and Beasts? Ontologies in Question." *Journal of the Royal Anthropological Institute* (N.S.).
Luhrmann, Tanya. 2012. *When God Talks Back: Understanding the American Evangelical Relationship with God*. New York: Vintage.
May, Rollo. 1958. "Origins of the Existential Movement in Psychology." In *Existence*, Rollo May, Ernest Angel, and Henri Ellenberger (eds.). New York: Basic Books, 3–36.
Merleau-Ponty, Maurice. 1962. *Phenomenology of Perception* (trans. Colin Smith). London: Routledge and Kegan Paul.
Orsi, Robert A. 2005. *Between Heaven and Earth: The Religious Worlds People Make and the Scholars Who Study Them*. Princeton, NJ: Princeton University Press.
———. 2012. "Afterword: Everyday Religion and the Contemporary World." In *Ordinary Lives and Grand Schemes: An Anthropology of Everyday Religion*, Samuli Schielke and Liza Debevec (eds.). New York: Berghahn Books, 146–161.
Piette, Albert. 1996. *Ethnographie de l'action*. Paris: Métailie.
———. 1999. *La Religion de Pres. L'Activite Religieuse en train de se faire*. Paris: Métailie.

———. 2005. *La Fait Religieux: Une Theorie de la Religion Ordinaire*. Paris: Economica.
———. 2009a. *Anthropologie Existentiale*. Paris: Editions Pétra.
———. 2009b. *L'Acte d'Exister: Une Phenominographie de la Presence*. Paris: Socrate.
———. 2010. *Propositions Anthropologiques Pour Refonder la Discipline*. Paris: Editions Pétra.
———. 2011. *Fondements a une Anthropologie des Hommes*. Paris: Hermann.
———. 2012. *De l'Ontologie en Anthropologie*. Paris: Berg International.
Plato. 1908. *The Dialogues of Plato*, vol. 3 (ed. B. Jowett). New York: Scribners.
Poster, Mark. 1975. *Existential Marxism in Postwar France: From Sartre to Althusser*. Princeton, NJ: Princeton University Press.
Ramos, Alcida Rita. 2012. 'The Politics of Perspectivism." *The Annual Review of Anthropology* 41: 481–494.
Ricoeur, Paul. 1970. *Freud and Philosophy: An Essay on Interpretation* (trans. Denis Savage). New Haven, CT: Yale University Press.
———. 1992. *Oneself as Another* (trans. Kathleen Blamey). Chicago: University of Chicago Press.
———. 1998. *Critique and Conviction: Conversations with François Azouvi and Marc de Launay* (trans. Kathleen Blarney). New York: Columbia University Press, 1998.
Rossi, Ino. 1983. *From the Sociology of Symbols to the Sociology of Signs: Toward a Dialectical Sociology*. New York: Columbia University Press.
Sacks, Oliver. 1986. *The Man Who Mistook His Wife For a Hat*. London: Picador.
Sartre, Jean-Paul. 1968. *Search for a Method* (trans. Hazel Barnes). New York: Vintage.
———. 1973. *Existentialism and Humanism* (trans. Philip Mairet). London: Eyre Methuen.
———. 1981. *The Family Idiot: Gustave Flaubert, 1821–1857* (trans. Carol Cosman), 5 vols. Chicago: Chicago University Press, 1: 1, 7–8.
Shielke, Samuli, and Liza Debevec (eds.). 2012. *Ordinary Lives and Grand Schemes: An Anthropology of Everyday Religion*. New York: Berghahn.
Smith, Jonathan Z. 1982. *Imagining Religion: From Babylon to Jonestown*. Chicago: Chicago University Press.
Stiegler, Bernard. 2009. *Acting Out* (trans. David Barison, Daniel Ross, and Patrick Crogan). Stanford, CA: Stanford University Press.
Taves, Ann Taves, 2009. *Religious Experience Reconsidered: A Building Block Approach to the Study of Religion and Other Special Things*. Princeton, NJ: Princeton University Press.
van de Port, Mattijs. 2011. *Ecstatic Encounters: Brazilian Candomblé and the Search for the Really Real*. Amsterdam: Amsterdam University Press.
Viveiros de Castro, Eduardo. 2012. *Cosmological Perspectivism in Amazonia and Elsewhere*. Masterclass Series 1. Manchester: HAU Network of Ethnographic Theory.

Chapter One

Conversion and Convertibility in Northern Mozambique

Devaka Premawardhana

Recent scholarship on Pentecostalism in the global South gives the impression of a singular trajectory of inexorable growth. In this chapter, I offer a counternarrative, not in denial of the widely reported statistical evidence but in affirmation of the ambivalence with which individuals behind the statistics experience novelty. In so doing, I bring existential insights to bear on such themes as rupture and discontinuity, which already, but inadequately, suffuse studies of Pentecostal conversion. Ethnographic evidence from northern Mozambique suggests that the "backsliding into heathenism" Pentecostal leaders decry is experienced locally as a capacity, a capacity for mobility and mutability, for shifting places and altering identities. The refusal of ordinary men and women to settle has long frustrated government administrators and religious reformers alike. It threatens to bewilder scholars as well unless we learn to think beyond the classificatory schemes outsiders so readily deploy and insiders so assiduously avoid.

* * *

"There is no question that Africa is on the move." So said United States President Barack Obama on a 2013 visit to Cape Town. He was remarking on continent-wide economic gains, gains that promised to eradicate poverty, curtail endemic diseases, and overcome legacies of misrule (Obama

---

Notes for this chapter begin on page 51.

2013). *The Economist* and *Time* magazine have also purveyed this message, both in recent years and both under the headline "Africa Rising."[1] Skeptics point out that Africa's new wealth is far from fairly distributed (Dulani, Mattes, and Logan 2013) but operative for the narrative's proponents and critics alike is the picture of a "traditional" past—marked by stability and continuity—against which a "modern" present introduces rupture and change. Although scholars (e.g., Fabian 1983) have long discredited the conceit of people outside history, versions of this picture persist, and not only in political speeches and media reports.

In this chapter I problematize the antinomy between continuity and change by exploring, on the basis of ethnographic research in northern Mozambique and with reference to existential anthropology, the frequently reported growth of Pentecostal Christianity.[2] I show that a lot can be learned by comparing this seemingly "modern" condition of contemporary Africa with another: the increase of population movements from rural to urban spaces. However, to appreciate what Pentecostal conversions share in common with urban migrations requires turning attention from such graspable entities as churches and cities to the indeterminate individuals who often relate passingly and partially to them. Converts' and migrants' fluid involvements with "modernity" refute teleological assumptions about its inevitability. Moreover, this fluidity has "traditional" roots: indigenous rituals, metaphors, and histories that shape actors by inculcating not conservative dispositions, but dispositions toward change. Thus if it is true that Africa is now on the move, now rising, now rupturing, this is largely because it has never been—nor is it likely to ever be—otherwise.

The "Modernity" of Rupture

Parallel to, if not responsible for, Africa's newfound ascent is what is seen as Africans' increasing mobility. Due to advances in media and transportation technologies, young people in particular decreasingly tether their lives to ancestral lands and customs. "More people than ever before seem to imagine routinely the possibility that they or their children will live and work in places other than where they were born: this is the wellspring of the increased rates of migration at every level of social, national, and global life" (Appadurai 1996: 6). These increased rates of migration, particularly rural to urban, are frequently reported as greater in Africa than anywhere else (cf. Potts 2012: 1–3).

It is not only physical mobility but imaginative mobility—across religious traditions as much as geographical zones—that captures scholars' attention today. There may be no more dominant narrative in the academic study of religion than that of Pentecostalism's "explosion" throughout the global South.[3] Commonly cited statistics (see Johnson 2013) report as many as 600 million Pentecostal and Charismatic Christians worldwide: not bad for a movement that began a little over a century ago. As with urban migration, in the story of Pentecostalism too Africa is often placed in the vanguard. A vast and growing literature (e.g., Meyer 2004; Adogame 2011) attests to its seemingly inexorable spread throughout the continent.

Not only are long-distance migration and Pentecostal conversion assumed to be general conditions characterizing contemporary Africa, they are sometimes paired as complementary expressions of underlying dynamics. No work presents this complementarity more clearly than Charles Piot's *Nostalgia for the Future* (2010). Piot's central thesis is that something dramatic, epoch-defining in fact, has changed quotidian life in West Africa: namely, the end of the Cold War. With the withdrawal of international support for dictators and chiefs, new sovereignties emerged that have spawned, in turn, new temporalities and subjectivities. Two expressions of this transformation are "the rapid spread of charismatic Christianity" and "the desire for exile" (Piot 2010: 17). Both reorient everyday life, turning attention from untoward pasts to indeterminate futures: Pentecostalism by demonizing village-based "tradition," visa lotteries by instilling hopes of escape to foreign lands. These two examples recall Charles Taylor's concept of "the great disembedding" in the history of the West. This is the quintessentially modern "ability to imagine the self outside of a particular context" and it finds expression in two practical concerns: "Should I emigrate? Should I convert to another religion/no religion?" (Taylor 2004: 55). Piot documents that Africans are increasingly asking and affirmatively answering both questions. Africa is evidently undergoing its own "great disembedding," its own entrée into modernity.

What modernity means is of course much contested, yet accompanying most uses of the category is an assumed break with what came before, i.e., the premodern or the traditional (cf. Puett 2006).[4] Among numerous misgivings Harri Englund and James Leach (2000) express toward the "meta-narratives of modernity" driving contemporary anthropology, one is precisely their exaggerated emphasis on rupture. Piot exemplifies this. Although not without gesturing toward continuities across periods, he eventually and unequivocally "wager[s] on rupture," declaring himself "committed to the idea that a threshold has been crossed," that "a seismic shift" and "a watershed greater than any in recent memory" have taken place (Piot 2010: 12–14). Likewise, for Arjun Appadurai, with "modernity at large"—with the widespread viability of disembedding—"the world in which we now live . . . involve[s] a general break with all sorts of pasts" (1996: 3).

Those words are echoed in the title of Birgit Meyer's influential essay, "'Make a Complete Break with the Past': Memory and Postcolonial Modernity in Ghanaian Pentecostal Discourse" (1998). In the case Meyer describes, to break with one's past means to sever ties with kin and to cease ancestral ritual practices. The global reach of this Pentecostal injunction has generated a decade's worth of ethnographic attention to and anthropological theorizing about Christianity. The most sensitive studies (Meyer 1999; Robbins 2004) demonstrate that this break with the past plays out paradoxically: the very process of demonizing and expelling ancestral deities also affirms their reality, presence, and power. Yet Pentecostalism's discourse of disjuncture and ritualization of rupture have led anthropologists of Christianity to retheorize how people relate the new to the old, and to do so programmatically, in terms that help legitimize their new anthropological subfield (Robbins 2003; 2007; Cannell 2006). Joel Robbins has forcefully argued that what blinds anthropology to the Pentecostal project of discontinuity is the discipline's "continuity bias," its view that "culture comes from yesterday, is reproduced today, and shapes tomorrow" (2007: 10). This bias finds expression in the tropes of syncretism, hybridization, and domestication, all of which suggest the new being received necessarily in terms of the old. Pentecostalism and the study of it demand something different. Rather than imposing anthropology's continuity bias on Pentecostals, Robbins uses "Christian models of time" (2007: 10)—evident in apocalyptic eschatologies and exorcism rituals—to dismantle the view that every act merely instantiates an a priori cultural framework. Piot, who draws heavily on Robbins, likewise concludes his book with a trenchant challenge to anthropology's fetishizing of cultural pasts (2010: 169–170).

Although not couching these critiques in the language of existentialism, an affinity suggests itself when Robbins faults anthropology's overly determinative concept of culture for leaving "no explicit room . . . for change and certainly not for radical change" (2007: 10). Change and futurity are key existential concerns. Friedrich Nietzsche's (1968: 479–481) elevation of becoming over being and Martin Heidegger's (1962: 305) view of the existing human as a "Being towards a possibility" express what Michael Jackson and Albert Piette, in their introduction to this volume, call "the surprising malleability and multiplicity of the human subject." Existential anthropologists would therefore not disagree with the claim made within the anthropology of Christianity that received models of cultural continuity woefully neglect novelty and surprise.

In her own study of Pentecostalism, Ruth Marshall offers yet another articulation of this critique (2009: 5–6). Differently from others, however, she does invoke existentialism, describing Pentecostalism's bridge-burning, aspirational qualities in terms of Hannah Arendt's principle of natality (Marshall 2009: 3). For Arendt, the miracle of birth expresses the capacity of all human action to initiate new beginnings, to release the future from bondage to the past (1971: 247). The evidence Marshall draws from Pentecostals in Lagos empirically grounds this existential point. Besides validating actors' own self-designation as "born-again" Christians, her work (like that of other rupture theorists explored here) offers a valuable critique of the social scientific view that people are bound and ultimately reducible to their formative contexts.

Beyond Pentecostal Explosion

Guided by the discontinuity turn in contemporary anthropology, I arrived in Mozambique in 2011 to study how urban migration and Pentecostal conversion correlate in one particular locale. I landed in Lichinga, the fast-growing capital of the northern province of Niassa. There, as many as fifteen branches of the Brazil-based Universal Church of the Kingdom of God (UCKG) had opened in the previous ten years: evidence, indeed, of Pentecostalism's "explosion" throughout the global South. Attending these churches, I regularly heard preachers enjoin worshippers to abandon the complex of persons subsumed under the moniker "tradition": ancestral spirits, ritual healers, and diviners. These must be renounced in favor of the true trinity: God, Jesus Christ, and the Holy Spirit—evidence, here, of the Pentecostal project of discontinuity.

It did not take long, however, before each of my initial observations demanded revision. In the first place, Pentecostalism's growth was far from "explosive." The most graphic illustration of this was written on the cracked, whitewashed wall of a two-story building across from Lichinga's municipal prison. During the time of my fieldwork, the building served as a storage and operations facility for a local non-governmental organization. A banner displaying the organization's Portuguese acronym ADPP (*Ajuda de Desenvolvimento de Povo para Povo*) occupied the top right corner of the exterior wall. However, in faded yellow letters that the banner only partially covered appeared the faintly visible words, "*Jesus Cristo é o Senhor*" (Jesus Christ is the Lord): the slogan affixed to UCKG buildings throughout the world. The narrative of Pentecostalism's boom is commonly expressed in terms of former cinemas, factories, and warehouses turned into churches. Here I encountered the reverse. In talking with UCKG pastors throughout the city, I learned further that this was not an aberration. Of the fifteen UCKG branches that had opened in Lichinga, as many as three had folded; others had moved into smaller buildings. Yes, churches were booming, but here, at least, some were also busting. It is not that Pentecostalism entirely lacked appeal. Indeed, as many pastors explained to me, every time a new congregation opened, masses of people would flood in. But within a few months, most would leave. Curiously, among those who left, many would appear again, but too irregularly to be counted by pastors as among the faithful.[5]

These observations may surprise those familiar with the literature on religion in contemporary Africa; they surprised me when the literature was all I had to go on. There is good reason for that. It has to do with distortions arising out of the way research decisions are made. Most scholars who set out to study Pentecostalism gravitate, understandably, to those places where Pentecostalism is vibrant, where people called (or whom we call) "Pentecostals" are most easily identifiable and readily researchable. This is one of a few occupational hazards that come with identifying oneself as an anthropologist of Christianity or as a scholar of Pentecostalism.[6] Consider the introduction to a volume of studies conducted under the auspices of the well-funded Pentecostal and Charismatic Research Initiative. Project director Donald Miller acknowledges that "statistics are difficult to assess because of the somewhat nebulous character of the renewalist movement" (2013: 9). He nevertheless goes on to cite a plethora of statistics backed up by two appendices, all of which corroborate the book publisher's claim that "Pentecostalism is the fastest growing religious movement in the world." Elsewhere in his introduction, Miller comments on "the privilege of overseeing a large research initiative on global Pentecostalism, which has allowed me to travel to places where one might not expect to see Pentecostal churches, such as Indonesia and Russia" (2013: 4). One wonders, however, whether he set out to visit places where, it happens, "one might not expect to see Pentecostal churches," or set out to visit Pentecostal churches that he knew he would see, and determined (particular parts of) particular countries to travel to on that basis.

The burgeoning anthropology of Christianity subfield likewise bolsters its legitimacy by screening for evidence, and championing the narrative, of Pentecostalism's "explosion." In one review essay the claim is made early on that the recent overcoming of anthropology's historical neglect of Christianity owes to "a tremendous expansion of Christianity in sub-Saharan Africa, Asia, and Oceania." There one finds in particular "Pentecostal and Charismatic groups whose members practice their faith in ways that make their commitments hard to ignore" (Bialecki, Haynes, and Robbins 2008: 1141). My research asks whether we ought not attend to places where Pentecostalism is *not* tremendously expanding, where the presence and practices of Pentecostals are in fact marginal to such popular Euro-American academic concerns as nationalism, neoliberalism, mass media, and the "resurgence of religion" in public life. Even in places where Pentecostals are relatively easy to ignore, would there not be a story worth telling, a story in part about Pentecostalism itself? Such questions are only recently being asked by anthropologists of Christianity (Robbins 2013), yet the fact remains that if one wanted to study Pentecostalism in Mozambique, one would not likely land in Lichinga. In my first weeks of fieldwork I wondered, indeed agonized over, whether I made a wrong choice of field site. I finally decided that there is no good reason this should be the case, for the ethnographic method, as I understood it, entails a commitment to people first and to abstractions like Christianity only insofar as they matter to those people.

Circular Migrations and Reversible Conversions

While noting Pentecostalism's uneven growth in the city of Lichinga, I also recorded stories of ambivalence toward the city itself. A friend named Gildon[7] told me that he needed a decent job to have money but, because examiners for the few available positions demanded bribes, he needed money to get a job. He turned to hawking tomatoes for scant pay in a crowded market, but later came to decide he would rather tend his own crops by returning to his *machamba* (smallholder farm) in his home district. Such a decision to reverse course is, against conventional wisdom, not uncommon in sub-Saharan Africa (Englund 2002; Potts 2010). Its commonality refutes what James Ferguson aptly calls the "myth of permanent urbanization" (1999: 41–43). I decided to track people like Gildon back to their rural homes, and ended up in the Makhuwa belt of southern Niassa province. The particular district to which I moved can require up to five hours of motor vehicle travel from Lichinga (many more during the rainy season when roads turn to mud). It could be considered a frontier society (Kopytoff 1987) given its marginality to centers of economic and political power. Its population density falls below the average for Niassa province, which is already distinguished as, by far, Mozambique's most sparsely populated region.[8] Although seemingly remote, the region has long been visited by global religions. At the time of my fieldwork, Muslim and Christian (Roman Catholic) adherents were present in roughly equal numbers, with nearly everyone also engaging in ancestral observances.

In the mid-1990s, Pentecostalism arrived in this district. Of the denominations present there in 2012, all but one confined their work to the district capital where attendees were almost entirely merchants and government workers from elsewhere in Mozambique. Only the Assemblies of God, African (hereafter AOGA), maintained satellite communities in the outlying villages.[9] These were sparsely and sporadically attended, one counting two married couples as its members, the largest—in a 700-person village called Kaveya—attracting never more than a dozen worshippers on the Sundays I visited. The Pentecostal churches in this region presented not only further counterevidence to the "Pentecostal explosion" narrative; my observations in them (and out of them) also clarified the limits of contemporary anthropology's enchantment with discontinuity. These limits became apparent through sustained participation in the everyday lives of ordinary individuals, individuals such as the young man, Abílio, who held the title of secretary at Kaveya's AOGA congregation.

Not long before my wife and I took up residence in Kaveya village, Abílio began a project, backed by a government loan, to install and operate a diesel-powered grinding mill. This was a tremendous technological import for a part of the world still lacking electricity, running water, and cell phone coverage. Kaveya already had a grinding mill, but Abílio identified a neighboring village ten kilometers away still without one. He moved his family and his project there. Sorghum or maize flour being the basis of *chima*, the pasty porridge that is a dietary staple throughout southeastern Africa, villagers eagerly welcomed the mechanized mills. Abílio counted on this fact to rise above the subsistence-level existence of nearly everyone he has ever known. Soon after installing the mill, Abílio summoned members of his Pentecostal church, back in Kaveya village, to inaugurate it. On an agreed upon day, the church members walked to Abílio's new home, and with the same vigor with which they prayed and sang on Sunday mornings, they blessed the grinding mill, imploring Jesus Christ to keep away all evil spirits who would love to see Abílio's project fail.

Four days later, it failed. The mill liner came undone and Abílio's enterprise for grinding grain ground to a halt. The following day, the village chief showed up at Abílio's compound to inform him that the recently deceased chief, named Mutikiniki, had been displeased. He was unhappy that Abílio arrived on his land and initiated a new project without first making the requisite sacrifices. Without delay, and without trying to conceal it from his fellow Pentecostals, Abílio gathered a different group to reinaugurate the grinding mill. At the *mutholo*-tree shrine in the forest behind his new home, Abílio and local ritual specialists bent low and rubbed sorghum flour between their hands, chanting their petitions to Mutikiniki. They requested from him restoration for the mill, clients for Abílio, and prosperity for the village.

News of this traveled fast, and eventually got to Pastor Simões, the district-level leader of the AOGA and officiating pastor at the church's main congregation in the district capital. He told me he was not terribly surprised, though still upset. After all, one of Abílio's responsibilities as secretary was to report to Pastor Simões when church members stray from the path. Here Abílio was the one straying. The next Sunday, Pastor Simões borrowed the motorcycle of a well-off congregant and journeyed the forty-five kilometers to Kaveya village. After leading the morning service, he called on the adult members to stay into the afternoon for a meeting. There Pastor Simões issued Abílio a reprimand (*repreensão*), an official church punishment that stripped Abílio of his leadership position and barred him from participating in church services. He was instructed to continue attending services but to do so without preaching, dancing, or singing, a severe punishment in a church of such intense and participatory worship (Maxwell 2006: 197–200).

For the next many months, Abílio continued regularly attending church services back in Kaveya, walking the twenty-kilometer round trip with his wife and their small child despite being still under reprimand. During that time, I regularly asked Abílio whether he regrets having broken his church's prohibition against ancestral sacrifice. Noting that the grinding mill is now up and running—possibly because of Mutikiniki summoned from the invisible realm, possibly because of the repairman summoned from town—Abílio answered no. He felt that he needed properly to propitiate the "owners of the land" (*donos da terra*) for his project to take off. Apparently the upward mobility to which he aspired required a certain degree of lateral mobility.[10] He therefore accepted without protest his punishment, conveying to me little sense of wrongdoing, no anguish over what he had done. He seemed almost surprised by my regular inquiries into his inner state. "Oh, Papá," he would say with a wide smile. "This is nothing." I was surprised by his nonchalance, a clear contrast with the moral anguish Robbins (2004) finds his Melanesian informants to experience in their Pentecostal projects of rupture.

Yet Abílio's response did recall something else: the equanimity of people I met throughout southern Niassa who had ventured out to urban centers—Lichinga, Cuamba, Nampula—only to return to their *machambas*. Unlike the Zambian labor migrants in Ferguson's study who went to mine towns with "expectations of modernity," the largely uneducated (in the formal sense) men and women of southern Niassa were not brought up on romantic tales of life in the city or of the professional achievements they could expect after years of schooling. The absence of modernist ideologies shaped the way people like Gildon approached their return to the countryside when life in the city proved unviable: without the sense of betrayal, humiliation, and shattered hopes that Ferguson (1999: 247) notes in his Zambian study. Gildon, in the context of migration, oscillated between the "modern" and the "traditional" as seamlessly as Abílio, in the context of conversion, seemed to.

Against the Singularity of Selfhood

How might anthropology better account for such fissures in the narrative of unidirectional ruptures and irreversible shifts? It turns out that Piot, despite purveying this type of narrative in his most recent work, provides therein an answer. Extending his thesis that both Pentecostal religiosity and long-distance migration independently bespeak discontinuity, Piot notes that the two phenomena even reinforce one another: "Not surprisingly, perhaps, prayer is routinely called on to enhance peoples' [sic] chances in the [visa] lottery. Entire Lomé congregations have even been known to engage in prayer . . . so that members will get visas." Yet, Piot adds, "The lottery fuels not only church attendance but also visits to spirit shrines. One selectee I know hedged his bets and did both, stepping up church attendance while also returning to the village to consult a diviner" (2010: 91). An important methodological shift has taken place from one passage to the next. It is a shift in focus: from ethnography to biography, from the general to the particular, from "entire Lomé congregations" to "one selectee." Although his book centers on wide-scale post–Cold War aspirations to break with such things as villages and spirit shrines, Piot in this brief but telling anecdote reveals what his theoretical model would disqualify: the circular and situational character of both migration and conversion.[11]

A flaw in much scholarly writing is its tendency to eclipse such variations in lived experience with overgeneralized explanatory theories, conceptual schemes, and metanarratives. A limitation of cultural anthropology specifically is its tendency to reduce human behavior, thought, and action to the cultural forces that shape them and the cultural representations that express them. The critique of culturalism—the presumed determinativeness and boundedness of "culture"—was powerfully made decades ago (see, e.g., Abu-Lughod 1991; Gupta and Ferguson 1992). Yet one need look no further than the thriving anthropology of Christianity for evidence that the problem persists. Robbins (2007) contrasts this subfield with the historical anthropology of Jean Comaroff and John Comaroff (1991; 1997). By focusing on the imbrications of Christianity and colonial capitalism in the South African missionary encounter, the Comaroffs fail to consider the content of Christianity in this particular setting, its significance "as a system of meanings with a logic of its own" (Robbins 2007: 7; see also Cannell 2006: 11–12). Yet it is precisely Robbins's systematic, logocentric conception of culture that anthropologists have done well to move beyond. Against "anthropologists today [who] commonly assert that all cultures are made up of bits and pieces of varied origin," Robbins insists on identifying that which uniquely characterizes Pentecostal culture (2010: 161–162). He ultimately settles on a negative definition—"a culture 'against culture'" (159, 161) in the sense that Pentecostalism is predicated on rupture with the past—but insists nonetheless that it is meaningfully spoken of as a whole. In his rejoinder, John Comaroff (2010: 529) argues that by "treat[ing] the faith primarily as culture," Robbins revives an ahistorical and immaterial notion of culture that is better off dead. I could not agree more with Comaroff in this critique (see also Englund 2007: 482; Hann 2007), though I do not endorse the alternative Comaroff and Comaroff offer, one that hypostatizes abstract and anonymous forces of another type, e.g., neoliberalism, commodification, and modernity (Englund and Leach 2000: 228–229).

Against all forms of reduction and abstraction, existential anthropology intervenes by reinserting the individual and refusing to infer lived experience from identities and epochs. Comaroff (2010: 528) would call this a "fetishism of the local" and a failure to deal with theory. Yet a phenomenological turn to lived experience need not imply a denial of either political economy or culture. It is simply a refusal to see the "macro-cosmic forces and determinations in the world" (Comaroff 2010: 528) as so forcefully determinative that people have nothing to do but acquiesce to them. Lila Abu-Lughod's (1991) call for "writing against culture" with "ethnographies of the particular" and Wilfred Cantwell Smith's (1962: 119–153) focus on "religious persons" prior to "religious systems" recognize that the discursive apparatuses of the human sciences can never succeed in erasing humans.

Along with identifying and characterizing "Christian culture," a parallel research priority in the anthropology of Christianity has been that of specifying what it means for such people as Abílio to be a "Christian self." Anthropologists and social theorists alike have long noted the role of Christianity, particularly Protestantism, in individualizing and interiorizing subjectivity (Cannell 2006: 14–22). Among those for whom selfhood is defined relationally, conversion to Christianity entails conversion not only to a religion but to modern notions of autonomous personhood (van der Veer 1996: 9; Bialecki, Haynes, and Robbins 2008: 1147; Keane 2007). An important challenge to existential anthropology arises from this point: if Christianity is what transmits the ideology of individualism, it may be misguided, ethnocentric even, to presume individuality in the people we study.[12] Inquiry can legitimately attend to processes of individualization, but not to individuals.

Yet just as surely as models of unidirectional conversion and migration oversimplify, so too do trajectories of individualization and the typology they assume. Against claims anthropologists once made about the mystical participations of "primitive" people, Godfrey Lienhardt highlights the eccentricities, slips of tongue, and clever calculations at the core of "traditional" African folktales. Without foreclosing relationality, these reveal an "African concern, also, on occasion, with individuals as individuals" (Lienhardt 1985: 143). Conversely, against claims that Pentecostals are autonomous individuals, numerous recent studies show that, postconversion, forms of sociality get newly produced (Coleman 2006; Engelke 2010; Haynes 2012) while others persist from the past (Lindhardt 2010; Daswani 2011). To honor such ambiguities, Simon Coleman recommends that we replace the language of trajectory (from relational to individual selves) with that of negotiation since "the spiritual, moral, and ethical movements involved in such negotiation are not one way and certainly do not seem inevitable" (2011: 244). Rather than reducing subjectivity to one relatively stable modality or another, determined by such "cultures" as African or Pentecostal, existential anthropology similarly calls attention to the variety of ways of being—egocentric *and* sociocentric—that remain available and negotiable whatever the cultural context (Jackson 2012).

By virtue of his leadership role in the church setting where anthropologists of Christianity are wont to find him, Abílio would be classified in scholarly accounts as "a Pentecostal," one among the 600 million constituting Pentecostalism's worldwide "explosion." But what does it mean for someone so eclectic in his religious practices to "be" Pentecostal? Can such labels do justice to individuals like Abílio and the unnamed visa aspirant in Piot's study? Is the behavior of either man emblematic of Pentecostal selfhood or of African selfhood, entirely and at all times autonomous or entirely and at all times relational? Though there may be heuristic value in speaking of a Christian, or modern, ideology of the self, care must be taken not to ontologize ideologies. To the extent they apply, they are best seen as applying episodically, in response to the changing circumstance of a person's life. So many of those whom I came to know over the course of my fieldwork limited their actions to neither a "Pentecostal" nor "traditional" frame, neither an urban nor rural one, neither an individual nor a relational one. Rather, they experimented with and oscillated between the various options available to them. If there is any essence to this kind of selfhood it would be its irreducible multiplicity, its intrinsic mobility. Existentialists have captured this paradox with terms such as the "journeying self" (Natanson 1970) and the "homo viator" (Marcel 1952).

Those among whom I lived might more playfully deploy the metaphor of the polygamous man. He must provide for the well-being of each of his wives and all of their children, a less than enviable role in a society so marked by scarcity. Given matrilocal residence patterns, discharging this responsibility requires that he spend much of his time walking, usually alone and sometimes all day, between the widely dispersed homesteads of his wives. Once, while returning to the district capital after an intensive week in the villages, I happened to cross paths with an acquaintance, a man I knew to have multiple wives. After exchanging greetings I asked whether he was also heading home. He replied with a hearty laugh. "The polygamous man has no home. He lives on the road!"

The Art of Not Being Settled

In both Lichinga and the rural districts, I met numerous migrants and converts engaging the paradigmatic "disembeddings" of modernity without regard for the unilinear teleologies associated with them. There is, besides this, another highly revealing commonality that connects migration and conversion. For in the Makhuwa language[13] as spoken throughout southern Niassa province, the words are virtually interchangeable. One would not know this relying only upon official Makhuwa-Portuguese dictionaries that render *conversão* as *opitikuxa murima*, literally "change of heart" (e.g., Filippi and Frizzi 2005: 1034).[14] Whenever villagers talked with me about changing religious affiliations or practices, they never used that expression. Much more common was the relatively mundane *ohiya ettini ekina, orowa ettini ekina* (literally, "leave one religion, go to another"): *ohiya* ("to leave") and *orowa* ("to go") being ways of designating all geographic dislocations. Conversion, it turns out, is expressed spatially and bodily; it is a migratory movement, as much physical as spiritual. This accords with one ancient Greek word for conversion, *epistrophe*, which connotes turning or returning, in contrast with another, *metanoia*, which suggests something more like rebirth and the transformation of interior attitudes (Hadot 1968).

The spatiality of change is actually a long-standing theme in Makhuwa thought and experience. Consider the myth of Namuli (Macaire 1996: 19–24; Lerma Martinez 2009: 40–43). Mount Namuli, the second tallest of Mozambique, is where all Makhuwa people trace their origins. Their forebears resided atop the mountain until disputes arose that resulted in different groups descending and spreading to surrounding regions. Makhuwa cosmogony, therefore, is a story of migration. Importantly, however, upon death one's spirit returns to and reascends the mountain. As commonly recited in songs and proverbs: "From Namuli we come, to Namuli we return."

Patterns of egress and regress permeate biographical narratives as well. When I asked Abílio to tell me about the times he has migrated in his life, he laughed and said, "I was born on the move." I took this as a metaphor for the many times he has moved, including his latest relocation to a village in need of a grinding mill. But he meant it literally. He was referring to events that have marked the collective memory of the community: their experience as refugees, flushed from their villages by rebel fighters who, during Mozambique's civil war (1976–1992), raided, pillaged, raped, and murdered in rural areas throughout the country (Vines 1991). This is, sadly, just one of the more recent historical circumstances that had many Mozambican peasants on the run (Lubkemann 2008). One could recount numerous state-making projects from precolonial and colonial (Isaacman 1996) to postcolonial times (Bowen 2000; Isaacman and Isaacman 2013): projects to enslave villagers, monitor them, control them, tax them, and conscript them. At least in the Makhuwa belt of Niassa province (Funada-Classen 2012), this long history of outsiders' attempts at control has met less military resistance than simple flight, one among other "weapons of the weak" (Scott 1985).[15]

In *The Art of Not Being Governed*, James Scott (2009) describes at great length this fugitive capacity among upland peasants of southeast Asia. He documents the array of techniques they and other self-governing people deployed against the efforts of states to consolidate them and confiscate their resources: living at a distance from the state center; practicing rotational, rather than fixed-field, agriculture; maintaining pliable social structures prone to fissure and reconstitution. All of these served as strategies of evasion, means of remaining illegible to state power, and they almost perfectly apply to the Makhuwa of Niassa province. They are also an itinerant people who have cultivated practices that facilitate flight in response to a long and continuing history of foreign invaders and their unwanted wars.

It should come as no surprise, then, that it is deep into the bush of this heavily forested region where most families construct their mud-plaster huts, in relative isolation from each other and in extreme isolation from the government's expanding infrastructure. That infrastructure consists mainly of rugged motor roads connecting the district capital to the countryside. Because these roads symbolize the rapidity of development that the contemporary, neoliberal moment prizes, the district government is currently engaged in a campaign to resettle villagers alongside them. Not coincidentally, it is on those roads that Pentecostal churches, even in rural outposts, have appeared.

The people among whom I worked are not averse to these contemporary changes. Whether from the rural district to the provincial capital, or from the forest to the road, many do in fact migrate; and, among those who do, many do in fact convert. However, to the consternation of government agents and Pentecostal evangelists alike, few do either with any sense of permanence. As in the example of Abílio, many who enter the churches continue sacrificing to the spirits; likewise, many who relocate to the main road continue cultivating far from it. Yes, people readily embrace opportunities for rupture, change, and new beginnings; but they do so on their own terms. In the case of the rural resettlement campaign, this is not by replacing their homes in the forest with new ones by the road, but by maintaining two distinct residences, even if many kilometers apart, and circulating between them: rainy seasons far from the road, dry seasons (after harvest) alongside it. This multiplicity of residences offers access to the best of both worlds: the main benefits of the road being schools, water pumps, and vehicular transport to the district hospital; the main benefit of the bush being abundant, fertile land that makes it possible, simply, to eat.

Maintaining one home far from the road also offers a site of refuge in case this resettlement campaign ends up as prior ones did. It is well remembered that after the Portuguese colonial government forced people to move to the roadside, war soon followed. Although that war resulted in Mozambique's birth as a nation, few in rural Niassa reported feeling their lives changed for the better. Following independence, the ruling government, adopting a program of socialist modernization, enforced a policy of compulsory villagization (Bowen 2000: 45–61). Soon after relocating to these communal villages, war again followed. This time it was Mozambique's civil war, a much different war but with a very similar feel for local peasants. It had nothing to do with them except for forcing them to live for over a decade as exiles: continually fleeing from rebel fighters, never able, and never foolish enough, to put down roots.

It is therefore not surprising that, today, most of those constructing second homes alongside the roads do so cautiously. They not only refuse to resettle permanently, they also seem little interested in building what government agents and development workers call *casas amelhoradas* (literally, "improved homes"): modern constructions using sturdy materials like baked bricks and corrugated zinc. Rather, for many, simple mud, bamboo, and thatch constructions known as *pau a pique* (Macaire 1996: 362–365) continue to serve just fine. Of course, such structures easily succumb to the rains, and must be abandoned or refurbished every five years. But that may just be the point. Unlike "modern homes," mud huts are easy to construct; and because the sunk costs of building them are negligible, they are not only quickly built, they are painlessly abandoned: architecture for the fleet-footed.

Although not nomadic pastoralists like other East African populations, the frequency of movement among many I came to know was striking. They seemed to get up and leave with the greatest of ease, most commonly in the case of marriage (and divorce), the depletion of soil fertility, a dispute with a chief, or a sorcery attack. There is a tendency to see those who live so itinerantly the same way we see hunters and gatherers: primitives of a bygone era. However, as Scott (2009: 327) maintains, people who choose nomadism are not a window into how "we" used to be before advancing up the civilizational ladder to agrarian states and then city-states. Rather, they are people who opt for the edges of "civilization" because they know that to be civilized means to be settled, to be settled means to be governed, and to be governed means to lack autonomy, freedom, and (what might be the same thing) mobility.

Dispositions toward Discontinuity

How does all this help us understand the contemporary state of Pentecostalism in northern Mozambique? I frequently asked pastors why it is so hard to retain members, why people like Abílio seem to enter and leave churches with such ease. "The problem," they would almost invariably reply, "is that people here are too rooted [*enraizado*] in tradition." It is a significant claim because if there is one thing that any newcomer to a village learns immediately, it is the importance of roots. Literally. Roots are essential components of the medicines prepared by healers, and root crops—cassava or manioc, especially—are the most common gifts with which strangers are sent off at the end of a visit. They are also a prime nutritional source for people who prize their mobility. Scott (2009: 195–196) describes manioc, yams, and potatoes as the ultimate "escape" crops. Unlike grains, they grow underground, invisible to the eyes of tax collectors;

and they can remain safely there for up to two years, to be dug up piecemeal as needed. They are illegible to state powers, just as the people who grow them aspire to be.

It was in conversation with Paulino, one of my research assistants, that I learned these features of roots. Sensing that Paulino had more to say, I pressed the discussion in a direction I hoped would shed light on the pastors' complaints.

"But what is it that roots us?" I asked. "Do we need to be rooted the way trees and plants do?"

"Of course," he replied without pause, "which is why we also have roots!"

He grabbed his forearm and I looked at him quizzically.

"Here," he said, pointing to his veins. "These are our roots."

In the Makhuwa dialects of Niassa province, while there is a word for veins (*misempha*), these are described as performing the function of roots (*mikakari*). Of course, in the way we tend to speak of roots, veins are decidedly not roots: my veins run through my body, but they do not anchor it to the ground. Yet in another respect, recognized in the Makhuwa metaphor, our veins do exactly what the roots of a plant do. They are the channels through which flow the sources of our vitality: lifeblood for us, soil nutrients for plants.

Continuing his lesson, Paulino said, "Our veins/roots [*mikakari sahu*] make our blood to circulate."

Then, dramatically bounding to his feet: "And that makes *us* to circulate!"

My observation about the new churches in northern Mozambique is not that people do not attend, but that they selectively attend. They move into the new churches, but they also move out, and when situations change and new needs arise they move back in. If they do this because they are too rooted in tradition, it is not in the pastors' sense of roots that fix, but in Paulino's sense of roots that mobilize.

Further suggested by this image is that being committed is not opposed to being fluid. Roots are not opposed to routes; roots *are* routes. The passing and partial pattern of religious participation I observed is often maligned, seen as a kind of backwardness not unlike foraging. It is disparaged as superficial, opportunistic, and inauthentic. A closer look, however, reveals that some people succeed in living eclectically without ceasing to live passionately. Refusing to equate fidelity with exclusivity, they engage with what Janet McIntosh (2009), in her study of Islam among the Giriama, calls polyontologism. Distinct from the overarching coherence presumed in the category of syncretism, polyontologism holds open pluralism and fluidity without discarding the sense of distinct, compartmentalized essences: "Religious plurality is not about reconciling Islam and Giriama Traditionalism into a new, systemic whole, but about drawing on both religions while continuing to mark them as distinct. More than one religion may be used, but they are juxtaposed rather than blended" (McIntosh 2009: 188). The multiplicity of states, identities, or positionalities one might assume in this model is not a simultaneous multiplicity but a serial one, akin to what computer scientists call toggling or multitasking, what linguists call code switching, and what psychologists call cognitive shifts. Entailed is an ability to fluctuate not only between multiple registers, but between periods of flux and periods of stasis (James 1950: 243).

The presence of fixity amidst movement, of roots amidst routes, tells us that credit can in fact be given to the anthropology of Christianity's rupture theory of conversion. As we have already seen, Pentecostal religiosity, with its Manichean worldview, is not well captured by anthropological models of hybridization and localization. It does, in fact, demand discontinuous conversion.[16] Among the Makhuwa, however, none of this is especially new. Various spheres of "traditional" life presume disparate domains and clear borders between them. A great deal of ritual effort is expended on establishing a plethora of distinctions: between men and women, the uninitiated and the initiated, the living and the dead, the village and the bush. Of course, these borders are regularly traversed. At initiation rituals, women mimic men, and men act like boys. At healing and sacrificial rituals, the dead join the living, and the living the dead. Men hunt for meat, women gather firewood, healers search for medicinal roots, and diviners seek out wisdom by regularly venturing out to and back from the bush. These transgressions demonstrate not the absence of borders but their permeability, indeed the way in which well-being is predicated on an interplay between closure and openness, containment and the refusal to be contained.

Pentecostalism plays on this double sense of borders. Preachers warn adherents to stay within the lines, not to "backslide into heathenism." Yet the ritual practices contradict the rhetoric. For while there is a discursive divide between Pentecostalism and everything outside of it, the experiential and embodied dynamics of Charismatic Christianity (Csordas 2012) reinforce more than they contravene the fundamental Makhuwa experience of the fluctuating self, a self whose well-being depends on transformations, and whose transformations often entail transportations. What is notable about the Makhuwa context is not so much the epistemological divide between Pentecostalism on the one hand and indigenous practices and beliefs on the other. What matters is that, despite the distinct domains, people move bidirectionally between them, oscillating as they always have with alacrity, nimbleness, and ease.

"Why do people convert?" This, the most common of analytical concerns, may not be the best question we could be asking. For it assumes that conversion is an anomaly. We generally conceive of religious conversion as the outcome of some calamity, whether personal or social.[17] What my research suggests is that what appears to outsiders as momentous shifts may be experienced by insiders as unexceptional. As Edmund Leach wrote about the effects of merging polities on Kachin self-perception: "It is only the external observer who tends to suppose that [such] shifts ... must be of shattering significance" (1954: 287). Ascribing shattering significance to religious change reveals at least as much about us as it does about those we work with. It bespeaks a bourgeois tendency to locate well-being in secure and stable identities, in tethering ourselves to something firm: brick homes, state centers, religious cultures. Yet might there be other ways to see things? Is it possible that there are people with a higher tolerance for "insecurity" and vulnerability, people for whom movement across borders, engagement with alterity, and exposure to the new are, despite their dangers, preconditions for well-being?

The normalizing of stasis over flux fits the substantive view of reality that we inherit from Plato's directive to fix our gazes on the eternal and the immutable. Since then, the Western intellectual tradition has had a hard time dealing with the phenomenon of change. One of its more recent models, from the philosophy of science, posits the existence of two durable paradigms within each of which "normal science" occurs; the shift from one to another is occasioned by "revolutionary science" (Kuhn 1962). What my project offers is the possibility of paradigms that collapse the distinction between the ordinary and revolutionary, where movements within paradigms are continuous with movements between them. These would be frameworks that facilitate their own piecemeal and experimental revision, that render transformations banal extensions of everyday experience (Unger 2007). In anthropological terms, the cultivated dispositions Pierre Bourdieu (1977) calls the *habitus* may not merely conserve the objective social order. Bourdieu at times gives that impression, coming close to asserting the determinism of social structures (de Certeau 1984: 56–60). Yet even if bodily dispositions more or less perfectly replicate structures, might certain structures have pliability and transformability built into them? Such structures would inculcate not dispositions *in spite of which* a "margin of freedom" (Bourdieu 2000: 234–236) remains, but dispositions toward mobility, dispositions toward discontinuity. In this case, people would embrace an experimental stance toward the world, not against their conditioning but because of it. The consequent collapse of such antinomies as structure and agency, roots and routes, continuity and discontinuity could also reconcile the two Greek words that create what Pierre Hadot (1968: 497) identifies as an internal opposition in the category of conversion. Suggested by the Makhuwa case is that a return to one's origin (*epistrophe*) might in fact be a return to a state of rebirth (*metanoia*); that to convert to one's true self is to convert to convertibility.

Next Moves

The lesson in all of this is that while scholars of Pentecostalism are right to point to discontinuity as a hallmark of Pentecostalism, it would be wrong to consider it uniquely so. The problem is not the foregrounding of radical renewal in and through Pentecostalism. It is the implication that there is something radically new about radical renewal. Pentecostal exceptionalism is another expression of what I have called the occupational hazards that come with identifying oneself as an anthropologist of Christianity. Robbins worries that anthropology's continuity bias, which necessarily excludes a "theory of truly radical cultural change," perpetuates the ethnocentric view of non-Western societies as stagnant. As a corrective, the anthropology of Christianity "recognizes that people really do learn new things and cultures really do change" (Robbins 2003: 231). This concern with novelty is commendable, existential even. But does the capacity to learn anything new require the presence of Pentecostalism or other aspects of "modernity"? Are there not endogenous engagements with alterity that prefigure (and inform) encounters with Christianity, such things as the experiences of migration, models of change, and rituals of transformation discussed in this chapter?[18] The notion that radical change initiates from such contemporary global forces as Pentecostalism may in fact be the ethnocentric position, as specious as journalists' and politicians' celebrations of Africa *now* being on the rise, *now* being on the move.[19]

Perhaps surprisingly, it is Pentecostal theologians who give the lie to Pentecostal exceptionalism. For Wolfgang Vondey (2010) and Nimi Wariboko (2012) in particular, Pentecostalism is but an expression of such existential universals as creativity, freedom, and play. Like Marshall (2009), Wariboko also draws extensively on Arendt's notion of natality, the capacity to begin things anew. However, unlike most social scientists of Pentecostalism, Wariboko refuses to confine natality to any single cultural or religious formation. This is in keeping with Arendt's use of the term; she presents it, after all, in a book titled *The Human Condition*, a point seemingly lost to those who associate "born-again" experiences exclusively with "born-again" Christians. Thus, although anthropologists of Christianity have valuably challenged anthropology's continuity bias and tendency toward culturalism, their assumption of Christian exceptionalism (see Hann 2007) with respect to discontinuity only recapitulates the problem. Despite recasting natality as "the pentecostal principle," Wariboko much better captures the existential point when he writes, "The pentecostal principle predates Pentecostalism and is likely to outlive it" (2012: 4).

I present my research as confirmation of this crucial insight. At least in northern Mozambique, Pentecostalism does less to introduce natality than to reinforce a preexistent capacity for it. With its dances and trances, exorcisms and ecstasies, Pentecostalism restages without displacing the fundamental Makhuwa experience of the self as mobile and mutable. In other words, despite rhetorical claims to the contrary, Pentecostalism is more an extension of than alternative to indigenous ways of being. This conclusion is not a simplistic return to discredited models of hybridization, domestication, and continuity; for what gets continued in this case is precisely the disposition toward *dis*continuity.

Resulting from all this should be a measure of skepticism toward what is surely one of the dominant narratives in the academic study of religion today, that of Pentecostalism's inexorable rise in Africa and elsewhere. The propensity for discontinuous change that contributes to the rise of Pentecostalism can also contribute to its decline. For just as the mobility of Makhuwa-speaking people draws them to the churches and finds reinforcement in the churches, it also facilitates exit *from* the churches. People are predisposed to convert. But once they do so they feel little need to stop.

What implications does this have for the anthropological study of Christianity? The argument I want to advance is that we, as scholars, need to find ways of being as polyontological in our thinking as the people we study are in their living. We need to cultivate a capacity to change directions, engage in multiple worlds, and see borders as bridges rather than walls. In my own work, I am less inclined to identify as an anthropologist of Christianity, a narrow specialization, than as a friend of Abílio, a man on the move. So I close by catching up with him.

In my final weeks of fieldwork, with the sugar-apple trees just coming into bloom, the time came to lift Abílio's reprimand. For the previous four months I saw him every week at church, but always seated silently in the back. This, again, was his punishment for propitiating the ancestors: no singing, no clapping, no preaching. In the AOGA church, the lifting of the reprimand is easily the most celebratory of occasions. It is called the ritual of liberation. That Sunday, for the first time since he came out to issue the reprimand, Pastor Simões, the district pastor, returned to Kaveya village. After his sermon, he called Abílio to the front, placed his hand atop Abílio's head, prayed his typically thunderous prayer, and declared the period of reprimand over. "You are liberated!" he yelled, and I joined the congregation in applause and ululations. Abílio smiled his broad smile and, as the voices of all gathered passed from cacophonic yells to euphoric songs, he grabbed the nearest drum. He pounded away for several minutes, then set the drum aside and ran forward to join the dancers. The intensity and integrity of Abílio's devotion were beyond dispute. Anyone there that day, hearing him praise God at full volume, watching him worship with all his body, would be hard pressed to say there is anything superficial about his faith.

Afterward, I approached the church deacon to learn his thoughts on what had just transpired. We clasped each other's hands and laughed heartily, still uplifted by the joyful mood.

"It looked like our brother was dead, and now he's come back to life!" I said.

"Yeah, yeah, yeah," the deacon replied, too animated to bother dissenting. Then, with the subtlest rephrasing, he corrected me: "He was bound, and now he's free!"

It was an important clarification. Undesired though death is, it is not resisted in northern Mozambique as intensely as it is in Western societies. Death—a passage rather than a cessation—actually conserves mobility, the fundamental property of the Makhuwa self. "From Namuli we come, to Namuli we return." It is therefore not so much that Abílio was dead and now "born again" as he was bound and now free, seated and now dancing, immobile and now mobile. There is a certain irony to the fact that the district pastor came all the way from the capital to officiate at this celebration. For we can know one thing for sure: Abílio, now back on his feet, will move again. What threatens to leave pastors—and scholars—as confounded as they have ever been, is that there is no telling where his next move might take him.

Notes

I thank Michael Jackson and Albert Piette for inviting my contribution to this volume, and Linda van de Kamp, Simon Coleman, and Don Seeman for offering helpful comments. The field research on which this chapter is based was financed primarily by the

Wenner-Gren Foundation for Anthropological Research, and also by Harvard University's Weatherhead Center for International Affairs and Committee on African Studies. Logistical and intellectual support came from the Centro de Investigação Xirima in Niassa, Mozambique, particularly its director Father Giuseppe Frizzi, I.M.C., and also from the Centro de Estudos Africanos of the Eduardo Mondlane University in Maputo, Mozambique.

1. "The Hopeful Continent" 2011; Perry 2012.
2. Pentecostalism is that branch of Christianity whose institutional origins trace back to the early twentieth century and that emphasizes such bodily expressions of piety as speaking in tongues and miraculous healing (Anderson 2004). Ethnographic studies of Pentecostal and other forms of Christianity that engage existential-phenomenological thought are few but growing in number; these include Csordas 1994; Lester 2005; Marshall 2009; Bielo 2011; Luhrmann 2012; Csordas 2012; and Seeman 2014.
3. No less a sociologist than Peter Berger has remarked that, "In all likelihood, Pentecostalism is the fastest-growing movement in history" (2012: 46), while prominent religion scholar Harvey Cox (2009: 197) has noted "the tsunami of Pentecostalism that is sweeping across the non-Western world."
4. Underlying this bifurcation of distinct epochs is a Foucauldian historiography. Concerned that what he calls "continuous histories" lend themselves to teleologies and totalities, Michel Foucault (1972) reconceives the history of science as a series of epistemic ruptures and discontinuities.
5. Ilana van Wyk (2014) has observed similar patterns in the Universal Church of the Kingdom of God elsewhere in southern Africa. She documents how church leaders' active discouragement of bonds of intimacy permits participants to approach the church pragmatically, to move in and out of it with relative ease.
6. In an essay on Christianity in the Senegambia region, Robert Baum similarly points out the distorting effect of research decisions: the belief of "commentators" in the decline of traditional religions has been reinforced by a tendency to study African religions in areas where massive conversion has already taken place" (Baum 1990: 371).
7. This is a pseudonym. To protect anonymity, I have changed the names of most individuals and locations.
8. The most recent census statistics, from 2007, place Niassa's population density at 9.5 people per square kilometer.
9. The AOGA is of Zimbabwean origin, but soon after its founding spread across national borders, particularly into Mozambique (Maxwell 2006).
10. In a similar vein, Linda van de Kamp (2013) describes the upward mobility of certain women in urban Mozambique and their willingness to "travel" across cultural and religious boundaries. Both forms of mobility, she argues, connect to the transnationalism of the Pentecostal churches these women are joining, and help explain those churches' success.
11. It should not surprise that Matthew Engelke's critique of an overly exclusive focus on discontinuity in conversion studies emerges from his detailed portrait of a single man. I share his view that "the array of churches and movements" upon which scholars tend to focus has caused the study of African Christianity to "suffer from a lack of detailed accounts of everyday followers" (2004: 84).
12. Pamela Klassen expresses this critique in her review of James Bielo's *Emerging Evangelicals: Faith Modernity, and the Desire for Authenticity* (2011). Challenging what I consider to be Bielo's valuable incorporation of phenomenological insights into the anthropological study of American evangelicalism, Klassen writes, "Granting autonomy to the people one is studying makes sense, but too much of a theoretical commitment to individual agency could be read as an evangelical Protestant conviction in itself" (2013: 679). For

reasons I will consider shortly, the limiting of individuality to Protestantism strikes me as fundamentally flawed, an example of the type of culturalism that anthropology would be better off without.
13. Makhuwa speakers, the most populous of all of Mozambique's indigenous-language communities, live throughout northern Mozambique's provinces of Niassa, Cabo Delgado, Nampula, and Zambezia. In the so-called Makhuwa belt of Niassa province, linguists have distinguished between many dialects of the Makhuwa language, including Xirima, Metto, Lomwé, and Interior.
14. That conversion here is presented as an internal affair may not be surprising given the authorship of this dictionary, as of many African-language dictionaries, by European missionaries and priests. Throughout northern Mozambique, Roman Catholic clergy have, often with admirable sensitivity, committed years if not decades of their lives to documenting linguistic and ethnographic data of the Makhuwa people.
15. In this respect, the Makhuwa of southern Niassa province may be contrasted with the Makonde of Cabo Delgado province, also in northern Mozambique. The Makonde, well known and respected for their military resistance to Portuguese colonialists, have repeatedly challenged outside aggressors and reformers, framing those challenges in the idiom of countersorcery (West 2005).
16. As argued and amply illustrated in an influential volume on religious change (Stewart and Shaw 1994), anti-syncretism is as viable a mode of religious being as is syncretism.
17. Some scholars of contemporary Christianity have helpfully attended to the ways in which conversion processes can run in reverse, deploying such terms as "deconversion" (Bielo 2011: 28–46), "temporary conversions" (Pelkmans 2009), "disaffiliation" (Gooren 2010), and "post-Pentecostal/Charismatic Christians" (Jacobsen 2011: 56). However, even here, the shift back is presented as definitive and extraordinary rather than situational, unexceptional, and likely to be reversed yet again.
18. Much more detailed explorations of how indigenous models of change inform Christian conversion can be found in Horton 1971; Rutherford 2006; and Vilaça and Wright 2009.
19. It suggests that G. W. F. Hegel (1956: 99) may have been right when he asserted about Africa that, on its own, "it is no historical part of the world; it has no movement or development to exhibit."

References

Abu-Lughod, Lila. 1991. "Writing against Culture." In *Recapturing Anthropology: Working in the Present*, Richard Gabriel Fox (ed.). Santa Fe, NM: School of American Research Press, 137–162.
Adogame, Afe (ed.). 2011. *Who is Afraid of the Holy Ghost? Pentecostalism and Globalization in Africa and Beyond*. Trenton: Africa World Press.
Anderson, Allan. 2004. *An Introduction to Pentecostalism: Global Charismatic Christianity*. Cambridge: Cambridge University Press.
Appadurai, Arjun. 1996. *Modernity at Large: Cultural Dimensions of Globalization*. Minneapolis: University of Minnesota Press.
Arendt, Hannah. 1971. *The Human Condition*. Chicago: University of Chicago Press.
Baum, Robert M. 1990. "The Emergence of a Diola Christianity," *Africa* 60 (3): 370–98.
Berger, Peter L. 2012. "A Friendly Dissent from Pentecostalism," *First Things* (227): 45–50.
Bialecki, Jon, Naomi Haynes, and Joel Robbins. 2008. "The Anthropology of Christianity," *Religion Compass* 2 (6): 1139–1158.

Bielo, James S. 2011. *Emerging Evangelicals: Faith, Modernity, and the Desire for Authenticity.* New York: New York University Press.
Bourdieu, Pierre. 1977. *Outline of a Theory of Practice* (trans. Richard Nice). Cambridge: Cambridge University Press.
———. 2000. *Pascalian Meditations.* Stanford, CA: Stanford University Press.
Bowen, Merle L. 2000. *The State against the Peasantry: Rural Struggles in Colonial and Postcolonial Mozambique.* Charlottesville: University Press of Virginia.
Cannell, Fenella. "Introduction: The Anthropology of Christianity." In *The Anthropology of Christianity*, Fenella Cannell (ed.). Durham, NC: Duke University Press, 1–50.
Coleman, Simon. 2006. "Materializing the Self: Words and Gifts in the Construction of Charismatic Protestant Identity." In *The Anthropology of Christianity*, Fenella Cannell (ed.). Durham, NC: Duke University Press, 163–184.
———. 2011. "Introduction: Negotiating Personhood in African Christianities," *Journal of Religion in Africa* 41 (3): 243–255.
Comaroff, Jean, and John L. Comaroff. 1991. *Of Revelation and Revolution,* vol. 1: *Christianity, Colonialism, and Consciousness in South Africa.* Chicago: University of Chicago Press.
———. 1997. *Of Revelation and Revolution,* vol. 2: *The Dialectics of Modernity on a South African Frontier.* Chicago: University of Chicago Press.
Comaroff, John. 2010. "The End of Anthropology, Again: On the Future of an In/Discipline," *American Anthropologist* 112 (4): 524–538.
Cox, Harvey. 2009. *The Future of Faith.* New York: HarperOne.
Csordas, Thomas J. 1994. *The Sacred Self: A Cultural Phenomenology of Charismatic Healing.* Berkeley: University of California Press.
———. 2012. *Language, Charisma, and Creativity: Ritual Life in the Catholic Charismatic Renewal.* New York: Palgrave Macmillan.
Daswani, Girish. 2011. "(In-)dividual Pentecostals in Ghana," *Journal of Religion in Africa* 41 (3): 256–279.
de Certeau, Michel. 1984. *The Practice of Everyday Life* (trans. Steven Rendall). Berkeley: University of California Press.
Dulani, Boniface, Robert Mattes, and Carolyn Logan. 2013. "After a Decade of Growth in Africa, Little Change in Poverty at the Grassroots." http://www.afrobarometer.org/files/documents/policy_brief/ab_r5_policybriefno1.pdf (accessed 24 December 2013).
Engelke, Matthew. 2004. "Discontinuity and the Discourse of Conversion," *Journal of Religion in Africa* 34 (1/2): 82–109.
———. 2010. "Past Pentecostalism: Notes on Rupture, Realignment, and Everyday Life in Pentecostal and African Independent Churches," *Africa* 80 (2): 177–199.
Englund, Harri. 2002. "The Village in the City, the City in the Village: Migrants in Lilongwe," *Journal of Southern African Studies* 28 (1): 135–152.
———. 2007. "Pentecostalism Beyond Belief: Trust and Democracy in a Malawian Township," *Africa* 77 (4): 477–499.
Englund, Harri, and James Leach. 2000. "Ethnography and the Meta-Narratives of Modernity," *Current Anthropology* 41 (2): 225–248.
Fabian, Johannes. 1983. *Time and the Other: How Anthropology Makes its Object.* New York: Columbia University Press.
Ferguson, James. 1999. *Expectations of Modernity: Myths and Meanings of Urban Life on the Zambian Copperbelt.* Berkeley: University of California Press.
Filippi, M. F., and G. Frizzi. 2005. *Dicionário Xirima-Português e Português-Xirima.* Maúa, Mozambique: Centro de Investigação Xirima.
Foucault, Michel. 1972. *The Archaeology of Knowledge: And the Discourse on Language* (trans. A. M. Sheridan Smith). New York: Pantheon Books.

Funada-Classen, Sayaka. 2012. *Origins of War in Mozambique: A History of Unity and Division*. Somerset West: African Minds.
Gooren, Henri Paul Pierre. 2010. *Religious Conversion and Disaffiliation: Tracing Patterns of Change in Faith Practices*. New York: Palgrave Macmillan.
Gupta, Akhil, and James Ferguson. 1992. "Beyond 'culture': Space, identity, and the politics of difference," *Cultural Anthropology* 7 (1): 6–23.
Hadot, Pierre. 1968. "Conversion," in *Encyclopaedia Universalis*. Paris: Encyclopaedia Universalis France, 979–981.
Hann, Chris. 2007. "The Anthropology of Christianity per se," *European Journal of Sociology* 48 (3): 383–410.
Haynes, Naomi. 2012. "Pentecostalism and the Morality of Money: Prosperity, Inequality, and Religious Sociality on the Zambian Copperbelt," *Journal of the Royal Anthropological Institute* 18 (1): 123–139.
Hegel, Georg Wilhelm Friedrich. 1956. *The Philosophy of History* (trans. J. Sibree). New York: Dover Publications.
Heidegger, Martin. 1962. *Being and Time* (trans. John Macquarrie and Edward Robinson). New York: Harper Perennial Modern Thought.
"The Hopeful Continent: Africa Rising." 2011. *The Economist*. 3 December.
Horton, Robin. 1971. "African Conversion," *Africa* 41 (2): 85–108.
Isaacman, Allen F. 1996. *Cotton is the Mother of Poverty: Peasants, Work, and Rural Struggle in Colonial Mozambique, 1938–1961*. Portsmouth: Heinemann.
Isaacman, Allen F., and Barbara Isaacman. 2013. *Dams, Displacement, and the Delusion of Development: Cahora Bassa and its Legacies in Mozambique, 1965–2007*. Athens: Ohio University Press.
Jackson, Michael. 2012. *Between One and One Another*. Berkeley: University of California Press.
Jacobsen, Douglas G. 2011. *The World's Christians: Who They Are, Where They Are, and How They Got There*. Chichester: Wiley-Blackwell.
James, William. 1950. *The Principles of Psychology*, vol. 1. New York: Dover.
Johnson, Todd. 2013. "Global Pentecostal Demographics." In *Spirit and Power: The Growth and Global Impact of Pentecostalism*, Donald E. Miller, Kimon H. Sargeant, and Richard Flory (eds.). Oxford: Oxford University Press, 319–328.
Keane, Webb. 2007. *Christian Moderns: Freedom and Fetish in the Mission Encounter*. Berkeley: University of California Press.
Klassen, Pamela E. 2013. "Review of *Emerging Evangelicals: Faith, Modernity, and the Desire for Authenticity*, James S. Bielo," *American Anthropologist* 115 (4): 678–679.
Kopytoff, Igor. 1987. *The African Frontier: The Reproduction of Traditional African Societies*. Bloomington: Indiana University Press.
Kuhn, Thomas S. 1962. *The Structure of Scientific Revolutions*. Chicago: University of Chicago Press.
Leach, Edmund. 1954. *Political Systems of Highland Burma: A Study of Kachin Social Structure*. Cambridge, MA: Harvard University Press.
Lerma Martinez, Francisco. 2009. *O Povo Macua e a Sua Cultura*, 3rd ed. Maputo: Paulinas.
Lester, Rebecca J. 2005. *Jesus in Our Wombs: Embodying Modernity in a Mexican Convent*. Berkeley: University of California Press.
Lienhardt, Godfrey. 1985. "Self: Public, Private. Some African Representations." In *The Category of the Person: Anthropology, Philosophy, History*, Michael Carrithers, Steven Collins, and Steven Lukes (eds.). Cambridge: Cambridge University Press, 141–155.
Lindhardt, Martin. 2010. "'If You Are Saved You Cannot Forget Your Parents': Agency, Power, and Social Repositioning in Tanzanian Born-again Christianity," *Journal of Religion in Africa* 40 (3): 240–272.

Lubkemann, Stephen C. 2008. *Culture in Chaos: An Anthropology of the Social Condition in War*. Chicago: University of Chicago Press.
Luhrmann, Tanya. 2012. *When God Talks Back: Understanding the American Evangelical Relationships with God*. New York: Alfred A. Knopf.
Macaire, Pierre. 1996. *L'héritage Makhuwa au Mozambique*. Paris: Harmattan.
Marcel, Gabriel. 2010. *Homo Viator: Introduction to the Metaphysic of Hope* (trans. Emma Crauford and Paul Seaton). South Bend, IN: St. Augustine's Press.
Marshall, Ruth. 2009. *Political Spiritualities: The Pentecostal Revolution in Nigeria*. Chicago: The University of Chicago Press.
Maxwell, David. 2006. *African Gifts of the Spirit: Pentecostalism and the Rise of a Zimbabwean Transnational Religious Movement*. Athens: Ohio University Press / Oxford: James Currey.
McIntosh, Janet. 2009. *The Edge of Islam: Power, Personhood, and Ethnoreligious Boundaries on the Kenya Coast*. Durham, NC: Duke University Press.
Meyer, Birgit. 1998. "'Make a Complete Break with the Past': Memory and Post-colonial Modernity in Ghanaian Pentecostalist Discourse," *Journal of Religion in Africa* 28 (3): 316–349.
———. 1999. *Translating the Devil: Religion and Modernity among the Ewe in Ghana*. Edinburgh: Edinburgh University Press.
———. 2004. "Christianity in Africa: From African Independent to Pentecostal-Charismatic Churches," *Annual Review of Anthropology* 33: 447–474.
Miller, Donald E. 2013. "Introduction: Pentecostalism as a Global Phenomenon." In *Spirit and Power: The Growth and Global Impact of Pentecostalism*, Donald E. Miller, Kimon H. Sargeant, and Richard Flory (eds.). Oxford: Oxford University Press, 1–19.
Natanson, Maurice. 1970. *The Journeying Self: A Study in Philosophy and Social Role*. Reading: Addison-Wesley Pub. Co.
Nietzsche, Friedrich. 1968. "Twilight of the Idols." In *The Portable Nietzsche*. New York: Viking Press, 463–563.
Obama, Barack. 2013. "Remarks by President Obama at the University of Cape Town." http://www.whitehouse.gov/the-press-office/2013/06/30/remarks-president-obama-university-cape-town (accessed 24 December 2013).
Pelkmans, Mathijs. 2009. "Temporary Conversions: Encounters with Pentecostalism in Muslim Kyrgyzstan." In *Conversion after Socialism: Disruptions, Modernisms and Technologies of Faith in the Former Soviet Union*, Mathijs Pelkmans (ed.). Oxford: Berghahn Books, 143–162.
Perry, Alex. 2012. "Africa rising," *Time*, 3 December.
Piot, Charles. 2010. *Nostalgia for the Future: West Africa after the Cold War*. Chicago: University of Chicago Press.
Potts, Deborah. 2010. *Circular Migration in Zimbabwe and Contemporary Sub-saharan Africa*. Oxford: James Currey.
———. 2012. *Whatever Happened to Africa's Rapid Urbanisation?* London: Africa Research Institute.
Puett, Michael. 2006. "Innovation as Ritualization: The Fractured Cosmology of Early China," *Cardozo Law Review* 28 (1): 23–36.
Robbins, Joel. 2003. "On the Paradoxes of Global Pentecostalism and the Perils of Continuity Thinking," *Religion* 33 (3): 221–231.
———. 2004. *Becoming Sinners: Christianity and Moral Torment in a Papua New Guinea Society*. Berkeley: University of California Press.
———. 2007. "Continuity Thinking and the Problem of Christian Culture: Belief, Time, and the Anthropology of Christianity," *Current Anthropology* 48 (1): 5–38.
———. 2010. "Anthropology of Religion." In *Studying Global Pentecostalism: Theories and Methods*, Michael Bergunder et al. (eds.). Berkeley: University of California Press, 156–178.

———. 2013. Interview with Leslie C. Aiello, *The Wenner-Gren Blog*. http://blog.wennergren.org/wp-content/uploads/2013/04/Joel-Robbins-Interview.mp3 (accessed 30 December 2013).

Rutherford, Danilyn. 2006. "The Bible Meets the Idol: Writing and Conversion in Biak, Irian Jaya, Indonesia." In *The Anthropology of Christianity*, Fenella Cannell (ed.). Durham, NC: Duke University Press, 240–272.

Scott, James C. 1985. *Weapons of the Weak: Everyday Forms of Peasant Resistance*. New Haven, CT: Yale University Press.

———. 2009. *The Art of Not Being Governed: An Anarchist History of Upland Southeast Asia*. New Haven, CT: Yale University Press.

Seeman, Don. 2014. "Coffee and the Moral Order: Ethiopian Jews and Pentecostals against Culture." Manuscript submitted for publication.

Smith, Wilfred Cantwell. 1991. *The Meaning and End of Religion*. Minneapolis, MN: Fortress Press.

Stewart, Charles, and Rosalind Shaw (eds.). 1994. *Syncretism/Anti-Syncretism: The Politics of Religious Synthesis*. London: Routledge.

Taylor, Charles. 2004. *Modern Social Imaginaries*. Durham, NC: Duke University Press.

Unger, Roberto Mangabeira. 2007. *The Self Awakened: Pragmatism Unbound*. Cambridge, MA: Harvard University Press.

van de Kamp, Linda. 2013. "South-South Transnational Spaces of Conquest: Afro-Brazilian Pentecostalism, *Feitiçaria* and the Reproductive Domain in Urban Mozambique," *Exchange* 42: 343–365.

van der Veer, Peter. 1996. "Introduction." In *Conversion to Modernities: The Globalization of Christianity*, Peter van der Veer (ed.). New York: Routledge, 1–21.

van Wyk, Ilana. 2014. *The Universal Church of the Kingdom of God in South Africa: A Church of Strangers*. Cambridge: Cambridge University Press.

Vilaça, Aparecida, and Robin Wright (eds.). 2009. *Native Christians: Modes and Effects of Christian Christianity among Indigenous Peoples of the Americas*. Burlington: Ashgate.

Vines, Alex. 1991. *Renamo: Terrorism in Mozambique*. Bloomington: Indiana University Press.

Vondey, Wolfgang. 2010. *Beyond Pentecostalism: The Crisis of Global Christianity and the Renewal of the Theological Agenda*. Grand Rapids, MI: William B. Eerdmans.

Wariboko, Nimi. 2012. *The Pentecostal Principle: Ethical Methodology in New Spirit*. Grand Rapids, MI: William B. Eerdmans.

West, Harry G. 2005. *Kupilikula: Governance and the Invisible Realm in Mozambique*. Chicago: University of Chicago Press.

Chapter Two

Both/And

Michael Lambek

> "Existential anthropology is less a repudiation of any one way of explaining human behavior—academic, scientific, religious, humanist—than a reminder that life is irreducible to the terms with which we seek to grasp it." —Michael Jackson and Albert Piette, "Anthropology and the Existential Turn"

> "All problems pertaining *to* humankind are ultimately problems *for* humankind." —Claude Lévi-Strauss, "Anthropology and the 'Truth Sciences'"

> "Insofar as life's essence goes, transcendence is immanent to it (it is not something that might be added to its being, but instead is constitutive of its being)." —Georg Simmel, "Life as Transcendence," in *The View of Life*

In this chapter I accept the invitation to redescribe my previous work as existential anthropology. Along the path of retrospection an interest in what Michael Jackson and Albert Piette call irreducibility stands out. I have addressed or recognized the issue as one of the incommensurability of traditions (hence their irreducibility to one another) and indeed the incommensurability intrinsic to the relation between any cultural terms, models, practices, or tradition and the world. I described this with respect to the articulation of Islam with spirit possession on the island of Mayo-

---

Notes for this chapter begin on page 80.

tte in the western Indian Ocean and with ancestral practice in northwest Madagascar. If one cannot choose between incommensurables, it is because each is insufficient by itself. Hence it becomes a matter of both/and rather than either/or. I raise the question of whether any single cultural model or tradition could ever be sufficient to address existential concerns and indeed whether an existential anthropology could be, according to its own lights, theoretically sufficient. However, to acknowledge the uncertainty of both/and (that logically encompasses the alternative of either/or) is to take an ironic stance. Insofar as it is associated with Kierkegaard, a position of irony is an existential one.

Ethnographic Introduction

Before Michael Jackson contacted me, I had not thought of my work as existential. I have read too little existential philosophy to make serious claims in this direction and I have not consciously been influenced by what I did read. I am happy to accept what I take to be a compliment, but as with any gift, it remains to be seen how to make it part of one's life.

I take the invitation to participate in this volume as being one to join a conversation with the editors, a form of mutual acknowledgment, in my language; perhaps a reciprocity of being, in theirs (Jackson 2005: xvi). I have to record at the outset my awe at the erudition and eloquence of some of the editors' recent essays, which I read only after having completed a draft of this chapter. Their invitation affords me the opportunity to revisit and redescribe some of my work as existential. What is the difference such a description or redescription makes? What horizons does it expand and conversely, what are its limitations?

One of the lessons of existentialism has been to oppose speaking of human life with respect to essences. There is by now a large literature denouncing essentialisms of various kinds, but it seems to owe its impetus more to Foucault than to Sartre and it does not explicitly complement its anti-essentialist stance with a pro-existentialist one, or its rejection of essences with a positive account of existence. That is to say, it is much clearer about what it opposes than what it advocates. Perhaps one of the goals of an existential anthropology is to fill this gap. But a challenge for existential anthropology is how to build a structure or body of knowledge on its original insights without, as it were, objectifying them. Moreover, existential anthropology cannot ascribe to itself an essence without risk of self-contradiction, or at least paradox. Hence to be viable, I think, existential anthropology must be explicit about its limits and bring such concepts as paradox, irony, and doubt to the fore. This would be an existentialism that takes the unbearable lightness of being (and the ultimate slightness of any explicit system of thought) as seriously as its weight.

With homage to Kierkegaard, I describe my approach to matters of theory as one of both/and. No doubt this resonates with something internal, but it is a lesson learned explicitly through fieldwork. The people whom I first studied in Mayotte juggled three traditions of knowledge that I referred to as Islam, cosmology, and spirit possession.[1] The traditions did not contradict one another and were not mutually exclusive, but nor did they did fit precisely together in the sort of totalizing structure elucidated by influential anthropologists (on both sides of the Channel and both sides of the Atlantic) at the time of my fieldwork. They were incommensurable to one another and articulated in practice according to the particular interest, skill, and circumstances of individuals. I drew on Alfred Schutz's distinctions of focus that he labeled expert, well-informed citizen, and man on the street (1964). The point is that these do not describe distinct roles or stable statuses so much as relationships or modes of attention toward specific bodies of knowledge that people shift among according to a variety of circumstances. The co-presence of the three traditions and the shifts in peoples' relations to them illustrate what Jackson and Piette describe as the fact that life is irreducible to any one set of terms. As the circumstances arise, one adds other sets of terms or shifts perspective as necessary. No one system is able to address completely and consistently the existential questions that Clifford Geertz (1973a) asserted were central to religion. For anthropology the lesson is that we need to recognize that no one system is ever fully complete or fully consistent; there is always something that escapes even the most elegant models.

The neighboring and related people I have encountered in northwest Madagascar enjoy an even more open society than do those in Mayotte, one in which Islam and Christianity rest easily alongside what can be called ancestral practice and no one need be defined as adhering exclusively to one tradition or another. Needless to say, this is a world or perspective that is very different from the expression of the Abrahamic traditions in so many places in the world today (and at times throughout their history), characterized by "fundamentalisms" of one kind or another, the defense of mutually exclusive loyalties and claims, and sometimes sectarian violence. Citizens of northwest Madagascar participate in a fully bilateral kinship world, one in which they can inherit from, and identify with, multiple ascendants from both the father's and mother's side and sometimes receive a specific call from one ancestor or another. This is a matter of identifying simultaneously with *both* sides (hence from ascending generations, with four or eight distinct persons or "kinds of people") rather than exclusively with either one side or the other. Insofar as one ascendant may have been Muslim or Christian and another not, and given widespread exogamy, one can imagine the various ways this can play out in practice. In effect, Malagasy do not become fully and finally identified as exclusively one "kind of person" (*karazan'olo*) until their burial, and even then the identity can be contested and the corpse moved from one place or kind of burial to another (cf. Astuti 1995). I find the tension between both/and and either/or modes of identity, belonging, or practice of central interest for how we exist in the world, and one way to think about its irreducibility.

For reasons or causes that were not preconceived and had little to do with explicit concerns with method or goals, the conduct of my first fieldwork in 1975–1976 turned on close relationships with people who were particularly intelligent and kind, and whom I encountered in a village of Kibushy (Malagasy) speakers on the western Indian Ocean island of Mayotte. The two most important figures for me, Bourha Mwaha and Mamazaza Oramby, a husband and wife, were not only singularly reflective, but they also *lived* their thought in a way that was initially surprising to me, namely by frequently becoming possessed by spirits who acted and spoke through their bodies and in their place—that is, in different and distinctive voices—but were somehow integrated in the totality of their lives. I followed their relationships and their work as they treated other people who were bothered by spirits or about to become possessed by them and I worked also with several other mediums. Drawing upon Paul Ricoeur's and Geertz's analogies of the text, I interpreted performances of spirit possession as articulating or addressing existential concerns rather than merely reflecting them (Lambek 1981).

Although I never wrote about it in quite this way, it seemed also to me that the question of human existence rose to a very high pitch each time a medium reached the threshold of losing consciousness and emerging as someone else, especially when someone entered trance for the very first time. This was a moment of exquisite poignancy and terror, in which the thrownness of being was distilled into an experience of being thrown, headlong, into an unknowable chasm. Who or what would emerge beyond this plunge into darkness? What were the stakes?

That moment or sense of sheer contingency was condensed (for me) in the plangent chords of a boxy homemade guitar (*gabusa*) and the snatches of song that sometimes accompanied and supported the medium and welcomed the spirit, musically carrying and maintaining the transition. They sang in an antiquated language of loneliness, longing, and arrival. *Mila longo, fanahazo*—"seeking/wanting/needing kin, now [you] have them."

This concentration of emptiness and fulfillment was connected (for me) to the human sound and energy sparking bravely in the midst of a very black and silent night, the vastness of the starry sky, the audible sigh of the ocean, and the enormous distance that separated me from home. Intense yearning, the terror and anticipation of letting go, the threshold of no return. (That was in 1975; today the village has lights, paved roads, Internet, electric guitars, and amplifiers. But spirits still return to displace people.)

That letting go—at once so deliberate and yet so passive, immediately transitive and endlessly intransitive, empty and full, lonely and companionable, terrifying and comforting, intense and banal, remote and intimate, anticipated and unforeseeable—condenses extremes of human experience into a moment. It evokes the leap of faith that Kierkegaard kept approaching. To retreat from the experiential brink to the safety of the concept, is to forget, in Michael Jackson's terms (2005: xxix–xxx), the eventfulness of being, "an occasion, a happening, where something vital is at play and at risk, when something memorable or momentous is undergone, and where questions of right and wrongful conduct are felt to be matters of life and death."

But powerful as it is, that moment of "falling," "diving," "or being sucked" into trance fails radically to do justice to spirit possession.[2] People in Mayotte understand it rather as being taken over. Spirit possession is less about becoming no one than being subjected to and emerging as someone else. As my early writing (1981; 1993) tried to clarify, the coherence and meaning of possession are made possible by an underlying structure, a cultural script, code, or grammar. People don't just "happen" to go into trance or become possessed and they do not become possessed by just "anyone." Moreover, once possessed by a given spirit, all kinds of things are possible as the spirit interacts with others and as the spirit becomes a part of the interior life of the host. Hosts are never possessed by only one spirit but always find themselves in relationships with more than one (though never simultaneously in trance with each). The multiple persons and voices alternate with and speak past each other, but also to each other and with reference to each other, adding layers of voice and address. There is a conjunction of action and passion, or agency with patiency. Each event of possession establishes new criteria for constituting and understanding the relations between people and each event makes possible (but not necessary) subsequent ones. In this last respect, possession is hardly different from ordinary life, in which events, understood here, less momentously than the quotation from Jackson implies, as acts of commitment (to a person, relationship, course of action, etc.), form the backbone of ethics (Lambek 2010a). Events of this kind may be as ordinary as the utterance of "good morning" or the failure to do so.

As I began to write up what I had learned about spirit possession—and from it—it seemed to me that what passed for theory about such phenomena was radically insufficient, and part of that insufficiency stemmed from the weight that observers placed on the state of trance or dissociation itself. As Paul Johnson (2011; 2014) has recently noted, early European political philosophers began to speak of spirit mediums as "possessed" in much the way that slaves were and with much the same justification. Functionalist anthropologists did not do a great deal better, albeit moving in the opposite direction and shifting from underplaying moral responsibility to overinstrumentalizing the intentions of the possessed, as though they were all too conscious of their aims and ambitions.[3] I turned instead, slowly, and step by step, to philosophy, or rather to a series of philosophical thinkers (Ricoeur, Gadamer, Austin, Arendt, Cavell) in an effort to speak compellingly about the subject in a manner that would be nonreductive (or as little reductive as I could make it) and yet still address seriously the goals of comparison, analysis, and abstraction that motivate anthropology. I wanted, first, to speak about the resonance, interpretability, and public significance of possession above and beyond the private intentions of its participants, in much the manner that the analysis of literary texts moves well beyond the private motivations of authors. Second, I wanted to explore the links of possession to complex and often contradictory psychological processes of selfhood, identification, conflict, separation, and intimacy. Third, I wanted to describe the process by which the curers themselves drew on their traditions, learned to carry their knowledge with authority, and practiced their art. And fourth, I wanted to deepen my understanding of person, intention, effects, agency, and specific kinds of acts (like naming oneself as a spirit, extracting sorcery from a client's body, uttering a Muslim prayer over someone, or sacrificing to an ancestor), as much to further appreciate possession (or "religion") as to use possession to further think about these concepts. I even published an essay comparing the coming into presence of the spirits with Heidegger's concept of truth as unconcealment (2010c).

Experience

If "the focus of existential anthropology is the paradox of plurality and the ambiguity of intersubjective life" (Jackson 2013: 9), then both spirit position as practiced in Mayotte and my interests in it coincide. Indeed, plurality of voice and ambiguity of intersubjectivity are exactly what possession works with, evokes, explores, and addresses. And I certainly share the "commitment to explore *empirically* the lived experience of actual people in everyday situations" (ibid.). But if life is irreducible to the terms with which we seek to grasp it, it is not reducible to experience or behavior outside of those terms either. As Georg Simmel put it, human life is not only "more-life," in its vitality and continuous transcending of boundaries, but also "more-than-life" in its generation of objectified forms (Levine and Silver 2010: xvi; see also Simmel 2010: 103ff.). We do need to draw on the conceptual apparatuses available to us, both those of the people being studied and the ones developed in the intellectual traditions at home. All along it seemed that to speak about possession purely as experience would be not only impossible (strictly speaking, since I was never possessed and since the possessed do not or cannot speak directly about their own experience; for several reasons it is not an appropriate question to pose). It also appeared to be another way to reduce it, and moreover a singularly false, self-deceptive, and ethnocentric one, since "experience" is so often taken (in the West) uncritically as foundational and a sign (icon, index, and symbol) of authenticity. As Jackson has put it (2005: xxvii), "one must be wary here of a romantic phenomenology that would make direct, sensible experience a metaphor for authenticity." Recourse to "experience" too easily short-circuits culture and the work of interpretation.

"Experience" has been a central term in American thought, especially as a starting point for understanding religion. Indeed, as a conceptual category in the study of religion, "experience" is currently undergoing a revival, being itself "experience near," as it were, to many North American practitioners, to what charismatic Christians say and do, as well as New Agers, transnational Buddhists, and the like. But recourse to "experience" by anthropologists is often philosophically naive, ignoring such matters as the fact that the word is not even directly translatable into a language as close to English as German (Jay 2005). When we speak of experience, are we emphasizing its cumulative quality, as in wisdom (*Erfahrung*), or its immediate quality, as in insight (*Erlebnis*)? More troubling is the way experience (in the sense of *Erlebnis*) is drawn upon as bedrock, linking it to a kind of naturalism or biologism; this is evident in the current wave of interest in "affect." For anthropology perhaps *Erfahrung* is potentially the more interesting concept.

"Experience" (of both kinds) is also conceptually linked to individualism, which is very different from the sort of holism posited by Louis Dumont (2013) as characteristic of "nonmodern" culture. More strongly put, one could ask whether existentialism serves as an ideology corresponding to modernity and hence quite inappropriate for other contexts. Sartre's emphasis on freedom could also be linked precisely to the collapse of a transcendent whole. "Freedom of choice . . . is exercised in a world without wholes, or rather in a world where the assemblages, sets or empirical wholes that are still encountered are deprived of their orientating function or value function" (Dumont 2013: 308). Hence existentialism would be germane only in the absence of God, exactly the starting point for some existentialists. And yet, at the least, questions of human finitude might hold different salience in different kinds of cultural worlds, for example in northwest Madagascar where it is posited that members of the royal clan live on in a kind of sublunary half-life, regularly demonstrated by their manifestations in the bodies of the fully living (Lambek 2002; forthcoming).

Without completely accepting this idealist argument concerning a sharp divide between modernity and what precedes it, whereby "the whole has become a heap" (Dumont 2013: 309), or accepting the picture of stable and hierarchical human existence within holistic worlds, the more general points are first, that existence is not coterminous with experience and hence experience is insufficient to address existence, and second, experience never occurs in thought or practice in a pure unmediated form. Human experience is always shaped by language, culture, historical location, social position, and so forth,[4] as well as by personal conditions of character and personality, not to mention the temporal qualities of consciousness—complex interconnections of memory, anticipation, and immediate foci of attention. Pooling together these diverse factors, one can say that human existence is shaped as much by structure as by contingency or freedom and as much by relatively objective factors as by relatively subjective ones.[5]

Succession, Separation, Anxiety

One question for existential anthropology is how closely to link its insights with those of psychoanalysis. Among the panoply of psychoanalytic approaches, I am attracted, like Jackson, to object relations theory.[6] However, I want to turn here only to the fact of human restlessness, namely that humans seek new horizons and sometimes even to disrupt the happiness they currently experience (Lear 2000). I would link this restlessness to the anxiety of influence, evident in the existential fact that each generation must succeed the previous generation, but also, in a sense, secede from it, forging its own path. Psychoanalysis thus emphasizes the tragic side of what can also be seen as the positive self-transcending qualities of life itself.

Human beings, like all life forms, are characterized by generational succession. Among humans this entails a degree of conscious deliberation but also of unconscious process and conflict. It is a matter of managing simultaneously identification with and separation from the parental generation. And the parental generation has similar conflicts with respect to loving and socializing yet eventually also attaining a distance from the following generation. Necessary for human flourishing, such mutual and ideally slow and nuanced mutual detachment can also entail acts or experiences of rejection and even destruction. At least, this is how it is portrayed in myth, most famously in the Theban cycle, including the story of Oedipus, but also very widespread elsewhere. Similar kinds of events are found, for example, in the accounts of early Sakalava monarchs that form the basis of and inflect contemporary practice in Majunga.[7] At the same time, Malagasy emphasize the good that flows between generations and the importance of respecting and acknowledging ascending generations.

An effect of the collapse of transcendent hierarchy in, or as, "modernity" may be to heighten rather than reduce the saliency of the generational dilemma, making it not simply a psychological and social issue of relatively routine succession but also a necessity of "freedom" to select new ideas and values. The social effects of capitalism and displacement and disruptions caused by war, colonialism, etc., are often such that parents become ineffectual and the connection to powerful but benevolent ancestors is experienced as broken or lost.[8] But whatever the case—societal breakdown or the speedup of change—these matters are always part of the existential condition of human generation. The picture applies in kinship-based systems, such as the Tallensi when Meyer Fortes (1983) observed them. The Oedipally infused search for new horizons plays a significant role in the ebb and flow of social life and is presumably a diffuse motor of history.

In sum, the concerns of existentialism have obvious affinities with those of psychoanalysis. One could say that psychoanalysis has uncovered or clarified certain existential aspects of human being, notably the inevitable tensions between adjacent generations, as people simultaneously respect and identify with and struggle to separate from their parents; the basic human ambivalence characteristic of intersubjectivity, love and hate, intimacy and distance, introjection and projection; the ambiguity of discerning between conscious reason and unconscious force in what moves us to action or inaction; and the basic state of human restlessness, in which the urge to extend beyond what is known, safe, or good, can sometimes lead us to undo the very ideals and positive circumstances we live by. The trick of applying psychoanalytic models or insight is to do so in nonreductive ways, in a manner that recognizes, as existentialism does, that people can often do otherwise than what we expect of them or what they expect of themselves (whether for worse or for better), that existence as potential is always more than can be pinned down or determined by structure. At the same time, psychoanalysis has the virtue of being relatively nonjudgmental, of recognizing that people often cannot help being who they are. Offering the possibility of understanding, and perhaps forgiveness, ideally it also acknowledges the limits of its own therapeutic powers.

Put another way, psychoanalysis recognizes the state of ordinary unhappiness (as Freud contrasted it to neurotic misery). Human existence is not ideal and idealism can sometimes make things worse. The pioneers of the Israeli kibbutzim attempted to do away with the pathologies generated within the nuclear family by getting rid of private property, weakening conjugal and parental bonds, and establishing communal dormitories for children from birth. Today in Israel there is a whole generation of adults who not only left the utopian communities of their parents as soon as they came of age, but also now blame the communal dormitories for the unhappiness and insecurity they experienced in later life. As psychiatrist Eliezer Witztum pithily expresses it, the pioneers attempted to do away with the Oedipus complex only to replace it by separation anxiety (personal communication, Jerusalem, May 2013). It seems you can't win.

Fieldwork

Human restlessness is a manifestation of the fact that existence exceeds the terms in which society places it. That is true for anthropologists no less than their subjects. What we observe and write about others' experience, other worlds, is always filtered through our own existential condition, shaped in the context we call "fieldwork." Fieldwork has its roots in a kind of restlessness but finds its measure in a directed intensity, a heightened awareness and hungry inquisitiveness where every question seems to lead to a dozen more.[9] I remember my first arrival in Mayotte when all was fresh and new—the lush vegetation, the opulent smells, the colorful and noisy bird life. My senses were heightened to all of this in part because I could not yet speak the language and did not know what to say with the few words in my vocabulary. It was easier at first to appreciate nature than culture (all too soon I came to ignore the fact that I was living near a beautiful empty beach). During my first days I participated in an archaeological survey, assisting two colleagues who left for Madagascar soon thereafter. We were walking down a road that led across the interior of the island to a large colonial plantation. The road was empty and silent, a gash of red earth pushing through the heavy aromatic green foliage and tall trees on either side. Eventually there appeared a figure passing us in the other direction, an elderly man dressed in voluminous elegant robes and shielding himself from the sun with a bright red or green parasol—I no longer remember what color. Wherever he came from and wherever he was going, he seemed quite purposeful yet also at ease. He showed no signs of being surprised by the presence of three poorly dressed white people. We exchanged brief greetings and went on our respective ways.

There was an unexpectedness—even audacity—to the appearance and the self-enclosedness of this man, going about his business as if he had just stepped out of a painting or we had fallen down the rabbit hole. In the event, I came to reside in a village of Malagasy speakers where no one could afford to dress as elegantly as this gentleman and where people were suspicious of those who did. No doubt he was from the old Comorian elite, connected to the Swahili world, perhaps claiming the status of *sharifu* (descendant of the Prophet) and dressing appropriate to the status. I don't think I ever again in all my visits to Mayotte saw another person strolling under a parasol. Yet the image of this man, a kind of apparition, came to signify for me a certain horizon—the intrigue of the place, the autonomous progress of local life with its concerns often obscure to me and unconcerned about me, and my chasing after other people's business (could I "walk in their shoes" while moving in a different direction?). How easy it is for fieldworkers to mistake their own experience or concerns for those of the people they encounter.

I cannot speak for other ethnographers, but I am always attracted to what seems exotic or most different, for reasons of romanticism, no doubt, but also simply as a challenge of understanding the real. I have come to think that the progress of the ethnographer as interpreter proceeds along a path atop a steep ridge. To fall down one slope is to exoticize and down the other slope to render another life or world completely mundane and banal. The danger on one side is to exaggerate difference; the danger on the other side is to overlook it and to ethnocentrically reduce the other's world to one's own. Of course, good anthropology must look in both directions, not to mistake deep difference for superficial similarity, but equally, not to mistake deep similarity for superficial difference.

My first book (1981) began with a parable of encounter rather like the man under the parasol, and continued with a different image of walking to describe the work of understanding. Eschewing the metaphors of depth and digging—hence of suspicion and secrecy—I depicted coming to understand "another" culture as being akin to the work of climbing a mountain; when one got to the top one discovered that the view, albeit from a different angle, was not too dissimilar from the view atop one's own mountain. The more schematic a written ethnography, the more it dissolves the hard work of discovery, of working through difference, with its stops and starts and false trails. The activity of the ethnographer has always struck me as being less like that of the archaeologist or the decoder of secret files than that of the (fictional) detective, listening to everyone's stories, filtering the contradictory accounts, following diverse leads, and coming up with a reasonably coherent narrative. But another goal of ethnography, I think, is to discover or expand the recognition of human similarity and to rethink or redescribe evident cultural difference from the newly discovered horizon. In this I differ from Rane Willerslev (Otto and Willerslev 2013: 4–5), who argues that anthropology is comparative, and implies that the aim of comparison is only to demonstrate sharp differences in order to critique dominant theories. I am not walking or looking in the other direction than Willerslev so much as climbing one slope further.

My sense of similarity derives largely from the human, intersubjective experience of fieldwork, striving to converse, coming to know people, and realizing our common understanding. I have already mentioned the intelligence and kindness of my chief interlocutors (on what basis could I recognize this?) and the close bond we were able to form. I do not deceive myself in this and I am sure it is characteristic of many other fieldworkers as well.[10] One thing that struck me was our mutual discernment and diagnosis of unusual or difficult personalities.

Another image from my first year of fieldwork: stepping out of my house in the morning, after a night of heavy rain, the paths slick with mud and the figure of a woman staring at me from the opposite hillside. She was in late middle age, rather portly but with a striking angular face and I had often caught her looking intently at me. She seemed reserved or unfriendly and she was known to have a quick temper around her children and grandchildren. Later I remarked to my mentor and friend Bourha Mwaha that unlike most people this woman still had not gotten over my strangeness. On the contrary, he confided, undoubtedly she was sexually interested in me. Bourha continued that she was well known for having seduced most of the young men in the village. He said all this with a chuckle but otherwise matter-of-factly, offering no value judgment and no advice.

The woman was a second cousin and hence classificatory "sister" of Bourha's. In his revelation, Bourha ignored the cardinal social rule that one should never allude to sex or sexuality in the presence of or with respect to a sibling of the opposite sex. Not only did the confidence signal something about the quality of Bourha's relationship with me, it brought to a climax my growing realization that one of the reasons we got along so well was that we shared a way of understanding people. As I followed Bourha (called by the pseudonym Tumbu in previous work) in his healing practice (Lambek 1993), I observed that alongside his deep knowledge of spirit possession and sorcery extraction that were initially very strange or simply unknown to me, he had an acute psychological sensibility and that his appreciation of other people, their character and motives, was consistently insightful in ways that resonated with my own growing awareness. Transcending cultural difference, certain features of character are widely prevalent and widely recognizable. People who are overly dependent or overly autonomous, aggressive or narcissistic, depressive or envious—these are not all so very different from place to place and I could readily share an appreciation of other people with friends in Mayotte. These features speak, albeit in different vocabulary and with different parsing, to our common humanity and our common weaknesses as individuals.

I have been to Mayotte many times but the longest stay and the most vivid to me was my first. I was young then and the youth of the fieldworker should be taken into greater consideration in understanding the project and outcome of ethnography than we usually do. The age and the *inexperience* of the fieldworker do make a difference. Immature people are asked to carry out a task that requires great maturity, discipline, patience, and sensibility. Young fieldworkers following lab scientists or refugee claimants in urban environments today, and talking to their friends over Skype or on Facebook each evening, may be less displaced or lonely (or lonely in a different way) than people of my generation were, but if the fieldwork is to be worth anything they will have similar adventures along the ridge between the exotic and the mundane, and between recognizing and acknowledging difference and transcending it. Young fieldworkers are inevitably more naïve but also more adaptable and more open than older ones. Fieldwork is itself a part of maturation, and a moral education (Lambek 2012). In that initial year, I lived for the first time without electricity or running water, attended my first wedding and first funeral, saw my first dead body and observed intimate therapeutic consultations and the personal secrets of adults, walked along forest paths at night and traveled in sailing canoes in the daytime to distant Sufi-inspired performances of great beauty and to spirit possession ceremonies of rowdiness and fun. It is all too easy to mistake all this for sheer cultural difference. It is likewise too easy to mistake it for simple personal adventure or romanticism and to overlook its substance.

On the one hand, experience is right there in front of us, in our immediate encounter (*Erlebnis*) with others; but on the other hand, the existential, the *Ding an sich*, is to be grasped only through lengthy journeying (*Erfahrung*), much as a religious sage would say—and religious sages teach that insight can come in both ways, as a flash of enlightenment and as a lesson learned after long travail.

Questions of Ends

Before the question of the means for conducting anthropology is the question of its ends. The evaluation of a tool depends on what we want to use it for. What are we after? Is existential anthropology seeking something particular and unique? Or is it after something general to all forms of anthropological knowledge? Is its goal better (sounder, deeper, more interesting, more original, more comforting, more disruptive, or more potentially transformative) than other approaches? Is the aim of anthropology more generally to add to the encyclopedia of human knowledge about ourselves, to understand and converse with strangers, to become wiser about our common condition, to understand the emergence of modernity or its current impasse, or to speak truth to power?

A cursory look at recent journal issues suggests that much anthropology, at least in North America, has taken as its subject (or mission) the investigation and uncovering of the roots and contemporary expressions of exploitation, oppression, inequality, and resistance, as if these were the central features or conditions of human existence, or have become so. Sometimes this is phrased in an alternate language of subjection and governmentality. Anthropology claims a special expertise and a calling on behalf of the impoverished and marginalized because of its longstanding partisanship with the underrepresented. This is all worthy and no doubt a comfort to those who practice it, if not necessarily of comfort to their subjects. Sometimes it is effective in eliciting change and not just outrage or cynicism. Sometimes it serves the important ethical function of bearing witness and of making its readers aware and uncomfortable. The best of this work either scales up, linking instances of oppression to larger forces that one can call structural or historical, or else scales down, facing us with the experience of particular human beings who are subjects or victims but equally given to hope and reason about their condition. The immediacy of suffering and voice speaks to the mediacy of history and structural violence (i.e., the forces that lie behind the fact that we inhabit worlds "not of our own choosing").

One cannot argue with any of this, and other approaches sometimes appear to be expressions of mere class privilege or self-indulgence. But missing, one sometimes feels, are explorations of the worlds themselves in which people live or lived, in which they "make history" and themselves, and that were once the main subject of ethnography and analysis. Missing too sometimes are the larger scientific, historical, or philosophical questions about human existence that inspired anthropology in the first place. Moreover, it is often left open how to collate the picture of relentless oppression and exploitation with all the good that human beings (including the writers of these articles) do or want to do or wish that they could do. How is it that other well-intentioned people are caught up in projects whose effects run counter to their aims or who fool themselves that the good they accomplish (in making money, governing, asserting national or religious pride) outweighs its bad effects? How is it that the short-term goals that the world currently provides us run counter to long-term goals of sustainability and justice? A related question, evident to readers of the parallel and equally prevalent poststructural discourse, is to understand how arguments concerning subjection articulate with the authors' own strong sense of their individual self and agency. How is it that intellectuals are able to escape their subject positions and what is it that makes one person a critical intellectual and another person a mere subject? And further, are we cynically to consider hopeful people dupes of "neoliberalism" (that hypostatized monster), or conversely are we to bemoan the prevalence of hopelessness, cynicism, and their effects? Are we to read with preference authors who are earnest or authors who are cynical? How is an intellectual now supposed to combine the two?

I exaggerate, I know. But these are real and pressing (existential) questions.

Historical Ontology

I take the existential—like the Marxist, the poststructural, or the interpretive—to be one frame for anthropology, one perspective or transection, but not mutually exclusive to other frames and perspectives. To practice existential anthropology in a pure form would be, I suppose, to get rid of all the conceptual baggage. Any attempt to speak *about* the existential is bound to fall into the conceptual.[11] The only way to catch the existential directly in words is literary. The short story might be the quintessential form; writers like Alice Munro or Anton Chekhov (Narayan 2012) may be our best existential anthropologists (albeit without explicit concerns of cultural difference, range, and variety). In some hands the essay approximates the short story form; here I acknowledge Michael Jackson's capacious literary talents and original experiments with genre, along the lines of the great W. G. Sebald. But where would that leave anthropology as we know it? Do we abandon, as many poststructuralists have done, the compilation of "objective knowledge" that could be passed on from generation to generation in our texts? Do we risk telling the same story over and over?

Insofar as I now rationalize what I have done, describe the path that I have traveled, or look around the clearing in which I find myself, it is only to claim that anthropology ought to engage more deeply with philosophy, and for the mutual benefit of both fields. I do not want to specify which kind of philosophy that ought to be or to immediately express loyalty to only one abstracted version ("phenomenology," "existentialism," "ordinary language") to the exclusion of others. Drawing from my understanding of spirit possession, I prefer to take philosophy as an orchestration of distinctive, singular voices rather than a strict competition among paradigms. Put another way, I choose methodological pluralism (both/and) over mutual exclusion (either/or), though sometimes difficult choices are necessary and, as may be apparent, I do have limits, my rejected or abjected "others" of theory. Speaking more generally and anticipating further argument, a paradox or challenge both for theory and for practical political forms of cohabitation is that both/and pluralism must include (make room for) among its alternatives either/or exclusivism.

I consider anthropology to be located at the intersection of history and philosophy. History, in the sense that it is empirical, contextualist, and materialist, taking account of multiple places and times, of the range of human experience and modes of life, and understanding these as located with respect to time and place, hence changing over time and across space, according to a range of processes, forces, and contingencies, including prominently the political and economic. Philosophy, in the sense of addressing the large questions of human essence and existence, of what is and what can be known and thought, made and done. Anthropologists have become quite good historians (in this broad sense and even in approximating what historians mean by their own craft), but they could ask their questions with more philosophical sophistication than they generally do, taking into account the history of debates within their own tradition. (Only in France would one need to "recover" from philosophy or theory and regain experience [Jackson and Piette, introduction, this volume, drawing on earlier work by Piette]. It has also become a truism that Americans are only too ready to cut and paste the latest French theory.)

To our own philosophical tradition must be added the insights of those we study. Skepticism is not exclusive to the West; conversely, the search for transcendent experience or certainty may be particularly urgent in the west now. Jackson (1982; 2013) has drawn extensively on the wisdom of Kuranko and Warlpiri, working alongside the recognition by anthropologists like Paul Radin (1957), Mary Douglas (1973), or Kai Kresse (2007) of the prevalence of philosophical reflection in all kinds of societies.[12] Conversely, some philosophers have recognized the significance of the ethnographic record and share the anthropological problematic. To describe this intersection of our respective fields I like to evoke the title of philosopher Ian Hacking's 2002 book *historical ontology*.

Within anthropology, ways of asking the big questions fall roughly between two poles or into two camps according to whether the ultimate object of investigation is described as human nature or the human condition. With apologies for reverting to ideal types and to dualism, I suggest that the former camp treats humans (humanity) and human ideas, acts, and products as objects of study, the other camp as a subjects of study (and other persons as fellow subjects), here using the word "subject" not in the poststructuralist sense. The difference is developed in Giambattista Vico (1968) and subsequently German *Wissenschaft*. It has been a recurrent theme within anthropology, and central to our discourse. Indeed, recognition of the difference, or struggling over it, perhaps embracing both poles, is one of the things that characterizes anthropology as a particular tradition of conversation and distinguishes it from neighboring ones. Vico argued (1968) that as humans ourselves we can understand the humanly constituted world ("culture") from the inside whereas we understand the nonhuman ("nature") only from the outside, hence less directly or well. We can recognize what is true (*verum*) only in humanly constructed worlds, not in nature itself.[13] The dominant strain of modern thought has inverted the observation, arguing that the objective truth (*certum*) we learn about the natural world is on firmer ground and superior to the relatively subjective truth we can know about ourselves. Objectivists since Descartes strive for the necessary distance to study humanity scientifically.

At one pole, some objectivist thinkers try to resolve the central questions, as if they could be resolved once and for all, by relying on a concept of "human nature," a set or system of relatively fixed human attributes and forces, human essence as it emerged in evolutionary history. Those who start at the opposite pole, with the frame or central organizing metaphor of the human condition, speak rather of human capacities and limitations, of existence or being-in-the-world. The one focuses on neurons, and genes (and even memes) and what they produce or exclude; the other on consciousness (and hence, too, unconsciousness), intersubjectivity, judgment, experience, wisdom, doubt, insight, and tragedy. The former relates humans to the natural environments of which they are a part, including fellow members of the species and the other species to which they are connected; the latter to the social and meaningful (cultural) worlds they have created or inherited. The former looks for structure and system, cause and effect, and certainty, and adopts the very human terms of "rule" and "law" to apply to the extra-human world; the latter acknowledges incommensurabilities, uncertainties, and aporia as well as the "natural" dependence on the "cultural" to complete the organism (Geertz 1973c). The former is to the latter as theories of determinism or predestination are to theories of freedom. But that is only an analogy and most anthropologists of either camp are sophisticated enough to see that neither account is sufficient, complete, or exclusively correct. Freedom and determinism themselves are not mutually exclusive.

Some people think the two approaches can be brought together within a single consistent and encompassing scheme, model, or theory, but these are invariably the people who begin with nature. I would say that the human nature position is ultimately monist in aspiration (unity of science, consilience, physicalism), while the human condition position is inevitably pluralist, dualist, or dialectical, taking note of difference, conflict, and contradiction, hence suspect of unified theory (Hegel not withstanding). The human nature position at its best is cybernetic, system-discovering, and tidy rather than atomistic. The human condition perspective at its best is historical, pluralist, anti-anti-relativist, philosophically well informed, and elegant rather than chaotic or obscure.

It is possible that some intellectual projects manage to evade or transcend these distinctions, or fall right in the middle of the continuum. Perhaps this is the case for the tradition stemming from Simmel and G. H. Mead through Erving Goffman to ethnomethodology and contemporary conversational analysis (Sidnell 2010) or the phenomenography developed by Piette (n.d.).[14] However, although I cannot claim to have fully thought this through, my inclination remains to consider the two broad perspectives as neither fully consistent, i.e., capable of being integrated into a single unitary system, nor directly opposed and mutually exclusive (either/or). Rather, they are incommensurable to one another, unable to meet fully in all respects, speaking more often and inevitably past each other. They are characterized by distinctive goals and methods and in the end, by recourse to different kinds of truth or different relations to the truth. Hence there needs to be mutual recognition, neither one position attempting to encompass and incorporate the other, nor explicit dismissal of each position by the other. In fact, many scientists do recognize the value of an informed humanism and vice versa and each can serve to critique the excesses of the other and remind them of their limits. This is analogous to the way distinct traditions or cultures can meet, less as radically different and mutually untranslatable than as incommensurable and available for translation, though never perfectly, and hence able to converse while unable to dissolve fully within one another.

Ethics and Irony

More generally, do we opt for worlds, outlooks, or positions that are inclusive (both/and) or those that are exclusive (either/or)? I take this conundrum in describing the relations among models or theories of human life to be characteristic of human existence itself. That is to say, it is a feature of human existence that the resolution between both/and and either/or positions is inconclusive. I wrote an essay on the mind/body problem (1998) arguing that it is irresolvable, that it is intrinsic to human being. If we start from the position of body we see a unity of body and mind, as in the pervasiveness and interconnections of the neurological, cognitive, and hormonal systems or in embodied habitual practice (including possession by spirits), whereas if we start from the position of mind we see an inevitable distinction between mind and body, a feature that is characteristic of most human systems of thought about the subject (including possession by spirits) no less than our daily experience. So while some philosophers think that one must be exclusively either a monist or a dualist, taking an either/or position, I think there is a case to be made for simultaneously embracing both monism and dualism, a both/and argument. Among the evident paradoxes is the fact that the either/or position could be conceived itself as dualist and the both/and position as monist, or better, as nondualist.[15]

The problem or paradox is recursive. Thus, if you are trying to decide whether to accept my both/and model, you could frame the issue in one of two ways: either the both/and model or the either/or model is correct and/or both the both/and and the either/or model are correct. In the end this is an illustration of the principle of hierarchy as elaborated by Louis Dumont, namely that while the two positions remain opposed or continuously return to a state of opposition, one of them is stronger insofar as it encompasses the other. That is to say, the both/and position encompasses both itself and the either/or position, whereas the either/or position, by definition, cannot do so.[16] Its relative simplicity may account for the attraction of the latter.

I take this formal paradox to be not only an intellectual dilemma but also a practical one, which is to say an existential dilemma that is characteristic of political and ethical life. Politically it includes the dilemma of whether freedom of speech is to include the freedom to advocate against it, or whether freedom to express multiple points of view includes the freedom to preach intolerance.

Ethics describes matters of difficult judgment, hence frequently sites of indecision and anxiety, of being faced with having to choose either/or while wanting both/and, or conversely faced with both/and while wanting the simpler alternative of either/or. These problems lie at the heart of ethical life; indeed they are what constitute ethics as ethics. As Roy Rappaport (1999) articulated, one way the dilemma is addressed or averted is through ritual, which cuts through uncertainty and the problem of alternatives by enacting and demonstrating a decisive choice. If you participate in the ritual you have publicly committed to its terms of reference. You are accountable in a specific way. More broadly, every act we undertake or undergo is consequential and we have to live with the consequences. It is ethical to stand by our commitments and acknowledge the consequences; this is what "ethics" entails. But likewise, at times it could be right to add competing commitments or to acknowledge that the first commitment was incorrect and needs to be retracted.[17] In other words, the performance of an act, and especially one whose terms are so clear, public, incontrovertible, and consequential that we call it "ritual," is a matter of either/or (at a minimum, either we perform or undergo the ritual or we do not). But our practice subsequent to the act and lived in the shadow it casts forward is a matter of the continuous exercise of judgment (Lambek 2010a) and could be conceived as both/and (e.g., I am a committed monotheist and I pray to the saints / visit the doctor).

In some ethical systems, notably those deriving from the Abrahamic religions, the emphasis is on either/or in a strong sense such that acts like conversion are irreversible or mutually exclusive. Once you make a commitment (like Abraham to God) or commit an act (at the limit, sacrificing your child) you are accountable for it for the rest of your life and it characterizes who you are such that you cannot also be another kind of person.[18] This produces (or stems from, or is congruent with) what I have called (2013) a forensic concept of the person. It is also akin to the argument through essences described by Sartre (1963): once a thief always a thief. In other ethical systems the weight could be on both/and. Observing the doubling or multiplicity of voice and commitment that Malagasy kinship and spirit possession offer has led me to speak of the mimetic concept of the person, where identities, commitments, and responsibilities are contingent, multiple, alternating, flexible, and partially context dependent. Thus in northwest Madagascar one can be either a Christian or a Muslim and subscribe to ancestral practice with no sense of unease. The focus is on how different commitments take you in different directions and how to balance or move graciously between them rather than sternly along a singular and irreversible path. Phrased this way, these alternatives are ideal types and in fact, both in practice and in ideology, personhood in any society or religious tradition is likely to be constituted through both forensic and mimetic dimensions.

Since our local notions of ethics are so bound to the Abrahamic tradition, either/or, and forensic ideology, it may be necessary to point out the obvious: both/and is not always a matter of having one's cake and eating it too, because it encompasses both having one's cake and not having it, eating it and not eating it. It is both the freedom to do otherwise and the obligation to do what one does. Both/and comprehends both either/or and both/and.

The argument about ethics in practice applies equally to the way we study or think about ethics in theoretical terms. Alasdair MacIntyre (1990) has spoken of three rival versions of moral inquiry. In his view these are incompatible with one another and one must choose between them. By contrast, I have described (2011) how anthropology moves among all of them, recognizing them as incommensurable but drawing on each. Hence, too, when Cheryl Mattingly (2012) lucidly distinguishes between a first-person humanist Aristotelian virtue ethics and a Foucauldian poststructuralist one, she is right to do so—and yet I want to draw from both. Taken alone, either is too extreme, the one granting too much to the singular individual, the other too little. The situation I think is neither one of choosing between theoretical frameworks nor of combining them into a single paradigm, but of recognizing incommensurability. It is a matter of rejecting what could become essentializing ways of drawing upon the insights of strong thinkers like Aristotle or Foucault—or indeed Heidegger or Sartre—and hence of affirming this is what the correct (true!) approach is.

To define what existentialism *is* seems to me to already violate what I take existentialists to say. Jackson and Piette's introduction to this volume is of course anything but the "methodological suspension of theoretical concepts" they advocate. This illustrates what I take to be an inevitable paradox. It is a false idea, a category mistake, to think one can separate concepts from experience. But then one of the inherent features of the human condition is that we do live with certain category mistakes (or shortcuts); we cannot escape them, we cannot help ourselves. Human evolution is one that has not left us an easy fit with our environment or ourselves.

Our minds are not fully commensurate with our world. As Jackson and Piette finely say, "Existential anthropology is less a repudiation of any one way of explaining human behavior—academic, scientific, religious, humanist—than a reminder that life is irreducible to the terms with which we seek to grasp it."

To say that life is irreducible to any set of terms with which we seek to grasp it suggests retaining multiple sets of terms and not to give full loyalty to any one. Hence a lesson of existentialism could be to accept its set of terms only alongside some other incommensurable set or sets of terms, to carry out or be committed to existential anthropology mimetically rather than forensically as it were.

Thinking through spirit possession has also led me to highlight the place of irony in human practice and understanding and to draw on irony to offset strong models of forensic personhood and agency and strong models of both essence/determinism and existence/freedom. Irony, in my sense, is not simply a subversive or irritating mode of speaking but a manner of recognizing and living the human condition. As Kierkegaard (Chamberlain and Rée 2001: 28) puts it, "Just as philosophy begins with doubt, so a truly human life begins with irony."

Irony for me encompasses the recognition of uncertainty and of acknowledging at times that one does not know (what one wants, how to live, even who one is) or recognizing that one has multiple and possibly competing, contradictory, or incommensurable aims and claims, intentions, desires, or commitments.[19] Irony is the recognition, or the condition of recognizing, *both* the necessary either/or quality of life, but where one cannot readily make up one's mind or lacks the full set of criteria to do so rationally and with full assurance, *and* the both/and quality of life—that surpasses the choices we make and comprehends both knowing and not knowing. Irony acknowledges the mimetic dimension of personhood—both being someone and doing something *and* not being that person or doing that act. And further, it entails recognition of being simultaneously both free and determined. One of my essays (2003) is called "Rheumatic irony," after a man whose highly situated experience of rheumatism (which he only suffered at military base) eventually prevented him from following his express wish to be a soldier. Another essay (2010b) is called "How to make up one's mind." Sometimes one has to make up one's mind but at other times virtue or realism lies in not doing so, in acknowledging the impossibility of doing so fully, of being of two (or many) minds. Ethics is the exercise of judgment entailed in navigating this territory. Irony includes the fact that as I sit writing these sentences I am not aware of which thought or sentence will follow next.

Polyonymity

The recognition of the value of multiple voices generated through spirit possession, the centrality of doubt and irony in human experience, the juxtaposition of irony to an ethics of stern and decisive commitment (of which sacrifice is the exemplary case), and the very use of the terms either/or and both/and all appear to put me in the neighborhood of Kierkegaard,[20] said by some historians of the subject to be the founder of the existential tradition in philosophy. Beginning to look around that neighborhood, it seems to be an interesting if uneasy place to inhabit. Kierkegaard's forensic seriousness combined with his mimetic play with genre and voice (more robust, original, risk-taking, and courageous than anything that characterized anthropology's "writing culture" phase) is certainly edifying. He wrote of what he called *polyonymity* and described himself as "a collaborator who has helped the pseudonyms to become authors." (Kierkegaard in Chamberlain and Rée 2001: 280, 283). Into how many voices is "Michael Lambek" distributed? Is he fooling himself; are they not but a single voice, perhaps a voice that is certain only of uncertainty? (To reprise the last sentence of one of my books (1993): "In conclusion, inconclusion.") More charitably: uncertain (skeptical) of certainty.

Perhaps I am an existentialist.

Notes

1. See Lambek 1993. Mayotte is an island in the Comoro Archipelago; a colonial backwater when I first encountered it in 1975, it has recent that has recently become a Département of France. My research in Mayotte and elsewhere has been generously supported by the Social Sciences and Humanities Research Council of Canada, in recent years in the form of a Canada Research Chair. Thanks to Michael Jackson, Albert Piette, and Don Seeman for their responses to earlier drafts.
2. It also fails to do justice to life, which is constituted as much intransitively (states of being) as it is transitively (decisive acts).
3. For an incisive review, see Boddy 1994. Lewis continued to dismiss all approaches other than his own functionalist attempts to view both possession and shamanism "as social rather than specifically cultural phenomena, exploring which social categories of people are most vulnerable to spirits, and what social consequences follow from this. We also examine how the character of possessing spirits relates to the social circumstances of the possessed" (2003: xiii).
4. The classic formulations are Geertz 1973 and Sahlins 1976.
5. Jackson 2005 addresses all this very well.
6. Jackson 2005 has discussed the importance of the Oedipus complex, drawing it out to encompass self-formation more broadly, hence loosely in line with recent trends in psychoanalysis like object relations theory.

7. On the widespread, see, for example, Sahlins 2012; on Sakalava, see Lambek 2002 and 2007.
8. A poignant illustration is Ashforth 2000. *Madumo* illustrates as well how the subject positions of witch and victim of witchcraft can readily become fused.
9. My wife, anthropologist Jacqueline Solway, has said she never feels more alive than in the field.
10. I describe the ethical limits of such relationships in Lambek 2012.
11. Indeed, insofar as the editors themselves are advocating an existential anthropology on theoretical grounds, they are professing rather than actually practicing it. They need to do so in order to be fully part of the conversation that constitutes anthropology.
12. Jackson 1982 and 2013; Radin 1957; Douglas 1973; Kresse 2007.
13. Vico 1968 [1744], as discussed in Rappaport 1999: 19–21 and 295–296. The distinctions are refracted in various ways in the work of Boas, Evans-Pritchard, and Geertz, among others, and especially in the shrill reactions their respective forms of interpretivism have provoked.
14. Piette offers very insightful discussions of Bateson, Goffman, and Simmel in developing his own original observational approach. But this places him toward the "human nature" pole of my opposition; as delineated in this essay, his interest appears to lie neither in culture, nor in what people say, nor yet in the continuity of peoples' lives from situation to situation. Indeed, he writes that his focus is on "the gestures or attitudes that do not have any signification for the individual himself" (n.d.: 31). However Simmel, notably in *The View of Life* (2010 [1918]) and especially in the essay "Life as Transcendence" (2010: 1–17), lies at the "human condition" pole. Other distinctive articulations of explicitly comprehensive or unitary positions by anthropologists include those of Lévi-Strauss, Bloch, and Rappaport, while historical materialism appears to oscillate between more naturalist and more humanist formulations.
15. My thanks to philosopher Kristen Brown Golden (pers. comm.) for the concept of nondualism.
16. Where I differ from Dumont is that his view of encompassment is resolutely structuralist, characterized by holism, a comprehensive and consistent structure of relations, and an ordered hierarchy, whereas I include things that are incommensurable with one another, hence a good deal more open and messier.
17. See Cavell 1976 and 1996 on the tragic consequences, respectively, for Lear and Hippolytus of not doing so.
18. However, different branches of the Abrahamic tradition take different stances on whether and when one can be absolved of sin or when, in legal terms, conviction, confession, and punishment are sufficient to offset or remove guilt.
19. In reaching and explicating this position I have been helped enormously by Nehamas 1998. See also Lear 2011.
20. On the other hand, I am quite unlike Kierkegaard insofar as the problem of faith is not my personal problem.

References

Ashforth, Adam. 2000. *Madumo: A Man Bewitched*. Chicago: University of Chicago Press.
Astuti, Rita. 1995. *People of the Sea: Identity and Descent among the Vezo of Madagascar*. Cambridge: Cambridge University Press.
Boddy, Janice. 1994. "Spirit Possession Revisited: Beyond Instrumentality," *Annual Review of Anthropology* 23: 407–434.

Cavell, Stanley. 1966. *Must We Mean What We Say?* Cambridge: Cambridge University Press.
———. 1996. *A Pitch of Philosophy.* Cambridge, MA: Harvard University Press.
Chamberlain, Jane, and Jonathan Rée. 2001. *The Kierkegaard Reader.* Oxford: Blackwell.
Douglas, Mary. 1973. *Natural Symbols.* London: Barrie & Jenkins.
Dumont, Louis. 2013. [1980] "On Value: The Radcliffe-Brown Lecture in Social Anthropology," reprinted in *Hau: Journal of Ethnographic Theory* 3 (1): 287–315.
Fortes, Meyer. 1983. *Oedipus and Job in West African Religion.* Cambridge: Cambridge University Press.
Geertz, Clifford. 1973a. [1966] "Religion as a Cultural System." In *The Interpretation of Cultures*, Geertz. New York: Basic Books, 87–125.
———. 1973b. *The Interpretation of Cultures.* New York: Basic Books.
———. 1973c [1962]. "The Growth of Culture and the Evolution of Mind." In *The Interpretation of Cultures*, Geertz. New York: Basic Books, 55–83.
Hacking, Ian. 2002. *Historical Ontology.* Cambridge, MA: Harvard University Press.
Jackson, Michael. 1982. *Allegories of the Wilderness: Ethics and Ambiguity in Kuranko Narrative.* Bloomington: Indiana University Press.
———. 2005. "The Struggle for Being." In *Existential Anthropology: Events, Exigencies, and Effects*, Jackson. New York and Oxford: Berghahn Books.
———. 2013. "The Scope of Existential Anthropology." In *Lifeworlds: Essays in Existential Anthropology*, Jackson. Chicago: University of Chicago Press.
Jay, Martin. 2005. *Songs of Experience: Modern American and European Variations on a Universal Theme.* Berkeley: University of California Press.
Johnson, Paul Christopher. 2011. "An Atlantic genealogy of 'spirit possession,'" *Comparative Studies in Society and History* 53 (2): 393–425.
Johnson, Paul Christopher (ed.). 2014. *Spirited Things: The Work of "Possession" in Black Atlantic Religions.* Chicago: University of Chicago Press.
Kresse, Kai. 2007. *Philosophizing in Mombasa.* Edinburgh: Edinburgh University Press.
Lambek, Michael. 1981. *Human Spirits: A Cultural Account of Trance in Mayotte.* Cambridge: Cambridge University Press
———. 1993. *Knowledge and Practice in Mayotte.* Toronto: University of Toronto Press.
———. 1998. "Body and Mind in Mind, Body and Mind in Body: Some Anthropological Interventions in a Long Conversation." In *Bodies and Persons: Comparative Perspectives from Africa and Melanesia*, M. Lambek and Andrew Strathern (eds.). Cambridge: Cambridge University Press, 103–123.
———. 2002. *The Weight of the Past: Living with History in Mahajanga Madagascar.* New York: Palgrave Macmillan.
———. 2003. "Rheumatic irony: Questions of agency and self-deception as refracted through the art of living with spirits." In *Illness and Irony*, Michael Lambek and Paul Antze (eds.). New York: Berghahn Books, 40–59.
———. 2007. "How Do Women Give Birth?" In *Questions of Anthropology*, Rita Astuti, Jonathan Parry, and Charles Stafford (eds.). London: Berg, 197–225.
———. 2009. "Fantasy in Practice: Projection and Introjection, Or the Witch and the Spirit-Medium." In *Beyond Rationalism: Rethinking Magic, Witchcraft and Sorcery*, Bruce Kapferer (ed.). New York: Berghahn Books, 198–214.
———. 2010a. "Towards an Ethics of the Act." In *Ordinary Ethics*, M. Lambek (ed.). New York: Fordham University Press, 39–63.
———. 2010b. "How to make up one's mind: reason, passion, and ethics in spirit possession." In *Models of Mind*, Marlene Goldman and Jill Matus (eds.), special issue of *University of Toronto Quarterly* 79 (2): 720–741.

———. 2010c. "Traveling Spirits: Unconcealment and Undisplacement." In *Traveling Spirits: Migrants, Markets, and Mobilities*, Gertrude Hüwelmeier and Kristine Krause (eds.). London: Routledge, 17–35.

———. 2011. "Anthropology's Ontological Anxiety and the Concept of Tradition," *Anthropologica* 53 (2): 317–322.

———. 2012. "Ethics Out of the Ordinary." In *ASA Sage Handbook of Social Anthropology*, vol. 2, Richard Fardon et al. (eds.). London: Sage, 141–152.

———. 2013. "The Continuous and Discontinuous Person: Two Dimensions of Ethical Life," *JRAI* 19: 837–858.

———. Forthcoming. "After Life." In *An Anthropology of Living and Dying in the Contemporary World*, Veena Das and Clara Han (eds.). Berkeley: University of California Press.

Lear, Jonathan. 2000. *Happiness, Death, and the Remainder of Life*. Cambridge, MA: Harvard University Press.

———. 2011. *A Case for Irony*. Cambridge, MA: Harvard University Press.

Levine, Donald, and Daniel Silver. 2010. "Introduction." *The View of Life*, Georg Simmel. Chicago: University of Chicago Press, ix–xxxii.

Lévi-Strauss, Claude. 2013. "Anthropology and the 'Truth Sciences.'" *Hau: Journal of Ethnographic Theory* 3 (1): 241–248.

Lewis, I. M. 2003. *Ecstatic Religion*, preface to the 3rd ed. New York: Routledge.

MacIntyre, Alasdair. 1990. *Three Rival Versions of Moral Enquiry*. Notre Dame, IN: University of Notre Dame Press.

Mattingly, Cheryl. 2012. "Two Virtue Ethics and the Anthropology of Morality," *Anthropological Theory* 12 (2): 161–184.

Narayan, Kirin. 2012. *Alive in the Writing: Crafting Ethnography in the Company of Chekhov*. Chicago: University of Chicago Press.

Nehamas, Alexander. 1998. *The Art of Living*. Berkeley: University of California Press.

Otto, Ton, and Rane Willerslev, 2013. "Introduction: 'Value *as* theory': Comparison, cultural critique, and guerilla ethnographic theory," *Hau: Journal of Ethnographic Theory* 3 (1): 1–20.

Piette, Albert. N.d. "Phenomenography of Details: What Is Anthropology?" http://www.academia.edu/2086786/Phenomenography_of_Details_What_is_Anthropology_.

Radin, Paul. 1957. *Primitive Man as Philosopher*. New York: Dover.

Rappaport, Roy. 1999. *Ritual and Religion in the Making of Humanity*. Cambridge: Cambridge University Press.

Sahlins, Marshall. 1976. *Culture and Practical Reason*. Chicago: University of Chicago Press.

———. 2012. "Alterity and Autochthony: Austronesian Cosmographies of the Marvelous," *Hau: Journal of Ethnographic Theory* 2 (1): 131–160.

Sartre, Jean-Paul. 1963. *Saint Genet*. New York: New American Library.

Schutz, Alfred. 1964. "The Well-Informed Citizen." In *Alfred Schutz, Collected Papers*, vol. 2, *Studies in Social Theory*, Arvid Brodersen (ed.). The Hague: Martinus Nijhoff, 120–134.

Sidnell, Jack. 2010. *Conversational Analysis*. Boston: Wiley-Blackwell.

Simmel, Georg. 2010. [1918] *The View of Life*. Chicago: University of Chicago Press.

Vico, Giambattista. 1968. [1744] *The New Science* (trans. T. Bergin and M. Fisch). Ithaca, NY: Cornell University Press.

Chapter Three

Reading Bruno Latour in Bahia
Or, How to Approach The "Great, Blooming, Buzzing Confusion" of Life and Being Without Going Mad

Mattijs van de Port

Much of my anthropology ponders the existential given that the world does not comply with our narrations of it. Life-as-lived is always in excess of life-as-imagined. And thus, we wake up one day to find that the world is not the place we took it to be, to find the sign-posted paths toward the future crossed, or to find a different pair of eyes staring back at us when we look in the mirror. Existential anthropology, in my understanding, is not the description of the stories people live by (as exemplified in what was once called symbolic anthropology), nor is it the description of being (as exemplified in the current attempts to design a "posthuman" perspective, which no longer privileges the human species). It is the description of the tensions—both horrific and pleasurable—that the gap between life and its cultural representations generates, and the imaginative and performative work to which these tensions give rise.

This chapter, based on fieldwork in Bahia, Brazil, exemplifies and explores this leitmotif. Using examples as different as spirit possession, lovemaking, and the act of reading Bruno Latour, it discusses modes of accessing radical otherness, the knowledge practices whereby people reach beyond common understandings as to what constitutes reality, so as to encounter a greater, more all-encompassing Real. Troubled by my own frightening recollections of such borderline adventures, I ask how my Bahian friends manage to cross the limits without going mad. They reveal

Notes for this chapter begin on page 101.

to me that "opening up to all of the world" is never as total as it sounds, and always already implies forms of closure. Indeed, we are all engaged in a nonstop performance of balancing acts, which seek to calibrate the dangers and pleasures of encountering the-rest-of-what-is. This renewed awareness of the pivotal role of boundary work in human world-making leads to a critical reflection on tendencies in current anthropology to privilege tropes of openness over tropes of closure.

Introduction

It happened almost twenty years ago, on the shadowy side of the Rua Aurea, not too far from the Terreiro do Paço, in the Portuguese capital Lisbon. A panic attack. I do not remember anything in particular that triggered it, but I vividly recall the accelerated heartbeats, the dizziness, the profuse sweating and the fear that engulfed me. An intense, all-consuming fear, but of what I did not know. I leaned against a dark grey wall to recover from the dizziness, then stumbled into a shop—the first door within reach, which gave access to a stationery store. I bought a box of color pencils.

In the days after the attack I was in the grip of the thought that I might go mad. "What had happened to me? Am I going mad?" I kept asking myself, only to tell myself, "no, of course not, don't be an idiot." Yet another inner voice would undermine such attempts to calm myself by saying, "well, that's exactly what other people who *did* go mad were telling themselves. But people *do* go mad, you know. Madness is of this world!"

It took a day or two for this second voice to quiet down. In a way, however, this all-too-lucid insight that "madness is of this world" has stayed with me. So when my dear friend David, who never really stopped being a hippy from the Height-Ashbury in San Francisco, insisted that one day we should go on an LSD trip—"That is exactly the kind of mind-expanding experience you keep writing about!" he keeps saying—I appreciated the gesture but told him, "no thank you." Or when Pai Luis, the Candomblé priest who consulted the cowry-shell oracle to divine my guardian spirit, told me that my Oxóssi "would never descend from his throne" to take possession of me, I was quite relieved, no matter how pityingly the priest looked at me for my having to miss out on such a marvelous experience.

Now, you may think that I am opening up to you by putting my recollections of this frightening, and somewhat embarrassing episode of a psychic breakdown on paper. But believe me, I am not opening up. Not really. For the act of writing is to invent forms for experiences that in and of themselves are ill-containable, boundless, fluid, formless, always in excess of the words we use to pin them down. The act of writing is to create frames: word-frames, sentence-frames, paragraph-frames, chapter-frames, book-frames. It is to punctuate the flow of being with full stops. The act of writing, I would say, is an act of closure.

Letting the World In, Shutting the World Out

Last summer I was in Salvador da Bahia, Brazil, doing research for a film[1] on the many ritual practices to "close" the body that I had encountered in that setting. I interviewed friends and acquaintances about the use of protective amulets and talismans, the taking of ritual herbal baths, but also such mundane acts as the donning of sunglasses or headphones, or the buttoning up of one's shirt all the way up to the collar. Such ongoing activities to close the body—*fechar o corpo*, as Bahians say—reveal an understanding of bodies as being both permeable and vulnerable. As I will elaborate below, my interlocutors were highly ambivalent as to how to evaluate this given. On the one hand, they considered an open body to be a prerequisite to establish a more intense and fulfilling engagement with the world. On the other hand, they recognized that there is a limit to how much openness a human being can handle. And thus they sought to harness their bodies against malevolent spirits and energies; protect it from the gaze of others; seal it off from the influences of bad luck and misfortune, not to mention bacteria or lethal viruses.

My intrigue with this never-ending concern of finding the right balance between opening and closing the body—between "letting the world in" or "shutting the world out"—is grounded in an observation that, over the years, has become the leitmotif of my anthropology: the stories we live by, and on which we so depend to make communicable our sense of ourselves and the world, fail to capture the experience of our selves and the world in its entirety.[2] As Slavoj Žižek famously argued, getting to know the world discursively is a process "which mortifies, drains off, empties, carves the fullness of the Real of the living body" (1989: 169), and we are forever haunted by "the remainder, leftover, scraps of this process of symbolization" (ibid.). I call this inerasable, menacing remnant of our reality definitions the-rest-of-what-is. *Fechar o corpo* is an attempt to keep the-rest-of-what-is at bay. So is the act of writing. Or, for that matter, the buying of a box of color pencils after a panic attack. For when this reality-surplus threatens to mess up received understandings as to what is of this world and what not, we have no other option but to fortify the boundaries of the normal, and thereby keep our world and our selves from disintegrating.

Whereas Lacanian thinkers such as Žižek tend to stress the traumatic aspects of the-rest-of-what-is—its maddening threat to the daydreams we call normality—mystically inclined truth-seekers make another assessment of it. They court this realm beyond the horizons of the known, hoping that an ecstatic encounter with what William James once called the "great, blooming, buzzing confusion" (2007: 488)[3] will bring mind-expanding revelations about life and being.[4] And that is indeed what I see many of my Bahian friends doing: in the possession ceremonies of the Afro-Brazilian religion Candomblé, in the ecstasies of the Bahian carnival, or in the raptures of their lovemaking, they open themselves up to that which is Other, intuiting that it is by moving beyond the horizons of their imagination that they will enrich their experience of being.[5]

In the film project I was working on that summer, I sought to evoke my Bahian friends' desire and fear for a reality that is larger then the one they know. However, as things go in contemporary academic lives, I could not use my summer break to fully focus on the research for the film. There was other work to be done, as I had committed myself to the organization of a special issue on the reception of the work of Bruno Latour in anthropology. So in between my filming activities I had to proofread incoming contributions, (re)read some of Latour's work, and ponder his radical revisions of what a science of the social might entail. The situation made for the occurrence of an exciting dialectic between mystical and scientific modes of inquiry—knowledge practices that are usually rigidly kept apart. With the comments and observations of my Bahian friends still echoing in my head, I couldn't help but notice just how much Latour's work is permeated with metaphors of opening and closing. In his thinking and writing, he seeks to open the body of thought underlying conventional research procedures, so as to keep the "great, blooming, buzzing confusion" of life and being in full view. And indeed, if mystical modes of knowing are characterized by what one author has called "an unrelenting resistance to procedures that ground the Real in stable or discrete conceptual or experimental objects" (Brammer 1992: 29), then Bruno Latour certainly qualifies for the label.

Unsurprisingly, I soon found the lines between my two projects blurring. Bruno Latour's instructions on how to go about grasping the real of life and being began to speak to my interlocutors' ways of expanding their knowledge, and vice versa. And yet, for all of the intriguing and unexpected similarities, reading Latour in Bahia also taught me that there is a huge contrast between Latour's rigorous ways of opening up to the-rest-of-what-is, and those of my interlocutors. This contrast, I will argue below, does not so much concern the *propositions* as to what it takes to know the really real. It concerns—if I can put it this way—the *"doing"* of this knowing. In the case of my Bahian friends, opening up to the rest-of-what-is occurs in a wide variety of practices that seek to manipulate the boundaries of the body, so producing extraordinary forms of consciousness. In the case of Latour, an awareness of the-rest-of-what-is follows from a different, but no-less-embodied and -experiential practice: the act of reading an academic text. The task I will set myself to accomplish in this essay is to discuss the contrast between these different modes of knowing, and ponder its implications for anthropological research.

The Pleasures and Dangers of Porous Bodies

Bahians tell each other—and their anthropologists—that an open body brings some of the best one can experience in life, and some of the worst. In the thoroughly religious society that is Bahia, it is an open, welcoming body that allows for intimate encounters with divine beings. In Candomblé initiation rituals, for instance, the body of the initiate is quite literally opened by cutting the skin with razorblades: incisions are made in the body and on top of the shaven head of the initiate to give the spirit full access to the body of its devotee. Spirit-possession ceremonies spectacularize this openness in theatrical ways: dressed in transparent, lace fabrics, as if to highlight the permeability of the boundary between themselves and the world, the initiates flaunt their capacity to receive *orixás*, *caboclos*, and *exus*[6] into their bodies. The actual moment of the arrival of the spirits also underscores the porosity of the initiates' bodies: in what often comes across as a dramatic struggle between spirit and self, the initiates clench their fists, and their faces get contorted as they close their lips tight, and squeeze their eyes shut. Some make a gesture of covering their ears, at which point the priest who is leading the ceremony usually comes running toward them to shake the silver rattle close to their heads. The piercing, metallic sound suffices to break what was left of the mediums' resistance to the arrival of the spirit. Once the spirits are incorporated, yet another striking performance of the permeability of the body may be witnessed: bystanders typically hold out their spread hands when approached by one of the dancing mediums, a gesture that turns their body into an "antenna," ready to receive *axé*, the life-giving energy the spirits emit.

When I asked a friend, who is in the initiation process, whether he felt it was scary to open his body so as to become possessed by something other, he smiled at the suggestion. "No way!" he sighed, "I think that it is the most wonderful thing in the world . . . really, to have the orixá inside your body . . . that is fantastic!"

The celebration of an open, porous body is certainly not exclusive to Candomblé and other Afro-Brazilian religions. Salvador's many baroque churches, for instance, are full with statues of bleedings saints, offering their open wounds up for contemplation, or insistently holding their stigmata out to you. And whereas Charismatic Catholics and Pentecostals are keen to avoid a vocabulary of "possession" (which they associate with the demoniacal), they in fact seek a very similar, bodily intimacy with the Holy Spirit. Stretching their arms toward the heavens, and singing such hymns as *"venha ser o fogo dentro de mim"* (come be the fire inside of me), *"vem fluir dentro de mim, santidade, santidade"* (come streaming inside of me, holiness, holiness), *"o meu corpo es a morada tua"* (my body is your dwelling), they too turn their bodies into receptacles for divine presence.[7]

Beyond explicitly religious settings, it is an open body that is capable of taking in the beauties of the world. Body language is again revealing. When facing the wide blue expanses of the Atlantic Ocean, looking up the towering heights of Salvador's Baroque churches, or listening to some moving ballad performed on a stage, people typically spread their arms as if to open their chests and let beauty "in." My friend Adriana gave me another striking example of the way she keeps her body open to the beauty of the world. When I asked her whether or not she was in the habit of using headphones, she answered: "I use them rarely. I like to be connected to the sounds of places, of people. You know, I even like to close my ears [presses her fingers against her ears] to then open them again, so as to be more aware of these sounds. Sometimes I go out on the veranda to do that. That is such a special moment! You hear the sound of insects, of birds, of the leaves, of the wind. And also of the city, you know. The honking of the cars. The people. I think that sounds reveal a lot about places, about my city. So I use my headphones very little."

Last but not least, it is an open body that allows for intimacy with one's lover. "Your presence enters through the seven holes in my head," is how singer Caetano Veloso puts it in a famous love song, which in Portuguese sounds a lot better, and when Caetano sings it even more. Interestingly, these seven "holes" are as much entrances to the body's interior as they are exit gates to all-of-the-world—which drastically modifies the notion of intimacy. For if the intimacy of lovers is conventionally thought of as the couple withdrawing into some secluded space, shutting out the rest of the world, in Caetano's love song[8] it is quite the opposite:

Entra pelos sete buracos da minha cabeça,	It enters through the seven holes in my head,
a tua presença	your presence
Pelos olhos, boca, narinas e orelhas,	Through eyes, mouth, nostrils, and ears,
a tua presença	your presence
Paralisa meu momento em que tudo começa,	Calls the moment in which everything begins to a halt
a tua presença	your presence
Desintegra e atualiza a minha presença,	Disintegrates and actualizes my presence
a tua presença	your presence
Envolve meu tronco, meus braços e minhas pernas,	Wraps my torso, my arms and legs
a tua presença	your presence
É branca verde, vermelha azul e amarela,	Is white-green, red-blue, and yellow,
a tua presença	your presence
É negra, negra, negra	Is black, black, black
Negra, negra, negra	Black, black, black
Negra, negra, negra,	Black, black, black
a tua presença	your presence
Transborda pelas portas e pelas janelas,	Flows out of doors and windows,
a tua presença	your presence
Silencia os automóveis e as motocicletas,	Silences the cars and motorcycles
a tua presença	your presence
Se espalha no campo derrubando as cercas,	Spreads out over the fields, tearing down the fences
a tua presença	your presence
É tudo que se come, tudo que se reza,	Is all that one eats, all that one prays,
a tua presença	your presence

For all of their appreciation of a body that is able to open itself up to (or even merge with) the world, my interlocutors also made it clear to me that this permeable, receptive body is a vulnerable body; and in need of constant protection. It is accessible to demons, to the danger of witchcraft, or to the harm that the evil eye and other bad energies may inflict.

In Candomblé circles, where openness to otherness is cultivated in the form of possession, stories abound about people having gone mad, or committing suicide, for having failed to protect themselves adequately.

Marcelo explained that to be able to open yourself and receive the orixás you have to close your body in all kinds of ways. You cannot eat certain things, you cannot drink or smoke at certain moments, you cannot make love: "Anyone in Candomblé has this obligation to purify the body, to close the body. You only leave the body open when you are inside the temple, and there are even rituals in the temple where you have to be closed. There are works you have to do for the *eguns*, which are the spirits of the dead that require you to be closed. We have various clothing items, which signify that the body is closed. They really close it, you know, they tie it."

In love lives, one's openness to the other easily brings pain and despair, urging one to close one's body, or "lift the shield" (*levantar o escudo*), as some Bahians would say. "Don't you try to mess with me," it says in a love song by singer Maria Bethânia,[9] "for I do not walk alone." And then, to the thundering sound of the drums, she enumerates the whole army of spiritual and imaginary beings she has gathered around her to harness her self against the pain a lover has been capable to inflict on her. Among them Zumbi, the legendary runaway slave hero; several orixás, especially those known to be warriors; Jesus, Mary, and Joseph; the hands of the *benzadeiras* that healed her body; and the indigenous shamans called *pajés*—a powerful crowd indeed. Yet the way Bethânia invokes these bodyguards in her song, with a voice that alternates between expressing utter frailty and a boastful overestimation of self, testifies to the impossibility of her attempt to "close her heart and throw away the key."

Urges to protect oneself by closing the body find expression in a rich repertoire of practices. People wear talismans, scapulars, or *contra-egum* bracelets against the threatening spirits of the dead. Small infants, thought to be particularly vulnerable, wear a broche with a *figa*, the image of a clenched fist, which symbolizes the strength of one's *fé* (faith). Many ask protection from the armor-plated saints one finds on Bahian altars, or else visit a *rezadeira*, a woman who has the gift to close a body. Younger, urban generations wear t-shirts with the prayer to Saint George printed on them, saying: "I'll walk dressed and armed with the weapons of St. George / So that my enemies, while having feet, don't reach me / while having hands, don't touch me / while having eyes, don't see me / and not even a single thought they have can make me suffer."

João told me about his escapular, a small necklace that has two images of a saint—one to be worn on your chest, the other one on your back. His body, sandwiched between saints, was thus made invulnerable for evil forces: "When I just obtained my escapular, I was using it for months. I drive a motorcycle, and it would happen that on the road, all of a sudden I would feel here [touches his chest] to see if indeed I was wearing it. *Ahh* [sighs with relief], I'm protected! It even happened that I returned home when I noticed I had forgotten to put it on. But although I have these syncretistic beliefs, I must say that after some time I lost this strict observance of going out with my scapular on. I think, oh well, I'm already protected, and I'll continue my journey."

João's lenience was not, as I first thought, because of a lesser concern over spiritual protection. Quite to the contrary, João told me that he now sees a Candomblé priest who regularly performs a ritual to close his body.

Other practices to close one's body are less explicitly situated in the realm of popular religiosity. Adriana already mentioned how headphones close the body and immunize the user from her surroundings. Talking about the way he uses his sunglasses, Alex told me: "Well, I obviously use my sunglasses to protect myself from the insane clarity of the light in this city. But, well . . . this week I wasn't doing well, you know. I really wasn't well . . . and so I found myself thinking, I'll go out with my sunglasses on. I live in this building from quite some time, I know the people who work here, and I always say *bom dia*. And these sunglasses, because I really wasn't doing well, prohibited people to notice it. I think sunglasses have this capacity: you weapon yourself to face the big city, and you protect yourself from the gaze of others."

The thing that struck me most in the way people talked about the opening and closing of their bodies is that these practices are never-ending balancing acts. Far from armor-plating themselves against the dangers of an open body, they seek to reach a livable degree of vulnerability. They are willing to take a risk: seeking to avoid the worst, they also seek to keep themselves open to the best that life can bring. "I know I should be using a condom, and usually I do," Vinícius told me. "But there is nothing better in lovemaking than the meeting of the flesh (*carne tocando na carne*)." Adriana was quite explicit about the balance that must be sought between opening and closing the body.

> For me, this closing of the body is somewhat paradoxical. Because you close yourself to open yourself up. You protect yourself so as to be able to throw yourself—with more security and less protection! For example, look at a group of capoeira players. The *capoeirista* who plays most daringly, who has the most beautiful performance, he certainly did a ritual to close his body. He knows that he need not be too concerned with the kicks of the other, and so he can put more into his own kicks. I am fascinated by this seeming contradiction, because it is not a contradiction. When I do a ritual in a Candomblé temple to close my body, then certainly I am not only closing my physical body. I am, above all, closing my ethereal body, my spiritual body. Knowing that I have a certain protection, the relation that my physical body has with the world can be looser

(*seja mais solta*). And so I do not have to be so cautious, with the world and with people. This is fantastic, don't you think? You close yourself to be able to open yourself up. You close something so that not everything can access you, but this enables you to throw yourself more easily into the world. So you are not invulnerable, simply because you did a ritual to close your body. These rituals don't make you invulnerable. They make you more daring.

Adriana articulates what most of my Bahian friends were saying in one way or the other: we can't take in all of the world, but we certainly want to keep ourselves open to the-rest-of-what-is, to connect ourselves with that which lies beyond the horizon of our knowing. Marcelo and Adriana are both in Candomblé, where they actively look for this kind of engagement with otherness. Alex is not in Candomblé; in fact, in our interview he declared himself to be an atheist. Yet then he added: "but I am a Bahian atheist, who is capable to see miracles." So he too wants to sensitize himself to all that is being shut out in the process of trying to make sense of things. He too wants to replenish his consciousness with all that he is not being conscious of. He too wants to see wonders and miracles.

"Opening up" in the Work of Bruno Latour

My notes—as preliminary as they are—on these practices of opening and closing the body resonated well with the work of (and on) Bruno Latour that I had to read for the preparation of the special issue. As stated, I was struck just how much Latour's philosophy is permeated with the attempt to open up received ways of knowing in the social sciences. His radical revisions of what a science of the social could be are one sustained effort to crack open the black boxes of sociological and philosophical forms of inquiry. He urges researchers to give up on the securities of being in the know, and promotes a radical uncertainty as the more profitable starting point for inquiry. Likewise, the concepts he introduces are first and foremost "crowbars": tools that were devised to keep openness at a maximum, so as to enable the researcher to witness how realities come into being.

Take the way he describes the central notion of the actor-network. The two parts are essential, hence the hyphen. The first part (the actor) reveals the narrow space in which all of the grandiose ingredients of the world begin to be hatched; the second part (the network) may explain through which vehicles, which traces, which trails, which types of information, the world is being brought *inside* those places and then, after having been transformed there, are being pumped back *out* of its narrow walls (Latour 2005: 179–180).

Clearly, this whole idea displays a deep affinity for the permeability of boundaries. Whatever we recognize as an entity—an actor—is bounded, yet via the network each actor may be filled with all-of-the-world. Reading these lines in Bahia, I was immediately reminded of those spectacular trompe l'oeil ceilings that one finds in the baroque churches of Salvador, where clouds, angels, and a distant light seek to bring the infinite outside *into* the architectural structure, or indeed, transport the congregation out of the building. Just so, I was reminded of Marsanne Brammer's understanding of mystical practices as "the dismantling of objectifying procedures, dismissing any claim that conceptual objects represent or contain either this experience or reality itself" (1992: 27). I wouldn't go as far as to characterize Latour's work as a brand of intellectual mysticism (I doubt he would be happy with such labeling), but (re)reading Latour in Bahia highlighted his preoccupation with opening up to the-rest-of-what-is. For here is a thinker who seeks to give up on any a priori assumptions as to what constitutes reality, in order to follow the dense continuum of experience and the endless mediations through which reality takes shape.

In the light of mainstream academic modes of knowledge production, so much given to the power of definition, predictability, iterability, and being-in-control, it need not be surprising that some of the critiques of Latour's work have focused on exactly the infinitude of the actor-network, its endless expansion. Thus, I found myself reading about the problem of "infinite regress" (i.e., the problem of knowing where things end in terms of causality) and the problem of "indefinite extension" (the problem where things end in terms of geographical and spatial limits). In a famous passage in *Reassembling the Social* (2005: 141ff.) Latour has joked his way around these critiques in a characteristically trickster-like manner, by staging a dialogue between a professor and a student. The student is desperate to find out where to stop his Latourian analysis, but his professor keeps telling him that he cannot see the problem: the limits of his analysis are set by such givens as the number of words he is allowed to write, the size of his hard disk and the amount of data that can be stored on it, or else the amount of time that remains, given the deadline. The passage has been commented upon as exemplifying how Latour jokingly evades the tricky problem of infinite regress and indefinite extension (Lecomte 2013: 473). In Bahia, however, I kept thinking that Latour probably does not *want* us to stop the network. Indeed, maybe he simply wants to criticize academic pretentions to be able to conquer all of reality; maybe he wants to keep his model open to infinity, so as to keep alive an awareness that any totalizing representation of reality is lacking. Maybe, he is arguing against academic "hubris" (cf. Verrips 1988).

And yet, for all of the resonances between Latour's and my Bahian friends' understandings of "what it takes to know," there are striking differences to be noted as well. These do not so much concern the propositions to replenish one's understandings by opening up to "the great, blooming, buzzing confusion," but they concern the way in which this mode of knowing is to be *practiced*.

As stated, my friends in Salvador are engaged in an ongoing balancing act between opening and closing their body; allowing themselves to be vulnerable—up to a certain point. Theirs is a risky game. Driven by the desire to experience the best that life can bring, they risk ending up with the worst: fear, misfortune, pain, sickness, madness, even death. It is exactly this vulnerability, this riskiness, that I find absent in the work of Latour.

Latour wants to keep things open to the maximum. Time and again he exhorts researchers to open up, and to open up more. He shows little patience for balancing acts. Typically, closure is the weakness, the flaw of the Moderns, or the petty concern of his critics. Sneering at the conventional thought that research may profit from the limits set by a framework, he writes: "It is true that frames are nice for showing: gilded, white, carved, baroque, aluminum, etc. But have you ever met a painter who began his masterpiece by first choosing a frame?" (2005: 143). Latour can take this radical attitude, I realized in the Bahian setting, because for him the act of opening up contains little risk. The reader who follows him to that spectacular vantage point from where one can see how being unfolds may lose some certainties along the way, but not his sanity.

This then is the odd thing with my reading of Latour. It is not that I do not subscribe to his take on the way realities come into being and unfold—I pretty much do. But I have difficulties identifying with a perspective that is so oblivious to the dimensions of danger, vulnerability, risk, and fear that my interlocutors kept referring to. Certainly, the real of "reality" may well consist of those never-ending movements along the infinite networks Latour urges us to describe; a world where everything is in constant transformation, an irreducible fluidity, an unstoppable streaming. Yet it takes only a few steps out of the universe of Latour's writings to realize that no one lives reality that way. Not my Bahian friends, not me, and I venture to say, none of my readers either. In effect, Latour's unrelenting relativization of all closures, of all fixities, turns being—or at least, *human* being—into a nightmare.

Take for example my Bahian friend Lucas, who told me he is only able to sleep when he has wrapped himself all up, from head to toe, in a white sheet: "Oh well, this thing of covering myself in a sheet at night . . . you know, I was always very afraid of the dark. Maybe it was this thing of being half-asleep, when your mind is no longer fully in control. So when I was a kid, I always saw things, heard things, and that fear has stayed with me up until today. I don't sleep well in dark places, alone. And in a way, to wrap myself up in sheets, all the way up to my head, protects me from the dark. It turns everything under the sheet into *my* world."

Lucas's observation surely makes sense. For is it not that things and sounds lose their well-delineated form in the dark, and can thus be taken to be something other, anything other? That the night disintegrates well-established boundaries between what is possible and what is impossible? That the dark is bottomless? No wonder a sensitive person like Lucas needs to protect himself from this dark, shrinking the boundless universe so as to feel safe.

The spectacle that we see from the vantage point to which Latour takes us in his writings recalls the traumatic Lacanian Real, or what religious scholars call the *mysterium fascinans et tremendum*—dimensions of being that we may *want* to explore, but which we cannot fully enter if we don't want to go mad. This, I would say, raises an intriguing set of questions. For what is it about our mode of *knowing* that allows us to embrace Latour's vision as a persuasive portrayal of *being*, and then continue to go on living as if nothing is the matter, as if nothing has changed? How is it possible that we follow Latour all the way up to the point were we can face his nightmarish portrayal of being, while comfortably sitting in our chairs, and even enjoying the fine jokes he is cracking along the way? Why do the vistas he opens up not instill in us an utter sense of discomfort, despair, and fear? Why do I shy away from taking an LSD trip, or from the invasion of otherness that is spirit possession, but *not* from reading Bruno Latour? The answer that readily presents itself is that this has to do with our academic practices of knowing, with the academic modes of address, the particular way in which we are engaged as readers.

The Act of Reading an Academic Text

Roland Barthes (1975), Wolfgang Iser (1972), and many others have taught us that, "it is the convergence of text and reader that brings the literary work into existence" (Iser 1972: 279). There is no reason to assume that academic texts are not subject to the same principle. Therefore, if we want to understand how it is that we can embrace Latour's portrayal of reality as persuasive, and yet go on living our lives as if nothing has changed, then we need to attend to the act of reading. A brief exposition of my own reading-experiences of Latour's work, last summer in Salvador, may be illuminating here.

I confess that Latour is no easy read for me. In Bahia, which must be one of the noisiest places on earth, I often had to use earplugs to get the kind of concentration that his texts require. There must be no one around—nothing must distract me. To enter Latour, one might say, I had to leave Bahia behind. Once I find myself inside the universe of his text, I find myself in academia. From the footnotes to the references, from the witty little jokes to the layout of the printed text, from my underlining of sentences to the turning of the pages, the practice of reading Latour brings me back to familiar terrain. Nothing is ever really strange or radically other in this world—or comes close to the baffling, open-ended strangeness of a possession ceremony in a Candomblé temple, for instance. Or to the strangeness of being invaded by fear without being able to say what it is that is so frightening. Nothing is strange, because in the world in which I sojourn when reading Bruno Latour the comforting signs of a secure and familiar world are always in sight. Year, page number, footnote, heading, subheading. Stretches of text may be opaque or impenetrable, but they are never nightmarish. Insights may be brilliant, but they are never devastating.

This capacity of the text to keep me in my academic comfort zone is reinforced by the mind-work I have to perform reading Latour. As an anthropologist, with no thorough philosophical training, I have no choice but to mobilize all my intellectual capacities in order to stay attuned to the development of the argument, to follow the author along, sentence by sentence, paragraph by paragraph, chapter by chapter. Reading Latour, "I'm all head," as the expression goes. Against all phenomenological insights that there is no such possibility of being "all head," I can only observe that all of my consciousness is up there under my skull, trying to process the abstractions, working hard to make something out of the complicated twists and turns of the arguments. Wherever Latour is taking me on the level of ideas, at *this* level, the level of reading, I'm deeply in academia: tied to its conventions of world-making; my body, emotions and affects numbed; "all head."

And then there is the particular pleasure-economy of the universe of the text. The rewards that keep me going are the moments where I sense that I've grasped the argument—"Aha, so this is what he wants to argue!" These moments allow for a pleasant sense of mastery, of being in control. Even where Latour is arguing against the possibility of such mastery, the act of reading rewards me with exactly that sense of "seizing it," of "holding it firm" that the verb "to grasp" connotes. Sure, I get lost every now and then, but I've learned that if only I read on there'll be that moment of regaining control again.

So how am I being engaged as a reader? I'd say the Latourian text takes me out of the world and locks me up in the familiar environment of academia. It keeps me in my head. It constantly replaces my sense of not knowing with a sense of being in the know. Even when the very argument leads to an understanding that reality exceeds all knowing, the act of reading produces the satisfaction of having grasped just that. These then might well be the balancing acts the readers of Latour perform to make it possible to access the reality he holds out to us without going mad. What we access intellectually becomes, in effect, affectively neutralized in the act of reading. We don't go all the way. We don't give ourselves over to the reality the philosopher has created, with all of our mindful bodies or embodied minds. We have our own white sheets under which to hide. And it is only thus, I would suggest, that we are able to follow Latour into the maddening reality he describes.

Conclusion

I have suggested that mystical roads to knowledge and Latour's anthropological inquiries converge in the intuition that *meaning* does not exhaust *being*. This awareness of the limits of human sense-making has instigated mystics to search for the plenitude of the Divine in experiences that lie beyond what can be said, thought and imagined. For Bruno Latour, and researchers inspired by his work, this awareness has triggered attempts to design what some have called a "posthuman" perspective on being[10]: a "flat" ontology, which no longer privileges the human species (and hence human modes of sense-making), but puts humans and nonhumans on an equal par as actors in a network. As different as these quests for knowledge may be, all seem to be driven by a desire to open up consciousness to the-rest-of-what-is—to create an awareness of the infinite reality surplus that is produced by the closure that every single signifying act implies; to access and explore that which has to be repressed and shut out, silenced and tabooed for human constructions of reality to make sense; and to thus arrive at a more all-encompassing awareness of being, a deeper insight, of more profound way of knowing.

I would like to believe that this convergence is a sign that the radical separation between mystical and scientific ways of knowing, which Michel de Certeau (1992) traced back to the late sixteenth century, may be open for negotiation. De Certeau documented how academia invented "mysticism" as a separate category of truth-seeking, qualifying it first as "extraordinary," then as "abnormal," and soon as "delusive" and "occult." As Brammer succinctly phrased it, "Situated in the marginal, the unsayable, the unreal, or the unconscious, the locus of the mystical became the *elsewhere* according to which science defined itself by what it is not" (1992: 28). Unsurprisingly, then, there is still a derogatory sound to the adjective "mystical" when used in academic settings.[11] One can *study* mysticism as a phenomenon; one can ponder and explain its stubborn attempts to move "into depths of truth unplumbed by the discursive intellect" (James 2009: 206), but one cannot take serious its truth claims, let alone embrace it as a form of knowing that might actually add something to our knowledge practices.[12]

Now some may want to argue that the strength of the academy is that it allows for intellectual exercises and abstract thinking: that it is our cool and levelheaded analysis that has brought us valuable insights and understandings. And that we might leave it up to the artists, poets, mystics, and madmen to close in on the "great, blooming, buzzing confusion" and explore alternative, more experiential modes of knowing. However, to sign up for this division of labor—"the thinking is with us, the experiencing is with them"—is to stick to a hopelessly inadequate portrayal of what the mystics and academics actually do. Moreover, it is to miss out on the opportunity to arrive at what Michael Jackson and Albert Piette call an "existential anthropology," a discipline that seeks to "illuminate life as lived, rather than exploit the facts of experience as mere grist for some intellectual mill."[13] Let me by way of conclusion elaborate this latter point.

An anthropology that wants to speak of "life as lived" cannot afford to ignore how the "great, blooming, buzzing confusion" plays itself out in human lives. It needs to devise modes of report that are more welcoming to this presence, showing how it may both enrich and mess up our lives. I think it is fair to say that anthropology, more than any other discipline in the social sciences and humanities, has acknowledged this necessity. And yet, being an academic discipline, courting recognition and approval from other academics (not to mention funding agencies), there are strong pressures to weed out the blooming and dim the buzzing. To sketch the issue in John Law's felicitous phrasing, "Parts of the world are caught in our ethnographies, our histories and statistics, but other parts are not, or if they are, they are distorted into clarity ... if much of the world is vague, diffuse or unspecific, slippery, emotional, ephemeral, elusive or indistinct, changes like a kaleidoscope, or doesn't have much of a pattern at all, then where does this leave social science? How might we catch some of the realities we are currently missing?" (2004: 2).

It seems to me that one of the responses to this dilemma in current anthropology is the favoring of opening moves over acts of closure. Clearly, the interest in the work of Bruno Latour does not come out of the blue: Latour is as much an exponent of the anthropological search for reopenings, as an instigator of it. Ever more frequent, and ever louder, are calls to replace the metaphor of the boundary—dismissed as "one of the least subtle in the social science repertoire" (Strathern 1996: 520)—with metaphors of the open-ended network. There are suggestions to stop thinking of theory as a solid framework, capable of imposing its particular "sense" on the world, and to take it to be "an adaptable, open repository" of sensitizing concepts and ideas, which help the researcher to follow reality as it unfolds (Mol 2010: 9). The massive anthropological interest in bodies, embodiment, and phenomenology is at least partially inspired by the idea to "collapse dualities" (Csordas 1990: 7) such as body-mind, subject-object, and structure-practice, which again signals the wish to free reality from the discrete knowledge objects into which it had been stored. At another level, the current anthropological celebration of opening moves comes to the fore in instructions for researchers to be "transparent" about their subjective presence in the production of knowledge, in the promotion of interdisciplinarity, and in the exploration of alternative, less logo-centric media for scientific report. David MacDougall's ruminations on the possibilities of a visual anthropology offer a clear example of the latter. Stressing the capacity of moving images to transport a spectator to the elsewhere depicted on the screen, he argues that visual modes of communication allow for a mode of knowing that is less bound by "meaning" and brings the spectator closer to "being." Which, according to him, helps to explain the academic resistance to visual media: "It is the fear of giving ourselves unconditionally to what we see. It seems to me that this fear is allied to our fear of abandoning the protection of conceptual thought, which screens us from a world that might otherwise consume our consciousness" (2006: 8).

Having long advocated such opening moves, I delight in these new modes of thinking, the vistas they disclose and the experimentations they allow. I do, however, regret that laudable pleas for opening up reified notions and concepts are frequently building themselves up *against* all acts of closure. In current debates there is an ill-concealed normativity that qualifies boundary-making as being somehow "bad"; meaning as somehow "artificial," "unreal," or "imprisoning"; symbolization as somehow "not getting there"; mediation as somehow standing in the way for encounters with the im-mediate. William Mazzarella coined this tendency neo-vitalist, and showed himself to be critical of it, arguing that "by romanticizing the emergent and the immediate, this neo-vitalist position tends too briskly to dismiss given social formations as always already foreclosed" (2009: 348).

In line with Mazzarella's critique, I have sought to show that forms of "closure" always accompany the moves of opening up—and I have suggested that this is as much the case with the people we study as with ourselves. As Clifford Geertz once wrote, the acts of closure by which human sense-making operates are "not additive to human existence but constitutive of it" (in Ortner 2006: 119). Mindful of the lessons of Bruno Latour, we might want to substitute "constitutive" for "co-constitutive." But other than that, the reminder that "the thing we seem least able to tolerate is a threat to our powers of conception, a suggestion that our ability to create, grasp, and use symbols may fail" (Geertz 1973: 99), is best not forgotten. We should therefore resist the temptation to pit "the plenitude of being" against "the limitations of meaning." For an existential anthropology, which studies *human* modes of being in the world, it might be more fruitful to take the irresolvable tension between the quest for meaning and the ungraspability of being as a starting point for research. We might then show how people's actions are endless balancing acts, seeking to calibrate the dangers and pleasures of "letting the world in" or "shutting the world out." As Michael Jackson put it in the introduction to this volume, an existential anthropology might explore "the *tension and dialectic between* immediate and mediated experience, reducing reality neither to some purely sensible mode of being nor to the theoretical language with which we render existence comprehensible."[14] It does not invest in grand, absolutist statements, but in a description of the endless meddling and tinkering[15] and making-do that I have discussed in this essay. It is only because the capoeira player has closed his body that he is able to risk the more daring performance. It is only because the reader of Latour finds herself enclosed in the safety cage of academia that she can enter his portrayal of being in the act of reading. And when I stumbled into that stationery store on the Rua Aurea in Lisbon, I bought a box of color pencils, hoping a performance of normality might restore a framework that had just disintegrated. That is indeed, how lives are lived.

Notes

1. The film project is being realized together with video-artist Kostana Banovic.
2. I first explored this theme in my work on the war-ridden Serbia of the early 1990s. See van de Port 1998.

3. I thank my colleague Laurent Legrain for bringing this wonderful phrasing to my attention.
4. For a full discussion of this theme, see van de Port 2011.
5. The term "mysticism" has long been used to denote candomblé's religious practices, starting with Raimundo Nina Rodrigues late nineteenth-centry descriptions of the cult. Today, *misticismo* is one of the terms cult members use when discussing their religion.
6. Orixás, caboclos, and exus are different types of spirits with which the people from Candomblé maintain relationships.
7. See for instance de Abreu 2008.
8. The song "A tua presença morena" can be found on Caetano Veloso's album *Qualquer Coisa* (1975).
9. The song is called "carta de amor", and appears on the album *Oásis de Bethânia* (2012).
10. See for example Kohn 2013.
11. The hesitant reception of the work of George Bataille in academia, frequently compared with a mystical mode of understanding, is a case in point. Whereas Bataille's work is often addressed in academic writing, his insights are rarely allowed to do their disruptive work in the analysis as such. "Bataille locates in limit-experiences such as sacrifice, eroticism, and torture the instruments of an intolerable ecstasy he calls sacred. This immediate sacred experience rejects outside of itself any and all disciplinary forms of archival codifications—in short, any possibility of academization. For Bataille, the sacred is essentially and even vehemently nonacademic. How is a scholarly community ostensibly devoted to the second or third-order study of sacred things to approach such a figure?" (Gangle 2012: 1122). For a discussion directly relevant to anthropology, see Ewing 1994.
12. Intriguingly, my study of Bahian candomblé has taught me that many of these mystics are as resistant to academic knowledge practices, and perform their part in keeping up the divide. They dismiss words and dialogues as suitable vehicles for the *deep knowledge* they are after, arguing that discursivity brings you nowhere closer to "the mysteries," as words keep you locked up in what is already known. For an elaboration of candomblé attitudes vis à vis academic researchers, see van de Port 2011.
13. Introduction to this volume.
14. Emphasis added; for a booklength pondering of such calibrating acts, see Jackson 2012.
15. I borrow this apt image of "tinkering" from my colleague Annemarie Mol.

References

de Abreu, Maria José. 2008. "Goose Bumps All Over: Breath, Media and Tremor," *Social Text* 26 (3): 59–78
Barthes, Roland. 1975. *The Pleasure of the Text.* New York: Hill and Wang.
Berliner, David, Laurent Legrain, and Mattijs van de Port (eds.). 2013. "Bruno Latour and the Anthropology of the Moderns," *Social Anthropology* 21 (4): 435–447.
Brammer, Marsanne. 1992. "Thinking Practice: Michel de Certeau and the Theorization of Mysticism," *Diacritics* 22 (2): 26–37.
de Certeau, Michel. 1992. *The Mystic Fable: The Sixteenth and Seventeenth Centuries.* Chicago: University of Chicago Press.
Csordas, Thomas. 1990. "Embodiment as a Paradigm for Anthropology," *Ethos* 18 (1): 5–47.
Ewing, Katherine P. 1994. "Dreams from a Saint: Anthropological Atheism and the Temptation to Believe," *American Anthropologist* 96 (3): 571–583.

Gangle, Rocco. 2012. "Review of Jeremy Biles *Ecce Monstrum: Georges Bataille and the Sacrifice of Form*," *Journal of the American Academy of Religion* 80 (4): 1122–1125.
Geertz, Clifford. 1973. *The Interpretation of Cultures*. New York: Basic Books.
Iser, Wolfgang. 1972. "The Reading Process: A Phenomenological Approach," *New Literary History* 3 (2): 279–299.
Jackson, Michael. 2012. *Between One and One Another*. Berkeley: University of California Press.
James, William. 2007. *Principles of Psychology*, vol. 1. New York: Cosimo.
———. 2009. *The Varieties of Religious Experiences: A Study in Human Nature*. Seven Treasure Publications.
Kohn, Eduardo. 2013. *How Forests Think: Toward an Anthropology Beyond the Human*. Berkeley: University of California Press.
Latour, Bruno. 2005. *Reassembling the Social: An Introduction to Actor-Network Theory*. Oxford: Oxford University Press.
Law, John. 2004. *After Method: Mess in Social Science Research*. London: Routledge.
Lecomte, Jeremy. 2013. "Beyond Indefinite Extension: About Bruno Latour and Urban Space," *Social Anthropology* 21 (4): 462–478.
MacDougall, David. 2006. *The Corporeal Image: Film, Ethnography and the Senses*. Princeton, NJ: Princeton University Press.
Mazarella, William. 2009. "Affect: What is it Good For?" In *Enchantments of Modernity: Empire, Nation Globalization*, Saurabh Dube (ed.). New Delhi: Routledge.
Mol, Annemarie. 2010. "Actor-Network Theory: Sensitive Terms and Enduring Tensions," *Kölner Zeitschrift für Soziologie und Sozialpsychologie* 50 (1): 253–269.
Ortner, Sherry. 2006. *Anthropology and Social Theory: Culture, Power and the Acting Subject*. Durham, NC: Duke University Press.
Strathern, Marilyn. 1996. "Cutting the Network," *Journal of the Royal Anthropological Institute* 2 (3): 517–535.
van de Port, Mattijs. 1998. *Gypsies Wars and Other Instances of the Wild: Civilization and its Discontents in a Serbian Town*. Amsterdam: Amsterdam University Press.
———. 2011. *Ecstatic Encounters: Bahian Candomblé and the Quest for the Really Real*. Amsterdam: Amsterdam University Press.
Verrips, Jojada. 1988. "Holisme en Hybris," *Etnofoor* 1 (1): 35–56.
Žižek, Slavoj. 1989. *The Sublime Object of Ideology*. London: Verso.

Chapter Four

The Station Hustle
Ghanaian Migration Brokerage in a Disjointed World

Hans Lucht

As the walls of European immigration control grow higher, casting long shadows into Africa, so do the profits of human smuggling and the risks taken in the African borderlands. Brokers, connection men, and human smugglers are just some of the names for the new actors that have emerged in these new social spaces; convenient pantomime villains in the global north—objects of moral contempt and political outrage—but often figures of hope in the global south, where the desire and necessity to move to where better opportunities may be found is as strong as ever. Based on ethnographic fieldwork in Niger, this chapter discusses how the human smuggling networks that guide West African migrants across the Sahara Desert toward Libya are not organized by large-scale criminal networks, as popular belief has it, but by destitute and stranded migrants that somehow refuse to give up believing that there is more to be gained than their current situation offers; whose desire to find a life worth living has not been crushed under the weight of the many catastrophes they have encountered on the road. Using narrative ethnography, I explore this world of great poverty and danger associated with undocumented labor migration in the globalized world.

* * *

By a strange twist of fate, many of the migrants who find themselves stranded in the Sahel, unable to continue their journey from West Africa

---

Notes for this chapter begin on page 124.

to the Mediterranean, discover that their setbacks may be turned to good advantage, and their experiences of hardship made a form of symbolic capital. For they possess first-hand knowledge of the dangers that await those who need to leave their homes most desperately, and in the desert these connection men appear to the migrants as tricksters who control what they most desire, namely access to the outside world, and an answer to the universal human need to be "going places" when one's own world, one's own socioeconomic environment no longer offers such "existential mobility" (Hage 2005).

My focus in this chapter is on the connection men's hunger to make more out of this disjointed world than what has been given and, in the face of adversity, to leave behind the transit zones on the threshold of Europe, all the while waiting for the next move, the next piece of information, the next big deal, while brokering paths for their compatriots that will enable them to undertake the journey that they have failed to make themselves but refuse to give up.

This chapter also heeds the call of existential anthropology to explore the "dynamic relationship" between the given conditions that underpin human possibilities and the strategies and actions whereby individuals stake their claims to what is considered a life worth living in spite of all obstacles, which is, as Michael Jackson argues, the human need to experience oneself as an actor and not simply acted upon, which, again, is another way of framing the eternal human "struggle for being against nothingness—for whatever will make life worth living, rather than hopeless, profitless, and pointless" (2005: x); or, in Arthur Kleinman's words, "the always unequal struggle between where the world is taking us and where we aspire to go" (2006: 17). This dilemma is best captured in the reality of human struggle, in critical events, as Jackson and Albert Piette argue (introduction, this volume), though we should be careful not to assume that we will reach a synthesis between our analytical concepts and the vitality of life. Incidentally, as Clifford Geertz has pointed out, what appears more durable and longer lasting than impressive systems of thought is what detailed ethnographic description has to offer concerning the social and existential "truth" of a moment, to the extent that it depicts the ethnographer in the field having penetrated a situation, or rather, perhaps, having been penetrated by a situation (1998: 4–5). For not only the informants, but also the anthropologists—if these categories make any sense in the deep immersion of ethnographic fieldwork—struggle to make sense of the moment, and to give it direction, retrospectively influenced by various known and unknown sources, not all of them "rational" or scientific, but including such feelings as desire, inadequacy and fear of lack of control.

In fact, the scientist who seeks to catch the world off guard and to expose it may be in for an unpleasant surprise, as Jean-Paul Sartre has argued. In *Being and Nothingness*, Sartre discusses "knowing" as a form of appropriation with deep-seated sexual connotations that gives rise to an existential dilemma he calls the "Actaeon complex." In Ovid's beautiful but terrifying rendition of the Greco-Roman legend of Actaeon, the famous hero—after a day of "glorious" hunting, nets "stiff with blood" from the butchering, spears "caked" and knives "clogged in their sheaths"—wanders into the woods and stumbles upon the sacred cave of Diana. He pushes into it, drawn by fate and curiosity, and reaches a veil of branches that hides a pool, where, incidentally, the goddess and her nymphs are bathing after their own hunt. He tears away the veil and surprises the goddess. The naked Diana is enraged by this intrusion and since her weapons are not at hand she splashes water into Actaeon's face, magically transforming him into a stag. Upon fleeing the cave in panic, he is torn to pieces by his own band of fierce hunting dogs who no longer recognize their master, but see a beast deprived of speech. His friends, aroused by this last unexpected and majestic kill of the day, cheer on the dogs and call out for Actaeon to come and rejoice in the bloodshed. To Sartre, the story is symbolically concerned with the desire to possess outside reality, to reveal and expose it, to "violate it by sight." But in this act of exposure and appropriation, the object of desire ceases to exist independently of the scientist as hunter, who finds nothing remaining except himself—that is to say, his own inadequacy and shortcomings that have devoured and destroyed its object of desire. Now, the hunter has become the hunted, fleeing the dogs of insecurity. Only new possessions will soothe this craving, and yet nothing remains at the same time perceptually possessed and perceptually new and reborn like social life (Sartre 2005: 599–600).

Antiquity was no stranger to the disillusions of naturalistic verisimilitude, which made the onlooker—in the manner of Narcissus—pour all his desire and aspiration into what may look like reality, or even more like reality than reality itself, only for it to turn out to be a disappointing kind of mirror image into which one fatally sinks; indeed, the desire to possess realistic forms of one's own making, or even posses forms that eclipse empirical reality was so strong that classic literature is rich with evidence of *agalmatophilia*, a condition in which individuals derive sexual arousal from an attraction to statues (Elsner 2007: 1–2). This dilemma of appropriating without destroying is relevant not only to art but also to language, ideas and concepts, cosmologies and ontologies, as Jackson and Piette argue (this volume); a space should remain open to what we cannot grasp in order for the object of our desire/investigation to live and breathe.

Perhaps, to the fieldworker, the uncontrollable and sometimes incomprehensible nature of ethnographic inquiry with its peculiar blend of long-term intimate involvement and penetration of (and being penetrated by) empirical reality combined with an ideal of scholarly detachment, depicting both the psychical, psychological, and social "geographies" of human life and its conceptual and ideological forms offers this unstable plasticity that contains the seeds of its own understanding and always something extra or hidden.

With this predicament of ethnographic fieldwork in mind—which adds another dimension to the fact that "the meaning of all human experience remains ambiguous" (Jackson and Piette, this volume)—I return to Niger and the Ghanaian connection men in the desert. Building on the ruins of their own failed adventures, the connection men struggle to regain a momentum in life by offering themselves as experts on the migration journey to Libya. During my stay with them in Niamey in the fall of 2010, a critical event occurred that in hindsight revealed something qualitatively new about the human condition particular to this given field.

Pushing People to Libya Under The Radar

Together with my field assistant Sammy,[1] I had for some time been following two Ghanaian migrants, Bobby and Kantinka, who had originally intended to travel to Europe but got lost on the way, and now worked the Ténéré bus station in central Niamey. Their work consisted in hustling other migrants, or as Bobby used to say with a characteristic laugh, "We tell them stories. We are story-tellers" (see also Lucht 2013). Basically what they did was to greet migrants that came from Accra on the bus and direct them to the next bus to Agadez, and set them up with a "ghetto" in the desert (the name Ghanaians give to the halfway houses) where they await further transportation into the dangerous desert, and finally Libya. For these services they were paid both by the migrants themselves and by the bus station—where they had a kind of lose affiliation, meaning that they were tolerated and allowed to hang out and wait—and by the "ghetto bosses" who they supplied with a constant flow of new hopeful migrants, risking everything for Europe. Incidentally, the Ghanaian connection men call themselves "pushers"; in this context this does not imply supplying drugs but being agents of mobility who "push" their compatriots further down the road.

In the terminology of European nation-states, this form of people movement is classified as human smuggling or even human trafficking vis-à-vis the Palermo Protocol. But here the official legal discourse will be bracketed out in favor of an exploration of how the pushers understand and enact their roles as facilitators of mobility, and how migrants see them, not as criminals, but as agents of change that they approach at a certain price and risk; agents of change who play their part, legal or not, in the practical governance of the EU-African borderlands. As Maybritt Jill Alpes has argued in a paper on the work of Cameroonian migration brokers, it is too often assumed in political and public debates in Europe that our legal distinctions on mobility and the actors involved in it has any bearing on the choices of those who need to move the most (2013: 8).

The "pushers" both had long and painful migration stories behind them that were slowly unraveled over the months as mutual trust grew and they felt comfortable opening up. Bobby had been on the road for close to twenty years, a good part of his life, and spent many years in Tripoli trading and using heroin, when he finally caught a break and made enough money from a spectacular burglary to make an attempt for Spain. Bobby actually made it all the way via Morocco, though he got lost on the way, and spent hard time in jail, and was then deported back to Ghana (see Lucht 2013). He stayed less than half an hour with his family in Accra—he had stolen from them before he left for Libya, and knew he would not be welcomed—and decided to head directly back to Libya with a bag of marijuana, and rejoin the drug trade. The plan collapsed when he was arrested in Agadez and the dope was confiscated. He had to use the last of his money from the burglary to bribe the local police to let him go.

Looking back, Bobby considered this an act of divine intervention in the sense that he would have been killed in the drug game in Libya, like so many of his friends, unless someone had stopped him from going. Broken, he ended up in Niamey, and hooked up with another stranded Ghanaian, Osu, a senior hustler he knew from Libya. It was Osu who introduced him to the pusher work, and this had been Bobby's work for almost ten years while he waited for the right moment to travel to Israel. He was adamant that he would make it one day. He had already tried once but got caught by the Egyptian police and gone to jail, where he was tortured with electrical wires. But next time, he said, he would be careful to make no mistakes.

Kantinka came into the pusher work later, when, after a series of calamities on the road (he failed miserably as a stowaway in Abidjan, he was duped by a white captain in Dakar, and then he lost all his uncle's money on the road to Libya) he was eventually found by Bobby and Osu wandering aimlessly around the streets of Niamey, hair growing wild and clothes torn, begging for food and going through trash like a crazy person.

Kantinka didn't like to talk much about that time but quietly explained that the frustration got to him, and somehow he lost his mind.

The two other "pushers" took him in and trained him in the hustling, and when Osu left to set up his own "ghetto" in the desert, Kantinka took over his position at the station and had been hustling with Bobby ever since. He too had not given up on traveling despite all his misfortunes. He wanted to go back to Ivory Coast, and try a "secret" harbor one last time.

When they hustled, Kantinka was the nice quiet one, whereas Bobby, who was a natural Hausa-speaking street kid from the poor parts of Accra—Nima to be precise—came into the frame when extra pressure was needed, or when "his people" from the shantytowns arrived.

Over the course of our time with the "pushers," Sammy and I had been eager to talk to their senior colleague Osu, who had his own "ghetto" in the desert. Though we exchanged pleasantries in Guan over the phone numerous times, and Osu suggested that he would stop by for a chat the next time he was in town, it was clear that the chances of "landing him," as Sammy phrased it, were not great. Bobby was unsurprised. He said there was nothing in it for Osu.

Then, one day, Bobby and Kantinka suddenly received a call from Osu, who informed them that he was coming down from Arlit to pick up twenty-four Ghanaian migrants going to Libya. He asked them to be ready to receive "the boys" at the SNTV bus station when they arrived. This was obviously great news for our research and we all went to the station to look for the migrants. In what follows, I give an account of the events that transpired over the course of that day—and how it was understood and discussed in the weeks following—and how, for a brief moment, the ambiguous nature of the field was illuminated.

Osu Makes His Move

On the way to the station the pushers got the first sign that something suspicious was going on. Kantinka called Osu back and asked him to provide them with a name, so that when they welcomed the boys to Niamey, they'd have an angle on the situation. Without a name, there's no natural opening, no easy way to approach them, and they'll have to hustle from "nothing," as Kantinka put it. But, curiously, Osu hesitated to give them a name, and then, a few moments later, said he'd forgotten the name altogether. This did not make the pushers comfortable. First, he would never forget that name in a million years, which meant that either he was playing some kind of trick on them, or, and this was considered to be the more likely scenario, he didn't know the name but had received incomplete intelligence from "his people" at the bus station in Accra—he had "eyes" there watching people on the move—that a big group of migrants were moving to Libya, and then decided to rush to Niamey to grab them before any other ghetto boss could claim them. Arriving at the SNTV station, things got even murkier; the boys had been there but were all gone. They had, the pushers were informed, taken a car to Wadata Station, from where they apparently planned to leave for Libya in the morning. This was disappointing news for many different reasons, Bobby explained. First, it was important to approach the boys as soon as they stepped off the bus, and make use of that moment of bewilderment, when a person after a long journey sets foot in a new town, still weary and dazed and full of impressions, and therefore inclined to let his guard slip. Once the boys had settled down, bathed, used the toilets, found a mattress to rest upon, and adopted the cool but vigilant pose of a migrant on the move, it is much more difficult to get close to them; the moment when one could "strike" would be long passed, as Kantinka explained. Moreover, the fact that the group decided to leave SNTV and go for another station meant that either they had a connection man telling them what to do—obviously not Osu who was in the bus coming to Niamey, oblivious to the developments taking place—or they had an experienced leader among them, who was "controlling" them, pulling the strings. To be sure, the situation was fishy, and when the pushers reached the other station, and quickly picked the boys out from the crowd, they quietly left again without making any attempt to address them, or even let them know that they were also Ghanaian. "We only have one possibility to strike, so if they will not listen, and tell us to go away, that's it, you see," Kantinka said. Instead, they retreated to the Ténéré station, and assumed their regular places on the wooden benches in the main lobby, their "office space," as Bobby always said, in order to figure out their next move.

By now it was clear that Osu didn't know the boys, as he claimed over the phone, but to pull off the deal he had tried to play Bobby and Kantinka. He wanted to make sure that they or somebody else did not get to the boys first, handle them, and inform another ghetto boss in the desert, perhaps striking a better deal than the one he was prepared to offer. So he claimed that they already belonged to him, which would make it pointless for Bobby and Kantinka to try and connect them with another ghetto, since they don't usually interfere with which ghetto the migrants chose, as long as they get their share. However, having already laid claim to the boys, Osu would have an advantage in the haggling over what kind of price per head the pushers could be expected to take; the less hustling required on the part of the pushers the less leverage in the following negotiations. But if the group was not really Osu's, and this now seemed to be likely, then a different scenario was possible. The boys were up for grabs, and Bobby and Kantinka were free to handle them anyway they saw fit. This meant that the pushers were at liberty to find another place for them in Agadez, or to "give them to another ghetto." This was ideal, again, because the pushers were now in a strong bargaining position, and could, for instance, pit the ghetto bosses against each other to obtain the best possible price, whereas if the boys had already made up their minds to join a certain ghetto, the pushers' room for maneuver was much more limited. In this case, when information about which ghetto the group is going to was obtained, they would place a call to the boss of the chosen ghetto, and inform him or her that they had twenty-one boys coming—incidentally, Osu also got the count wrong—and they would be in the clear. Even if the ghetto boss had already made the necessary arrangements with the group, Bobby and Kantinka would still take their share, since there was always a next time, there were always more people coming through, and the ghetto bosses needed to be on good terms with the pushers on the road unless they wanted them telling would-be migrants that they were dangerous people, and that migrants lose their lives traveling with them, and that they should rather chose someone else if they'd like to make it through the desert. But what was not acceptable, from the point of view of the pushers, was to see a group leave Niamey without having obtained information enabling them to place the call to Agadez. To do that, the pushers needed "a key" to open the situation; they didn't feel comfortable walking into the station grounds and try to retrieve the necessary information without a name or a face or anything, especially since the migrants could have a strong person "controlling" them. They needed an "innocent person" in the station, as Kantinka explained, somebody who could walk in, fresh-faced, start a casual conversation, and get closer to the boys and extract the information—who their leaders were, and what ghetto, if any, they had decided on. Moreover, they didn't want the local station pushers, who dealt with the "French boys," to see them, and possibly claim their share of the deal. So, it was decided to send Sammy, who agreed. By now, we realized later, their hustle had become our hustle too.

 First, however, we all retreated to the Ténéré Station and waited until five o'clock in the afternoon, when the sun was less scorching, and the "Ghana boys" in the station would have finished resting in the shade, and were ready to stretch their legs a little bit. To be sure, Osu was now, unknowingly, on the way out of his own hustle, even as he approached Niamey, and made regular calls to inform the pushers of his ETA. This situation did not appear to worry the pushers; though they were on friendly terms—Bobby always talked warmly about him, and their years of struggling in Libya—this was business, and in business affairs Osu unfortunately tended to disappoint them. Bobby explained that he had not always lived up to his commitments and had sometimes forgotten, or neglected, their agreements, so though they would welcome him happily, like a good friend and "senior brother," they were not about to bend over backward to help him land the passengers.

We left the Ténéré Station at five, and walked to the nearby Wadata Station, cutting through a compound with little round traditional huts with thatched roofs, and a dry field packed with hundreds of white rams that somehow clashed with the West African metropolis. The rams were to be slaughtered for the approaching feast of *Tabaski*, a Muslim holiday commemorating Abraham's sacrifice of Isaac (though Muslims believe it was Ishmael, who was sacrificed).

As we approached the station, we found a place to sit on a bench in the shade across from the big iron gates, outside a barbershop, and watched Sammy disappear into the busy bus station. Kantinka strolled down the street to look for a satchel of water, but came back a few minutes later with good news. Sammy had called him to let him know that he had not only made contact with the boys but also established the fact that they were all Guan people from his home village of Senya Beraku. This piece of news swung the deal back in favor of Osu, who was also a Guan person and who spoke the Effutu. Having worked intensively with Guan fishermen in Ghana and Italy, this was, of course, a welcome surprise to Sammy and I. The pushers now discussed whether Osu had something up his sleeve; these boys were "his people," and he should surely be able to land them. Had he been pulling their leg all along, knowing that he already had them in the bag; that it was a done deal?

A few minutes later, Sammy came out of the station with an older man, Mr. Barnes, who Bobby at a distance identified as their leader. They walked directly across the street to greet us. Mr. Barnes, as it happened, was Sammy's cousin on his mother's side, and he shook my hand enthusiastically, and said that they needed me on my throne in Senya, alluding to the fact—something that Sammy had no doubt informed him on the way—that I was appointed chief fisherman of Denmark on my last visit to the village. We decided to withdraw to a nearby drinking place and sit down and talk, Mr. Barnes holding my hand, as custom demanded, as we walked along the dusty four-lane high street. As we were going, however, Mr. Barnes suddenly had a change of heart, and said he would rather just have the drinks, and return to the station. Sammy convinced him it would just be a quick drink and a chat, and Mr. Barnes again agreed to go along, but now somehow without any real enthusiasm, his shoulders dropped and he looked worried. When we reached the place, a lively intersection spot called Africa, Sammy called Osu, who was still in the bus, and handed over the phone to Mr. Barnes, so they could make further arrangements—Sammy made the assumption that the Senya group would be happy to travel with a fellow Guan person from Winneba, the neighboring city in Ghana. They spoke for a while, exchanging trivialities, but Mr. Barnes did not appear to be in the mood for chitchat, so he quickly hung up the phone, swallowed his Sprite, and declared he was ready to return to the station. Kantinka and Bobby, who were keeping a low profile, said goodbye to him, and left us, as we walked Mr. Barnes back, picking up a crate of cola on the way. Heading back, we talked a bit about the declining state of local fishing, and the eternal wanderlust of the young Senya Beraku fishermen.

At the station, the twenty-one Senya Beraku would-be migrants in transit to Libya were resting on mattresses in the shade of one of the station buildings. One of them remembered my last stay in the village and even witnessed when I took "my office." They were all very young, in their early twenties, and appeared happy to see us. We handed over the crate of cola, and wished them a safe journey. Sammy told them to get some rest before the bus left at dawn, and gave some general advice about the many dangers of the road, being a veteran of the road to Libya himself. There was another experienced guy among them, who seemed more alert and less jovial than Mr. Barnes, and who Sammy briefly introduced me to at the entrance, as we were leaving the station. He was called P. J. and had been to Libya by road eight times, he informed us. Unfortunately, he had no time to sit down and talk with us and excused himself because, as he said, he had a lot of things on his mind and stuff to prepare before the group left in the early morning.

The reluctance of P. J. was not a surprise to the pushers; unlike Sammy and I, they realized quickly that Mr. Barnes was not the real leader of the group but at best a kind of second-in-command, and any decision of whom they decided to stay with in Agadez would rest with P. J. If that was really the case, then maybe Osu had a problem, Sammy admitted. Because, speaking earlier with P. J., he had mentioned that Osu was coming down, ready to help them out. But much to Sammy's surprise, P. J. responded angrily that he knew Osu very well, and that he was the most dangerous of the Ghanaian connection men, "a real killer," and he would never undertake any kind of business with him. Bobby and Kantinka were not surprised. When Osu was based up in Arlit a lot of the people he pushed into the desert never came back. "He's a good hustler but the conclusion is poor," Bobby said, "and now even his own people reject him."

This crucial piece of information—that the most likely leader of the group, P. J., was not interested in doing business with Osu—opened the hustle up again, and Kantinka wanted to know from Sammy whether another name was mentioned. Sammy didn't know, he thought the whole thing was a done deal when he found out that the boys were Effutu-speaking people like Osu. Then Sister Macy, Osu's rival ghetto boss from Agadez, suddenly called Kantinka and said that she had twenty-one boys coming up, and she would like them to go and grab them, and make sure everything went smoothly. The only problem was that she was currently in Ghana, and when the leader of the group heard this he promised to call her back, and she was still awaiting his call. Shortly after, Sister Fay, another ghetto boss from Agadez, called with almost exactly the same request; she was also in Ghana but had handed over the job to her husband, who was only awaiting the final confirmation from the group. This meant, Kantinka explained, that someone from the group, probably P. J., had called both Sister Macy and Sister Fay only to find out that both ghetto bosses were in Ghana, and since he didn't know their people in Agadez, he had hesitated to make the final decision. This would possibly open the door again for Osu, he explained, who had the advantage that he would be there soon, personally, even ready to leave with them on the bus in the morning. The question was whether he would be able to talk to P. J. and convince him face-to-face that he was not the "killer" people said he was. So the ball was back in Osu's court.

The plan was to wait for him to arrive, and then we would all walk down to the station, and sort things out with the group. The pushers were happy with this. They had the information they needed; they now knew the names of the ghetto owners, who were in play, and whatever happened they would take their share, though Osu was not necessarily the preferred business partner due to his tendency to forget his obligations.

When Osu finally arrived, he did so in style; he was sitting on the back of a roaring off-roader driven by a very tall and very drunk man, who wore a leather cap. The tall man drove the motorcycle all the way into the bar, and parked it on the sandy floor next to our table. Osu himself got down, and greeted the pushers warmly with his characteristically hoarse but jovial laughter, his big belly hopping up and down. He was wearing a tight striped sky blue and white jersey, and a chain with a large gold medallion over the jersey. He was clearly older than the pushers, perhaps from a different generation altogether; when he laughed, as he warmly did all the time, a gold tooth was displayed in the upper row of teeth. The tall man was also a pusher, but at a different station, and made an awful impression. When he was not stupidly bragging about himself—his important position in the world, his diplomatic passport, his high education in both political science and law, and his many girlfriends—he went out of his way to insult Bobby and Kantinka, who he jokingly described as "little boys," and, unlike him, not able to handle women and important business. The pushers remained perfectly calm; they were not drunk, and apparently not unfamiliar with his rants. Later in the evening, he proposed a business scheme to them, in which he would get part of their hustle and he would allow them to take part of his hustle. He presented the idea as an outstretched arm to his junior brothers, when, clearly, he was eager to take a share of the big money he imagined them to be making.

Later, the tall man with the cap pulled me discreetly aside and asked why we were ignoring him, when he was, in fact, the most knowledgeable person in Niamey about migration, and it would be better for our work to talk to him instead of these useless boys, who he loved as junior brothers but whose insights were not to be trusted. We agreed to make an appointment with him, much to the amusement of Bobby and Kantinka, who informed us that he had been trying to persuade everybody that would listen not to talk to us, believing us to be agents from the European Union. When the tall, drunk man finally took off, nearly crashing his huge motorcycle into a car in the opposite lane of traffic, it was a relief to everybody.

The moment of truth arrived. Osu wanted to go and see the migrants. We went with him into the station, while the pushers stayed behind. Sammy approached the group, some sleeping, and some listening to the radio, and Mr. Barnes rose from his mattress and walked over to meet Osu, who was at his most pleasant and jovial, and they talked for a long time in Effutu. Osu offered him a good deal on the stay in Agadez and on the journey to Libya; a deal it would not be possibly to get elsewhere but that he was prepared to offer, given the fact that they were the same people. Mr. Barnes thanked him but said he couldn't make the decision; he had to ask someone else first. He went back to talk to P. J., who was apparently sleeping among the boys. But P. J. didn't get up, and Mr. Barnes came back, and said he was sorry, but their leader was sleeping, and he didn't want to wake him up. That was the end of it right there. Nobody believed P. J. to be asleep, rather he had been watching and listening in the dark, but did not want to talk to Osu face-to-face and allow him the chance to explain himself. So to avoid open conflict, the door was effectively shut in Osu's face.

Here, in Osu's failed hustle, the inherent potentialities and pitfalls of this sociopolitical field came to the fore in one critical moment, when what was at stake was suddenly drawn out in the open and became a "public" spectacle. Osu made his play, and was completely, categorically denied and humiliated in his attempt "to land" the Senya passengers for himself. The moment said a lot about the inner workings of the trans-Saharan migration chain; how it is directly linked to changes in global political economy, i.e, the tightening and expansion of EU border regimes and the logical restraints on regular and legal mobility that follows suit, and how new actors, the pushers, step in to inhabit these emerging social worlds of involuntary immobility, purveyors of that which is most desired, namely, "to go places." It shows how they are in a constant flux to navigate the changing environments and demands and the different actors they encounter, but also their own biographies—that to some extent are echoes of previous successful or failed hustles and to some extent out of control in the sense that the rumor is always out there—that come back to haunt them.

As soon as the hustle collapsed in front of our eyes, the whole enterprise appeared almost panic-stricken and doomed. Coming down from the desert and engaging the would-be migrants personally was not the conventional way a big ghetto boss would go about his business. It hinted of desperation, and suddenly showed Osu in a new less-convincing light. Clearly, as Bobby argued, if he couldn't persuade his "own people" then he might have a big problem; reputation was everything in the pushers' business.

They Spoiled My Name: Ghosts of the Past

A moment later, we were back on the street a few blocks from the station, eating fried fish in a Ghanaian street kitchen. Osu, who had suffered such a major defeat moments before, appeared determined not to let the disappointment get to him. He was on the phone with someone, laughing and talking, and a few minutes later a young and attractive lady was hanging on his arm and he was eager to find a hotel room. That, of course, meant we had to postpone the interview.

First, we went to the place where Sammy and I stayed, the shabby Hotel Moustache, but all the rooms were occupied, primarily by the prostitutes that worked the hotel courtyard. Sammy then took Osu and the girlfriend around town looking for another place, carrying his bags in respect, until finally they found a place at the outskirts of town. By now, Osu seemed to have forgotten all about the station hustle, or rather he had set his sights on a new hustle. He had come to Niamey primarily to talk to us, as a friendly gesture—meaning, of course, that he was our guest and that we should pay for him. Sammy later reported to me that, over dinner that night, Osu had eaten almost two whole chickens. The next morning, Osu arrived at our hotel. He was going back to the desert; he had a meeting in a certain village with somebody who owed him a large sum of money. This was money he had put down to cater for some stranded migrants, he explained, as he smoked a hash cigarette in a hotel room at the Moustache, while Bobby was stuffing blankets under the crack of the door and spraying them with perfume to disguise the scent. Osu's woman was still with him, eating meat from a black polythene bag, and casually spitting out pieces of bone on the floor.

Unsurprisingly, Osu was eager to downplay the incident at the station. It's just a business, he said. "Even your own brother, if he doesn't trust your business, he will go a different way. Maybe today it didn't come my way but maybe tomorrow it will come my way, you see?"

He explained that the migrants often plan the long journey from home, and they don't want to disappoint the people with whom they have made arrangements. That was a typical Ghanaian thing, he explained, since Ghanaians are God-fearing and are loath to "betray" other people: "So if they call somebody in the desert and say they are coming, and that person prepares for them, and the driver is awaiting them, they can't change the decision, even when they see their own brother. I understand that. Everybody knows me. They know me too. So they see me there but they can't go and change their minds. But I don't want to force them. I take a look at the thing and I think this is not my thing. I have to give them a chance, and maybe my own chance is on the way coming, you see?" He laughed loudly.

Pressed on the issue of the many unfortunate migrant deaths connected to his enterprise, Osu admitted that it may have played a part in their decision but the story was wrong. He connected the passengers to the drivers, and they connected them to the people that walk migrants over the mountains, and some of them were not good people, and something went wrong out there, and a lot of people died. It was an unfortunate situation but it was out of his hands, and moreover a journey like that would always be a risky business no matter what.

"Anything good, there's bad inside. They [the drivers] have good people and they have bad people. The bad people don't care for human beings, they care for money; sometimes the drivers themselves, they rob them. It's true. But the majority of passengers entered Libya. Only some of the drivers used to do that kind of fuck up, you understand what I'm saying?"

Because of the "fuck up," Osu explained, his name was unfairly "spoiled." He even tried to warn people, "But the moment your name is spoiled you can never get more passengers again."

To prove his point, Osu explained how he had even made a good living in Arlit, which he had left behind when it dawned on him what was going on in the road; that he was sending people to their deaths in the mountains. He had a nice house; a truck, and the police were not interfering with his business. But he turned his back on it all because it was "wrong" and he wanted to "do the right thing." He was now operating out of Agadez, sending people directly to Libya through the Ténéré desert—a road he felt was much safer. He couldn't change the fact that his notoriety still clung to him though he tried to live by the word of God.

We talked about his earlier life in Libya, and how he was into prostitution and selling drugs with Bobby, and became addicted to heroin. He was arrested during the riots in Tripoli in 2000 and spent three months in jail before being deported. Those three months were the hardest time in his life. In his cell there was no access to heroin so he defecated and vomited uncontrollably during what became an involuntary "cold turkey," but that he thought of as a test from God. He likened his time there to the trials of Job and prayed for the strength to change his life and leave the dangerous junkie and criminal activities behind.

When he was a child, Osu explained, his strict father had predicted a criminal career for him, and it had felt like an evil omen. One time, when he came home from hanging out in the street with some bigger boys who he ran errands for, buying cigarettes and the like, his father smelled smoke on him and called him a "criminal." The boy, shocked by those words, asked for an explanation, and the father told him that when he was not in, Osu acted like he was owner of the house, but when he came home Osu was like a snake on the grass: "You understand? A green snake on the green grass—you can't see it; it's a very secretive being."

In the Libyan jail, he felt the truth of those hurtful words that had been fully realized, and he prayed for the strength to turn everything around and leave his "dangerous" junkie life behind him. Since then, he had worked as a "travel agent" in Niger's desert. But his real dream in life, he added somewhat surprisingly for a big ghetto boss, had always been to live in a "cottage" in the countryside and work with "animal farming." He prayed that God would one day have sympathy for him, and give him the chance to open "a small poultry farm."

Shortly after Osu left, Sister Fay's husband called Kantinka, and let him know that he had finalized the deal with P. J. and the Senya Beraku group had agreed to live in his ghetto. The deal was done, or almost. Because the next day, Sister Macy's husband also turned up at the checkpoint in Agadez, ready to pick up the group, and Sister Fay's husband had to struggle to get them home. This didn't make Kantinka happy, and he called Sister

Macy's husband, and "blasted" him for not respecting the normal business procedure; the group was going to Sister Fay, it was a done deal, and he should better respect that. But, apparently, Sister Macy's people found the whole thing to be so unresolved that they might also show up at the checkpoint and see what was going on. Kantinka wouldn't have any of it. What would happen, he argued, if next time Sister Macy had a group coming, Kantinka called another ghetto, and told them to go and pick them up also? It would be chaos.

Flickering Light: A Penumbral Field

The following days and weeks, Sammy and I discussed Osu's station hustle, trying to figure what really happened and the ramifications for our understanding of trans-Saharan migration to Libya and Europe; sometimes we would bring Bobby and Kantinka into our discussion and those exchanges to a large extent inform the narrative above. It was clear that what we had seen and taken part in, and what Osu had contributed to in the short interviews he gave before leaving for the desert, shone at best a flickering light on an already enigmatic situation.

Osu, like Bobby and Kantinka, understood themselves as a form of "travel agents" at the service of the less fortunate; agents of a kind of "globalization from below" (Bayart 2007: 13) that kept aspirations alive in a world of growing restraint on geographical mobility, which, following Ghassan Hage, is a privileged avenue to "existential mobility" (2005: 470). It was telling that for Osu and his fellow ex-junkie Bobby, the pusher work represented a return to the word of God that he had strayed from during his "criminal" years in Libya. Whether he was responsible for people dying under his direction could probably never be resolved. He was correct to suggest that death in the desert is a condition of high-risk migration across the Sahara, which, again, is the only form of mobility available to the poorest of the migrants, who are, incidentally, those who need to move the most. For instance, in October of 2013, ninety-two bodies, including women and children, were discovered in the mountains close to Arlit in the region where Osu once had a ghetto, some decomposed, some half-eaten by animals (Nossiter 2013). The point is that the organization of the smuggling networks, the fact that they are not as well-organized and interconnected as some would like to think, but more decentralized and intermediary, makes it difficult if not impossible for the individual pusher to control what is going on in the desert when he or she has handed over his passengers to the next link in the chain. It was possible that bad people had "spoiled" Osu's name—and that he had stopped it when he realized what was going on—and it was possible that he had had his eyes on the money and not on the safety of his passengers, or as Bobby said, that he was a good hustler but gave a "poor conclusion," and he only stopped and relocated because the flow of people dried out when it was known that he was indeed dangerous.

The fact that Osu shed no tears at the mention of the many people, even townspeople of his, who had perished on the road, under his direction, should perhaps not be taken as proof of a cynical disposition, or that he was indifferent to the loss of his fellow human beings. Our short time with him did not allow us to search his true feelings on this issue; maybe if we had longer time with him he would have presented a more complex image of himself than the big powerful ghetto boss he preferred to project. Second, the seemingly casual acceptance of loss on the road did not necessarily reflect a cold-hearted disposition but, rather, a deep-seated understanding of human life as in a constant flux between giving and taking, between sacrifice and reward, between life and death. This form of "existential reciprocity" (Lucht 2011: 238–252) informs West African migrant journeys to the extent that most migrants and their travel agents know and resign themselves to the risk of death in the desert, not only as an unacceptable aberration or obstacle but a precondition of the desired advancement. By giving up everything, by putting one's life in the hands of powers beyond one's control (God or whatever name is given to the powers that one is sustained by), these powers are somehow morally obliged to respond, thus creating a moral structure and a sense of existential direction and empowerment in an otherwise unresponsive world. This is not to say that migrants are unaffected by the horrors of the road—they do everything to avoid those situations and are often traumatized by the nearness of death—but that the journey is underpinned by a logic of sacrifice and not by the lies or assurances of the pushers.

In the failed station hustle we caught a short glimpse of Osu in action, as he opportunistically attempted to take action in a fast changing sociopolitical environment, making use of his knowledge and the resources at his disposal—his great travel experience, his savoir faire, and the alleged quality of his connections to drivers—while at the same time struggling with a hidden enemy, the ghost of his troubled past, that threw a spanner in the works. This was a make or break situation, and this time he came up against obstacles that could not be surpassed, and he had to accept defeat. His attempts to retrospectively trivialize the matter could not disguise that this was a bad day at the office; he took a blow to his already crumbling position in the eyes of his fellow pushers when he failed to manage a hustle with so many things otherwise speaking on his behalf. Yet, rewriting and reworking the situation into a trivial matter, a mere ripple in the give and take of the big pusher "economy," he perhaps qualitatively altered the sense of the event. This is an important aspect of the existential imperative, however, that "going places" always entails meeting obstacles, and going around or above or under these obstacles or even changing course altogether, and having to deal with the loss without losing one's sense of purpose. Osu was not about to give up on life because of one bad hustle. Adroitly, he turned the loss around when suddenly the passengers had not been his main concern. He had come on our request to assist us in the work, and at least he managed to get two chickens and a hotel room instead of nothing.

To Sammy and I the event also gave cause for some introspection. We had both assumed that it would be better for the Ghanaian migrants to travel with a Guan person from Winneba if for no other reason, apparently, than he spoke Sammy's mother tongue and that he came from an area where I had conducted ethnographic fieldwork and was appointed chief some years ago. But turning up with Osu at the station, knowing what we knew now, it seemed like a questionable idea in the sense that we could have been seen as vouching for someone, who could have, in the worst-case scenario, sent these migrants to their deaths in the desert. The truth of the matter was that we were as eager "to land" the passengers for our own reasons as the pushers were for their reasons. But what our misguided involvement in the hustle revealed was something of importance to the understanding of the organization of the routes. Namely, that the migrants too have resources, and that the pushers for all their inflated egos and big plans sometimes came up against seasoned travelers with their own agendas, like the serious and elusive P. J., that were not easily talked into submission, something that we, looking back on the station hustle, were grateful for.

Going further into the debris of the event, there were a few things that kept returning in our conversation. One was Osu's troubled relationship with his father, who had called him a "criminal" all those years ago, demeaning and humiliating him as a small boy, and how Osu as a grown man apparently still struggled to come to terms with it—even to the extent that he would share the story with two strangers as the reason why he decided to change his life around. Michael Jackson has argued that, when no longer confined to its conventional sexual and patriarchal bias, "the struggle for existence finds its most dramatic and perhaps universal expression in the Oedipal Complex" (2005: 181). Here, to be freed from the yoke of his father's curse, to become his own man rather than simply living out the dark promise given to him in his childhood, Osu suffered in a Libyan jail and came out a changed person. In retrospect, what choice of life could represent a greater contrast to that of the metropolitan hustler—what could represent a greater reversal of that trajectory so unfairly bestowed on him—than the dream of one day living in a cottage and managing a small poultry farm?

Conclusion

In the station hustle it could be argued that the ambiguity of the event possibly hid as much as it revealed about Osu and the particular social and political world that he sought to bring into line with his own hopes and desires by playing the cards he had been dealt and suffering defeat. Those critical moments in human life are not easy to contain because they are largely undecided, elusive, and resistant to conceptual reduction, yet they speak about the existential imperative to make more out of this life than what has been given. To Michael Jackson, these critical events are always penumbral and they overflow the words and concepts we have at our disposal in describing and understanding them, yet they concern issues of the greatest importance to human life where something "vital is at play and at risk" (2005: xxix). This means accepting the limits of insight, giving up on possessing and appropriating empirical reality or even eclipsing it, and instead exploring how to understand or to "know" a given moment without squeezing the life out of it in the cold and ultimately frustrating embrace of concepts of our own making—however existentially important they are to *our* sense of mastery of the world we encounter.

There is an interesting parallel here to another time and world when the question of how to represent the ambiguity of human life was explored and experimented with. During the High Renaissance in Europe when iconic painters such as Leonardo and Michelangelo obtained a hitherto unprecedented level of technical mastery and realism—leaving behind for good the iconic representation of the Middle Ages—it was discovered that, strangely, a real connection to the representation of empiric reality is somehow lost if the gaze of the beholder becomes too invading or if too much of the celebratory optimism of the natural scientific revolution also associated with the Renaissance was allowed to disclose, in a frozen moment, the undecided and ever-changing nature of human life. The lifelike portrait, it was discovered, is not achieved through painful attention to every anatomical detail, though the great artists knew and mastered those better than anyone, or fixing people in a compromising situation, but through leaving something to the imagination.

To be sure, existential anthropology has little in common with the works of the High Renaissance, and especially with the bourgeois fetishism surrounding the famous paintings, yet there is a certain justification for this digression into the insights the search for a method has to offer—that is, the ambition "to capture" a moment while allowing it some freedom to live and breathe. This method is evident in the famous *Mona Lisa*. There are, of course, many ways to approach an image as celebrated and overdetermined as this one, but one cannot argue with the craftsmanship and realism of the portrait, or more precisely, the indisputable fact that Leonardo da Vinci's painting is successful in creating a sense of the subject, the young wife of Francesco del Giocondo, as being a real human being. Indeed, as Giorgio Vasari, Leonardo's contemporary biographer, as well as painter and architect, finds, "On looking closely at the pit of her throat one could swear that the pulses were beating" (1968: 266). Much has been written about the enigmatic nature of her smile, but one might agree with the art historian Ernst Gombrich that *Mona Lisa*, unlike the figures of the painters of the previous generation, who look "somewhat hard and harsh, almost wooden," looks very much alive: "Like a living being, she seems to change before our eyes and to look a little different every time we come back to her" (2007: 300). Though Leonardo mastered the anatomy of the human body to perfection, the exposure of every physical detail in the portrait is not the method here. On the contrary, the liveliness of the *Mona Lisa* is brought about by the exclusion of details. Because, as Gombrich suggests, "The more conscientiously we copy a figure line by line and detail by detail, the less we can imagined that it ever moved and breathed" (300, 302). Leonardo apparently sensed this predicament of realism and came up with a surprising solution to the problem of plastic imitation of life. By blurring the contours and mellowing the colors (the so-called *sfumato* technique) at the corners of the eyes, and the corners of the mouth, something all-important is left unresolved, hidden in the shadows, leaving it up to the imagination of the beholder to decide what's at stake (302–303).

In existential anthropology too, the truth of any given moment is not ours to expose, pin down, and possess, as Jackson and Piette argue in this volume. The real dilemma is rather how to at the same time "capture" the significant events in human life without snuffing out the pulse; how to do justice to "the full range of human experience, intransitive and transitive, fixed and fluid, rational and emotional, coherent and wild, real and symbolic" without sacrificing lived reality in the lifeless embrace with one's logical concepts.

Notes

1. This was the third research project Samuel and I had undertaken on undocumented migration—a fourth followed in 2013—and he had become indispensable to me as a translator and assistant, but also in my thinking and analysis, which he discussed and would weigh in on and make important contributions to.

References

Alpes, Maybritt Jill. 2013. "Migration Brokerage, Illegality, and the State in Anglophone Cameroon." DIIS Working Paper 2013:07. Copenhagen: Danish Institute for International Studies.
Bayart, Jean-François. 2007. *Global Subjects: A Political Critique of Globalization*. Cambridge: Polity Press.
Elsner, J. 2007. *Roman Eyes*. Princeton, NJ: Princeton University Press.
Geertz, Clifford. 1988. *Works and Lives: The Anthropologist as Author*. Stanford, CA: Stanford University Press.
Gombrich, E. H. 2007. *The Story of Art*. London: Phaidon Press Limited.
Hage, Ghassan. 2005. "A not so multi-sited ethnography of a not so imagined community," *Anthropological Theory* 5: 463–475.
Jackson, Michael. 2005. *Existential Anthropology: Events, Exigencies and Effects*. New York and Oxford: Berghahn Books.
Jackson, Michael, and Albert Piette. 2015. "What is Existential Anthropology." New York and Oxford: Berghahn Books.
Kleinman, Arthur. 2006. *What Really Matters. Living A Moral Life Amidst Uncertainty And Danger*. Oxford and New York: Oxford University Press.
Lucht, Hans. 2011. *Darkness before Daybreak: African Migrants Living on the Margins in Southern Italy Today*. Berkeley: University of California Press.
———. 2013. "Pusher Stories: Ghanaian Connection Men and the Expansion of EU's Border Regimes into Africa." In *The Migration Industry and The Commercialization of International Migration*, Thomas Gammelttoft-Hansen and Ninna Nyberg Sørensen (eds.). London and New York: Routledge.
Nossiter, Adam. 2013. "Scores of Migrants From Niger Found Dead in Sahara," in *The New York Times*, 31 October. http://www.nytimes.com/2013/11/01/world/africa/bodies-of-dozens-of-migrants-found-in-nigers-northern-desert.html?_r=0.
Sartre, Jean-Paul. 2005. *Being and Nothingness*. London and New York: Routledge Classics.
Sørensen, Ninna Nyberg, and T. Gammeltoft-Hansen. 2013. "Introduction." In *The Migration Industry and The Commercialization of International Migration*, Thomas Gammelttoft-Hansen and Ninna Nyberg Sørensen (eds.). London and New York: Routledge.
Vasari, Giorgio. 1968. "Life of Leonardo da Vinci." In *The Lives of the Artist*, Vasari. London: Penguin Books.

Chapter 5

Mobility and Immobility in the Life of an Amputee

Sónia Silva

> "Travel to see the elephant, old age is worthless" (*Kumona njamba kwenda, kukola chamokomoko*) — Luvale proverb

Samuzala lived through colonialism in Angola, the liberation war, the civil war that followed independence, forced displacement to Zambia, and a landmine accident resulting in amputation. At different points in his life, Samuzala was a trader, a migrant, a refugee, and an amputee. In engaging with Samuzala's life story, a narrative of movement, we learn that mobility and immobility are relative to one another; mobility and immobility are not absolute conditions, with complete immobility being the flip side of pure, unimpeded mobility. In everyday existence, mobile individuals experience stillness, and physically immobilized individuals experience movement. As humans, we exist in a universe created by the possibilities of stasis and mobility, a universe that sets limits to our existence but also opens up new horizons. By adopting an existential stance we are more likely to avoid stereotyping and reification. We are also more likely to privilege the lifeworld over concepts such as migration and forced displacement, and more open to giving voice to new understandings of collective phenomena from the perspective of those individuals whose lives and movements generate them.

Notes for this chapter begin on page 151.

* * *

Capturing the sense in the contemporary world that mobility is a never-ending source of excitement and enchantment, Noel Salazar and Alan Smart write, "Mobility is a central metaphor for the contemporary world, both in physical form and its imaginative implications" (2011: v). Mobility suggests a movement forward, an improvement, a conquest. In this narrative of progress, however, little thought is given to those who lag behind, unable to catch up with the fast runners. The world is divided into the highly mobile and the practically immobile. The highly mobile travel in motorized vehicles, bullet trains, and commuter jets. They have daily access to kiwis from New Zealand and coffee beans from Kenya, and, through the media, they are instantly fed news about events as these are happening in the antipodes. The less mobile, in contrast, continue to rely on their own feet and legs for locomotion, walking long distances on their way to work and school. For the highly mobile, progress is as real as mobility. For the less mobile, progress is a mirage. Lagging behind, made obsolete by the high-tech infrastructure of the wealthier nations, the less mobile are of little interest to the highly mobile, including many an academic expert on the topic of mobility in the contemporary world.

Let us slow down momentarily. Let us ponder not the manifold ways in which high speed affects the quality of movement and life (differences of speed are not immaterial), but ask instead whether speed, by itself, affects the significance of movement in human existence. Does one need to be a speeder to speak to the centrality of movement in human life?

The less mobile can be as obsessed with movement as the more mobile. The Inuit of Iglookit perceive the act of traveling as "a way of being," the Scottish Gypsy Travellers see their journeys as "engaged living," and Cape Verdeans and Jamaicans take migration to be a way of life.[1] For those who reside in northwest Zambia, where I conducted two years of ethnographic fieldwork, the ability to move in physical space is a fundamental dimension of personhood, and to grow up is to become a traveler, particularly for men. Slow travelers are not the remainders of the mobility formula. They are in movement as much as fast travelers.[2]

In what follows, I recount the life story of Samuzala, a Chokwe middle-age man from Angola whom I met in Chavuma, a rural district of northwest Zambia.[3] Samuzala never traveled by airplane or set foot in an airport. At different points in his life, however, he become a trader, a labor migrant, a refugee, and an amputee, experiences that offered him privileged glimpses into the place of mobility and immobility in human life.

Like all life stories, Samuzala's story is a tapestry woven with many threads. Some threads speak to his singularity as an individual with a story to tell, others to his identity as a Chokwe man from Angola who has lived all his life in the Upper Zambezi, a region shared by east Angola and northwest Zambia, and still others to the centrality of movement in human existence. Moderns may be convinced that modernity—*their* time—is the age of mobility. Mobility, however, as both a physical and existential imperative, is not theirs alone.

As will become evident, Samuzala organizes his narrative in temporal terms, moving from his childhood in the outskirts of Luena, the capital city of Moxico province in east Angola, to the time we met in Chavuma. As he moves through time, he refers to historical processes that have deeply impacted the entire Upper Zambezi region; namely, Portuguese colonialism in Angola as well as the armed conflict between the Portuguese military forces and the Angolan liberation movements of MPLA (Popular Movement for the Liberation of Angola) and UNITA (National Union for the Total Independence of Angola); the transition period from the end of colonialism and the colonial war in April 1974 to the formal granting of independence on 11 November 1975, a violent period in which the competing nationalist movements attempted to gain control over the entire nation; the thirty-year-long postindependence civil war waged between the government forces affiliated with MPLA and UNITA, now redefined as insurgency; and, throughout these violent phases of recent Angolan history, the forced displacement of countless Angolans to the neighboring country of Zambia.[4] Samuzala, however, does not present these processes as historical formations that succeeded one another on a chronological axis, disembodied and free-floating; instead, he describes them as a series of journeys undertaken on the face of the earth. Capturing this relation between movement and human existence, Tim Ingold writes, "The world of our experience is a world . . . that is continually coming into being as we—through our own movement—contribute to its formation" (2000: 242).

Yet scholars are often less interested in this continually emerging formation of collective phenomena through movement than in the resulting patterns. Think of migration and forced displacement. Scholars often refer to these population movements as social facts in the Durkheimian sense of collective phenomena endowed with "a reality existing outside individuals" (Durkheim 1982: 19). But are migration and forced displacement not best described as concepts on which we draw in an attempt to explain what are, necessarily, much fuzzier and multilayered processes? Provided that we never lose sight of fuzziness and complexity, those concepts are valuable tools for scholars and nonscholars alike. The moment we reify those concepts, however, not only do we lose touch with reality, but we turn those individuals who migrate and are forcibly displaced into a lesser, one-dimensional version of themselves: he or she the "migrant," he or she the "refugee" (Silva 2013a; 2013b). In a passage on refugees, Michael Jackson asks: "On what grounds can we claim that 'refugeeness' is a sui generis cluster of ostensive traits, or a specific field of human experience—as is assumed in almost every essay or monograph on the subject that begins by citing the number of refugees in the world today, both external and internal, and invoking the Geneva Convention Relating to the Status of Refugees" (2002: 81). Concepts are not isomorphic with human experience. By drawing on existential ideas we are more likely to avoid the ever-present risk of reification, a risk that all scholars are familiar with and yet continue to incur. We are also more likely to privilege the lifeworld over scientific concepts, and be more open to giving voice to new understandings of worldwide phenomena from the perspective of those individuals whose lives, as "singular universals," as Sartre put it, generate the collective phenomena that scholars define as their object of study.

It is from this perspective that we can begin to understand Samuzala's life story as he told it to me in the shade of an orange tree in August 1999. I was genuinely drawn to this man whose gentle manner and broad smile seemed incommensurate with the tragedy of a life lived in the midst of conflict and disruption. For this reason, I think, I expected him to dwell on the traumatic events that had made of him a refugee and an amputee. But what he offered is not a lesson about the history of Angola and a tale of suffering at the hands of others acting with impunity and no mercy, although it is that, too. Told in a stark, matter-of-fact style, his short life story is first and foremost a narrative of movement, a narrative that speaks of life as movement, and of mobility as an act against immobility, a cry of freedom.

A Life in Movement

> SAMUZALA: I spent my childhood (*unyike*) in Luena-Moxico [then Luso], playing and playing with the other children, collecting firewood and carrying it to the village men's shelter, learning from my father our village ways. The grown-ups cooked *shima* [thick porridge], scooped a bit of *shima* from the serving plate, shaped it into a ball, dipped it in the gravy, and gave it to us to eat. If you didn't go out to collect firewood, they would punish you. Our job was to bring firewood to the men's shelter. The men sent you out on small errands, "Bring water! Bring thick porridge!" what have you. In my youth (*ukweze*), I started cultivating fields and going out to cut poles to make rafters. Soon, I looked for a wife and moved to Luvuei [then Lumai, an Angolan town located in Moxico province].

In Luvuei, I continued cultivating cassava, going out to the fields to cut down trees, and catching fish in the rainy season. In the dry season, I filled a *chivulu* basket with small fish and carry it on my shoulders all the way to Léua, an Angolan town north of Luena where there is no fish. Those of us who were beekeepers carried honey and wax. In exchange for our merchandise, the Portuguese storekeepers gave us cloth, thread, needles, and other things. Sometimes they gave us money (*lishelenge*). A large *mutonga* basket filled with fish sold for 50 or 70. A small *mutonga* sold for much less, approximately 20. If you preferred, the Portuguese were willing to pay you with cloth. I still remember some of those types of cloth: *mahina akayishala* [striped cloth], *mbololo* [blue cloth with white edges], and *pandeziya* [fantasy cloth]. First they weighed your load. If it came to the price of one or two lengths of cloth, then they paid you with cloth. But they never forgot to add a handful of free small items on top—maybe salt or a razor—which they called *pasela*. We were trading nicely. There were no disagreements or arguments, no. And we were living well. On the way back home, we stopped in Luena to purchase clothes and other commodities for our wives and children. The wealthier among us were buying cattle. We had no money to open our own stores, but we were purchasing cattle, clothes, blankets, even bags (*jipongishi*).

Then I joined the Angolan roads company, JAEA [Junta Autónoma de Estradas de Angola]. Our work consisted in opening and clearing main roads in the southern part of Moxico province. We opened roads and covered them with gravel. My job was to clear the ground behind the graters (*mazembe*) by removing the remaining vegetation. We worked as a team and spent long periods of time on the road. This was our work. Our salaries arrived by plane at the end of each month. At first we were paid 500, then 800, and finally 2000. On the payment day, I always sent some money to my wife, who stayed with my older brothers in Luvuei. Opening and clearing main roads was strenuous work to be sure, but we were living well.

Everything changed when the MPLA took control of Luvuei. Everyone was afraid, even the Portuguese, who soon fled and dispersed. Having lost our jobs, some of us chose to remain in Luvuei, others to go back to the villages where we had come from, and still others to hide in the bush. But we all lived in fear of being caught by UNITA soldiers. We said to ourselves, "One day I will go to my fields to cultivate, and the UNITAs will catch me and take me to their bases (*jimbaze*) where they, the bush-people, live." If the UNITAs found you alone in the fields, they would catch you for sure, you knew that. So many of us fled.

My wife and I decided to walk to Zambia, where my mother and other relatives who had fled the colonial war in the late 1960s were already living. We took the Nyakulemba route. First we rested on the bank of the Lungwevungu River. Second, we rested by the Vundu Lagoon. Third, we rested in Nyambingila. It took us four days to reach my mother's village is Chavuma. In Chavuma, we lived our life as we had done in Angola, cultivating fields. That's all. Now and then Meheba officials [Meheba is one of the official refugee settlements in Zambia, located near Solwezi, the capital city of North-Western province] toured the area of Chavuma, looking for Angolans.

SÓNIA: When exactly did you come to Zambia?

SAMUZALA: When the MPLAs entered Luvuei in 1975. That war . . . It all began during colonialism with the whites saying, "The *vaturoji* are coming!" The term *turoji* [*turras* in Portuguese, an abbreviation of *terroristas*] referred to the bush-people, the liberation fighters who hid in the bush. The whites were telling us that the *turras* were coming to steal our things. They were urging men to join their military forces and fight the enemy in the bush. This war between the Portuguese and the liberation fighters started in the mid-1960s. Now, the whites have left Angola, colonialism has ended, but we, blacks, are still fighting. We call this war our second war, the war that started in 1975 when MPLA, supported by the Cubans, took over Luvuei. During the first war, the whites relocated people from the villages to their towns, and the liberation fighters took people from those towns to the bush. This war has long ended. The present war is our own war, the war of Neto and Savimbi [Agostinho Neto, one of the top political leaders of MPLA, became the first president of Angola after independence; Jonas Savimbi remained the leader of UNITA, now redefined as insurgency]. Some people liked Neto, other people liked Savimbi. As more and more people died, our hearts saddened. We said to ourselves, "We must flee, they will kill us with their axes and knifes." If you hid in the bush, the UNITAs would catch you and take you to their bases. If you sought refuge in Luvuei, the MPLAs accused you of being a bush-dweller, a UNITA supporter. Some people spent the nights in the bush because they feared being trapped and killed inside their own houses. People lived in fear. So they started to scatter (*kulimwanga*).

I came to Zambia and settled at my mother's village, as I was saying. I became a farmer, a fisherman, and a beekeeper all over again. Then, I became injured. You know that, VaSónia. I stepped on a bomb [landmine]. I had gone to Angola hoping to find good-quality bark to make a beehive. Little did I know that I would step on a mine. That mine was planted by MPLA soldiers. Many of us have been maimed and killed by those traps (*vijila*).

Yes, I thought so many things after the accident. But God gave me wisdom to become a basket maker. My first basket was very rough. It had no decoration, no beauty. I made it for practice (*yatusumbi*). Then I learned several designs, one after the other. I still remember when I sold my first basket, a winnowing tray (*lwalo*). I sold it to a local woman for 500 kwacha. I had earned 500 kwacha even though I was immobile like an old man. I felt proud and happy.

Today, I think many, many things in my heart. My wife and five children feel weak but do not complain. I think many things in my heart.

I have nothing else to say. *Twasakwililako mwane* (thank you).

Mobilities

As I listened to Samuzala, I was struck by the ease with which he interconnected a series of movements in his lifelong journey without ever ignoring their historical specificity. Samuzala speaks of many comings and goings, traced out in the process of performing daily tasks, fulfilling obligations, and seeking the company of others, the endless series of "to and fro movements that define the mundane patterning of all social life" (Jackson 2002: 32). Samuzala also speaks of other movements, often coded as migration and forced displacement in scholarly analysis, that occur when life-as-usual is interrupted and thrown off course by contingent forces and events. But he never allows those movements to crystallize and break away from the fluidity of the lifeworld. As Jackson observes, "In telling stories we testify to the diversity, ambiguity, and interconnectedness of experiences that abstract thought seeks to reduce, tease apart, regulate, and contain" (2002: 253). In retelling the stories that others tell us, we attempt to make whole and bring to life what we often divide and deaden in the process of analysis.

Scholars in refugee studies and forced migration are well aware that the distinction between migration and forced displacement is clearer on paper than on the ground. In dire situations, migration becomes a form of forced displacement, and prolonged forced displacement can amount to full-blown migration. In addition, notwithstanding the shared assumption that forced displacement is more forceful than voluntary migration—because it is more urgent and leaves no room for choice—"there is no clear-cut separation between choice and constraint, between forced and voluntary mobility" (Salazar and Smart 2011: v). Although in his life story Samuzala does not mention the reason why, as a young man, he chose to emigrate to Luvuei, he told me on another occasion that he was forced to seek employment in order to pay the colonial tax and satisfy the new necessities of daily life in colonial Angola. When, years later, he was forcibly displaced from Luvuei, he knew that it would be difficult for him to find employment as an Angolan refugee living in Zambia, but he hoped nonetheless that he would be able to rise above his condition as a refugee and make ends meet. For Samuzala, choice and constraint are the two sides of every act, be it migrating, becoming a refugee, or getting married.

While choice and constraint may become on occasion the topic of conversation (Why did you leave at that particular moment? Was it the right decision? Did you have a choice?), Angolan refugees more typically engage with those existential themes by speaking of movement as an act with particular resonances. They will, for example, refer to so-called forced displacement not by stressing the Western idea of forcefulness—or the germane Western notions of displacement and uprootedness (Malkki 1992)—but by employing a descriptive, movement-related term, *kulimwanga*, to become dispersed. War dispersed families and relatives, many of whom crossed the international border into Zambia and resettled on the west bank of the Zambezi River or in the larger towns located on the east bank, such as Chavuma, Zambezi, and Kabompo. Others headed willingly or unwillingly to the official refugee settlements set up by the Zambian government and UNHCR. "Dispersal" brings to mind not only the disruptive events that caused it, but also the collective experience and mental image of physical movement across the landscape as groups of relatives set off in different directions hoping to resettle in safer locations. "Dispersal" is primarily a movement concept.

Equally revealing of the emphasis on movement across the landscape, rather than forceful displacement through uprooting at the point of origin, is the description of dispersal as a form of movement imbued with particular emotional and experiential tonalities. In the Luvale language, these different tonalities are conveyed by means of two verbs: *kwenda*, to travel at one's pace, and *kuchina*, to run. In extreme situations, people had to run for their lives. I heard many stories of people who ran for the forest and hid there for weeks, months, and even years, wearing rags, bathing with mud, and relying on boiled honey, game meat, and wild fruits for survival. My good friend Armando left Luvuei when he was a child. He had been secluded with other boys in the male initiation camp (*mukanda*) for several months. One night they heard the sound of shooting. "I could not stay there waiting to be slaughtered," he said. "I left the camp, hid in the forest for three weeks and then ran toward the line [the international border]." Armando and the other neophytes were robbed of a significant part of their *mukanda* experience, including the final, much-anticipated "coming-out" ceremony, during which large crowds gather to celebrate and welcome the boys back into society as young men. The war had violently interrupted his initiation ceremony as well as his life. Armando told me that he ran to Zambia in the late 1970s. He only saw his mother again after the war ended in 2002.

Unknown numbers of Angolans were forced to make their way through the forests. On this account, Zambians jokingly refer to the Angolan refugees as Tree Log Jumpers (*Zomboka Mingowa*), Cutters of *Minbungo* (*Vateta Minbungo*, a type of vine that blocks movement), and Droppers of Head Pads (*Vambila Kata*). At times, Zambians employ these names pejoratively. Whereas edifying travel, *kwenda*, is understood as a poised, smooth, and enjoyable journey, running, *kuchina*, in fear is often described as hazardous and clumsy. Women balancing head pads on their head being a familiar image of verticality and composure, the name Droppers of Head Pads strongly conveys the idea of hasty movement provoked by shock.

But these are stereotypes. Whereas the media disseminates images of African refugees walking in long columns as orderly and obediently as cattle, some Zambians stereotypically describe Angolan refugees as small groups running through the forest in a panic, jumping over logs and fallen trees, and cutting *minbungo* vines as they go. In reality, though, the Angolan refugees moved in different modes and at different paces, according to the immediate reason that triggered their flight, and the distance between their point of departure and the international border. Many refugees never ran. Some refugees alternated between running and walking at different points in their journey. As for media images of defeated refugees walking in a column, they obscure the reality of forced displacement in different parts of Africa and the world. The numbers of Angolans who walked down the main roads toward the border were relatively small. Most refugees traveled in small groups down paths previously trodden for other purposes, such as trading, visiting relatives, and migrating for work. Apart from the larger influxes of the mid-1960s, mid-1980s, and late 1990s through the early 2000s,[5] the number of refugees in northwest Zambia increased in relatively small but steady increments, adding up to the estimated total of approximately 240,000 by March 2002 (UNHCR 2002: 6).[6]

This leads back to the problem of reification in the study of mobility. Was Samuzala a *migrant*? Was he a *refugee*? Did his identity ever shrink to the point that he became one of these labels? Migration and forced displacement always encompass a range of experiences and activities that far exceed the movement of migrating and fleeing proper. In the process of walking toward the border, many Angolans, including Samuzala, yearned to meet relatives who had migrated to Zambia during colonialism or had become refugees in an earlier date. They also hoped that those relatives would welcome them in their villages. Some refugees hoped to find employment at the CMML mission in Chavuma. The so-called refugee might be a refugee, a migrant, and a guest all at once. Movement and mobility are experientially dense. What appears to be a series of discrete, mutually exclusive types of movement is, in effect, a composite of experiences and intentions, a composite that is best translated by such generic movement-related terms as "travel," "journey," even "adventure."

Noting both the similarities between different travels and the experiential density of each type of movement is at least as important as recognizing the irrefutable differences between mundane and extraordinary types of movement. This focus on similarities has helped me reduce the risk of reification in my own work (Silva 2013a). It has also helped me come to terms with the fact that Samuzala and other Angolans in Chavuma did not describe their experiences of forced travel as negatively as I had expected. Whereas elsewhere, forced migrants described their movement in the language of displacement and uprooting from their original homeland—the Yaqui Indians' narratives of forced displacement from their fertile land in northwest Mexico are a case in point (Erikson 2003)—the Angolan refugees often opted to emphasize the similarities between so-called forced displacement and other forms of movement. Notwithstanding the real dangers of traversing war zones and hiding in forests, the Angolan refugees spoke of fleeing as a form of travel and even, in some cases, an adventure. Do not adventures need obstacles to overcome? Ramon Sarró (2007: 4) asked himself this question during his work with African immigrants in Portugal, some of whom described their migration experience as an adventure. At the very least this perspective has the important advantage of presenting migration, as Sarró does, "from the viewpoint of action, initiative and risk, instead of victimage, trauma and economic desperation" (2007: 2).

Let us recall Samuzala's adventures as a migrant and a trader. In spite of the meager salary received as an employee of the national roads company of Angola, Samuzala greatly enjoyed opening up roads through the vegetation, seeing the machines cut through thick branches without effort, and covering the bare ground with gravel. Together with his coworkers, he said proudly, they built roads from Luvuei all the way to the town of Lumbala N'guimbo in the furthest southeast corner of Moxico province. They slowly traveled long distances in the process of building roads so that others could travel those same roads at motor speeds. The spirit of adventure is also present in Samuzala's account of his trading ventures to Léua every fishing season. Walking a distance of approximately 155 kilometers on sandy terrain carrying a long cylindrical basket filled with fish on the shoulders is surely strenuous work, and selling fish to the Portuguese storekeepers in Léua may not conform to your usual image of a life adventure. Yet Samuzala nostalgically reminisced about his trips to Léua and the memorable transactions with the Portuguese storekeepers. In exchange for his fish, the Portuguese gave him money or lengths of cloth, always closing the transaction with a small gift known as *pasela* still used in trading today. Maybe they gave him a bit of salt, a razor, or thread and needles. "They always gave you *pasela*," Samuzala said. "Before you departed, they gave you some flour and perhaps some *carapaus* [the Portuguese word for mackerel], and closed the transaction by saying, 'Take this food for your journey.'" On his way back home, Samuzala would stop in Luena to buy clothes, blankets, and whatnot for his wife and children. Summarizing his trips to Léua, Samuzala said, "You placed the fish load on your shoulder and set off. You slept on the way. The moon changed. You passed Luena and headed to Léua. You traded your fish for money, and returned back home to tell your relatives about your travels (*kutwa mujimbu*)."

Life is not sliced up in chunks ready to be gauged and tagged by scholars. Present movements speak of past movements, and movements across regions, international borders, and even oceans speak of shorter movements from here to there. Movements of all kinds also speak of the traveler's thrill of adventure, from the first trip ever taken to the city to that most special, long forgotten moment when the seasoned traveler, then a toddler, took his or her first steps and, in a moment of courage, let go of the mother's finger.

Mobility

The importance of movement in human existence cannot be overstated. The physical ability to cover long distances at great speed has been critical for the survival of the human species since at least our Plio-Pleistocene hominid ancestors roamed the face of the earth (Jackson 2013: 227). Moving from phylogeny to ontogeny, the physical ability to crawl, stand up on one's feet, and take the first steps is as critical to the cognitive and psychological development of every child today as it was, I suppose, in the Plio-Pleistocene. In this light, it is hardly surprising that humans everywhere—and quite regardless of their mobility index—similarly see their life course in terms of distances trodden. This physical movement defines a biographical arch: as one grows up and becomes an adult, one's travels dramatically expand; as one ages and nears death, one's travels contract. One begins and ends with immobility. In between, one travels.

You do not need to have lived in Ancient Greece to understand the Riddle of the Sphinx. If asked to answer the famous riddle, "What goes on four feet in the morning, two feet at noon, and three feet in the evening?" any person in the Upper Zambezi, including Samuzala, will most likely answer, "*Vakemba, vakulwane,* and *tushinakaji.*" Nursing babies (*vakemba*) only feel secure and protected within reach of their mothers on whose backs they travel day in, day out. Toddlers and children (*vanyike*) do not venture far. Toddlers do not dare crossing the village perimeter. On realizing that their mothers have left for the fields in the early morning, leaving them behind, toddlers run down the village path in search of their mothers, crying and screaming with all their might, only to stop at the point in the path where, in their perception, the familiar space of the village meets the unknown. Children aged four or five do not venture much further unless accompanied by an older child or an adult. By the time they turn six or seven, however, children become physically stronger and learn to control their fear. They are now referred to as *tumbululu*. These *tumbululu* are often seen playing and roaming in groups. They venture out to the cultivated fields and surrounding woodlands, where they enjoy hunting for a type of rodent that lives in underground tunnels. Together, they skin, prepare, roast and eat their prey with the pride of hunters and the joy of children. Male and female *tumbululu* also collect small firewood for their mothers and fathers, as Samuzala describes in his life story.

Ukweze, or youth, ranges from early teenage years to early adulthood. The younger *vakweze* cycle down the motor road to the town of Zambezi or travel by bus to Solwezi, the provincial capital, but do not cross the plains and forests that separate them from the city of Luena in Angola, for example, unless accompanied by an older man. Traveling long distances within the boundaries of inhabited territory is true for both male and female *vakweze*. There is a gender difference, though. Whereas female travelers remain confined within inhabited territory throughout their lives—women remain *vakweze* in this regard—men travel anywhere in their adult years (*ukulwane*), a stage of life that stretches from young adulthood (*ukweze*) to early old age (*uvupu*). For as long as the physical ailments of late old age (*ushinakaji*) do not slow them down, men travel far and wide within and beyond inhabited space, visiting relatives, attending rituals, setting up fishing camps on the west bank of the Zambezi River, going on hunting expeditions in Angola, selling and trading with city-dwellers, searching for employment in the cities of the Copperbelt and Lusaka. Traveling in the Upper Zambezi, by foot or motor vehicle, is always a learning experience and a personal challenge. Traveling is also seen as an adventure, and here crossing the vast expanses of the Upper Zambezi is remindful of what is, perhaps, the most emblematic symbol of independence in the United States, the road trip adventure through the desert.

And just as much as men and women love traveling, they enjoy returning home and telling their relatives, friends, and neighbors about their travels, a custom known as *kutwa mujimbu*. After exchanging greetings and sharing the latest news about events and relatives, the traveler gives a detailed account of his or her journey to a rapt audience. During my visit to Chavuma in 2010, I happened to be present when my friend Maria came to greet Sapasa, her paternal relative, on her way back home from

Lumbala-Caquenge, an Angolan town located near the border. She had cycled down the main road to Lumbala on her own, carrying a load of commodities for trade: bathing soaps, *chitenge* cloths, small bottles of oil, and salt. Maria sat on a small stool facing a group of four Angolans who had meanwhile gathered to hear the latest news from Lumbala. She spoke of her trading ventures and the relatives and friends she had visited, some of whom had resided in Chavuma during the civil war. She spoke of the lack of services such as schools and health clinics, and of the shortage of basic goods such as soap and salt. She reported that elephants were destroying the cultivated fields in search of food, a clear sign, she said, that the elephants were suffering, just like people. Then Sapasa, a paraplegic middle-aged man who was born in Angola and spent most of his youth in a colonial settlement, or *aldeamento*,[7] in Lumbala, asked Maria about his old neighborhood. "Did you see my *bairro*?" he asked. Following a moment of silence, she mustered the courage to answer: "It is no longer there." "What do you mean?" Sapasa retorted nervously. "The only thing standing are dilapidated walls covered with bullet holes, *eh mwane*, thank you," Maria said. Sapasa's neighborhood as he remembered it had been wiped out from the face of the earth. In its place lay the ruins of a protracted conflict that destroyed both human lives and walls. Maria's travels displayed a mix of happiness and sadness, the same emotions that her story generated.

In *Routes*, James Clifford points out that the word "travel" "has an inextinguishable taint of location by class, gender, race, and a certain literariness" (1997: 39). The word "travel" brings to mind the exploration voyages of white, upper-class men of the caliber of Tocqueville, Vasco da Gama, Baron Alexander van Humboldt, and Cabeza de Vaca. It also brings to mind the leisure trips of present-day tourists and the work trips of white-collar professionals, trips in which long distances are traversed in the comfort of motorized vehicles, at least today. But walkers and bicycle riders like Samuzala and Maria are long-distance travelers too, and their "travel stories" speak as eloquently as European "travel literature" to the centrality of movement and adventure in human life. This is equally true of the CEO of a multinational who flies first class around the world, the wealthy Zambian businessman who travels across Zambia in the comfort of his air-conditioned, four-wheel vehicle, and the poorest villager in Chavuma who must rely on his or her legs and calloused feet to go everywhere. As Ingold (2007: 2) puts it, "wayfaring," no less than "transport," is a modality of travel.

To this egalitarian assertion, we should add the following: never base your judgment of mobility on appearance. Behind the semblance of indigence and simplicity in a rural setting of Zambia stand well-traveled individuals who have been to South Africa, England, Portugal, and Romania. A case in point is Mr. Chinoya. When we met in 2002, this middle-aged Luchazi man had just arrived from his fields, a hoe on his right shoulder and rags for clothing—hardly the picture of a seasoned traveler. Yet Mr. Chinoya, in addition to his long distance travels in the Upper Zambezi, had been to Lisbon and Porto, the largest cities of Portugal. The late Mr. Chivundo also comes to mind. In spite of his old age, Mr. Chivundo, a Luvale man, stopped by my house in Chavuma once a week to sell his *mafwo* (leaf vegetables) and drink a cup of sugar-filled tea. Again, like Mr. Chinoya, Mr. Chivundo was hardly the image of an international traveler, clad as he always was in a faded, several-sizes-too-short dark grey suit, a half-shredded nylon mesh for a hat, and a large basket of vegetables on his right shoulder. Yet Mr. Chivundo had spent several years in Johannesburg, South Africa, working in the mines. He knew all too well that mining is a dangerous and poorly paid job, yet he enjoyed interspersing mining stories with comical machine sounds produced with his mouth, and hilarious imitations of the bossy demeanor and stiff postures of the mine supervisors. And Mr. Chinoya and Mr. Chivundo are not the only well-traveled men hiding behind the appearance of poverty and peasantry. As one Luvale proverb reminds the high-browed: "Ask the peasant where to find the oil container" (*Hula watoma akulweze saji yamaji*).

Mobility Against Immobility

In the contest for power that followed the end of colonialism and the colonial war in 1974, the MPLA and UNITA nationalist movements turned violently against each other, unleashing what would become one of the deadliest and most disruptive civil wars fought on African soil in the twentieth century. East Angola, once again, became a strategic battleground. As traveling became increasingly dangerous, many east Angolans were forced to remain within the bounds of their townships, now under the control of the MPLA-affiliated national government. Samuzala explained:

> We were afraid, so we remained still (*kuliswata*). If you lived in town and decided to go somewhere, the UNITAs might catch you and ask: "You, town-dweller, where are you going? You, come with us!" They took many of us to the bush. People feared traveling, so they sat still. Traveling became too dangerous. Do you think that we were living in Angola as we are living here in Zambia? Uh-uh. We lived in fear. We always thought, "They might find me and punish me." Those who ventured out into the bush feared to be asked on their return

to town, "Why did you go to the bush, to the bush-people?" We traveled with fear. We lived in discontent. That is why we fled.

Samuzala chose to flee early on, in retrospective the right decision. By fleeing in 1975, he and his family escaped the protracted civil war waged by UNITA against the government, including, as Angolans in Chavuma always note, the atrocities committed in east Angola in the mid-1980s and the intense armed conflict that preceded the cease-fire in April 2002. By March 2002, as mentioned, approximately 240,000 Angolans had sought refuge in Zambia alone (UNHCR 2002: 6).

Unemployed and disillusioned, Samuzala and his family set off on their long journey to Zambia. They took the same route that countless other travelers had taken before them. On the first day, they crossed the Lungwebungu River to its southern bank. On the second day, they reached the Vundu Lagoon by the Kashiji River. On the third day, they reached Nyambingila, a small town in Zambia. On the fourth day, they passed through Nyakulemba, near the Kashiji River, then crossed the Zambezi River to its eastern bank. They rested for several days in Chavuma before proceeding to the village of Samuzala's father in Kabompo, an additional leg of some 250 kilometers that Samuzala omitted in his narrative. In the early 1980s, however, following his father's death, Samuzala and his wife and children moved again, this time to the village of his classificatory mother in Chavuma, where we met. He chose not to settle in the Meheba Refugee Settlement located south of Solwezi, the provincial capital, because, as he put it, he did not want to be trapped in the refugee settlement as he had been trapped in Luvuei.

In his life story, Samuzala does not paint an image of despondency. He recognizes that the civil war severely impacted the life of all Angolan refugees, but nowhere in his discourse are there signs of hopelessness and defeat. The concept of forced displacement is predicated on the bipolar distinction between those who hold power and those who are at the mercy of that power, having no choice but to flee. Robbed of the right to determine their present as well as their future, refugees become reduced to mere victims who head for the closest border almost by instinct. They become objects whose movement is a reaction to the action of others. Writing in 1973, E. F. Kuntz graphically expressed this view when he compared the movement of refugees to the movement of the billiard ball: "devoid of inner direction, their path is governed by the kinetic factors of inertia, friction and the vectors of outside forces applied on them" (1973: 131). This image of refugees, however, speaks more clearly to the cultural and intellectual predisposition to see necessity and freedom as mutually exclusive than it does to the ways in which refugees see themselves and perceive their act of fleeing. Hannah Arendt puts it thus: "Since action acts upon beings who are capable of their own actions, reaction, apart from being a response, is always a new action that strikes out on its own and affects others" (1958: 190).

We can say that the military conflict forced Samuzala to flee, leaving him no choice, and that his fleeing was therefore his reaction to a threatening situation that he could not possibly ignore or control. But, as Samuzala sees it, he was not forced to flee; he was forced to be still. What if the war continued for a long time? Was he going to condemn himself and his loved ones to a life of misery, fear, and immobility? Was he going to curl up in a corner and wait to be shot? For Samuzala, the experience of being stuck and immobile meant being unable, to use an English expression commonly heard in Zambia, to move freely. From his perspective, therefore, fleeing is not an instinctual response to aggression; it is instead his choice, his cry of freedom.

The existential significance of drawing together different collective phenomena under the umbrella of movement should now be clearer. Regardless of type of movement and degree of constraint, movement is seen as an act of freedom whose existential value can only be fully grasped in opposition to the prison of immobility. Worse than having to flee and become a refugee is to be forcibly immobilized. Consider, in this regard, Emmanuel Mulamila, a Ugandan man that Jackson met in Copenhagen in 2010 and whose life story he recounts in *The Wherewithal of Life*. In conversation with Jackson, Emmanuel describes the many forms of physical and psychological abuse that he and his younger siblings underwent at the hands of their aunt in Uganda, the reason why he ran away from home. In Emmanuel's words, "It was from that period that I stopped being immobile, I stopped being home. That's the time I realized that if life got too hard for me, I had the alternative to leave." Moved by Emmanuel's story, Jackson asked himself "whether this was what people do in an impasse, with all passages blocked. Desperate to recover some sense of freedom in mobility, they hit the road" (2013: 32).

Immobility

In Chavuma, Samuzala channeled his energies into clearing fields, hunting, and fishing. Life was harder than in Angola, but with determination and hard work he was able to make a living and raise his five children. He sold game meat and smoked fish to other villagers in Chavuma, using the profit to purchase goods such as salt, soap, and clothing from the local stores, and then selling these goods to the Angolan civilians and UNITA soldiers who came to the weekly market held in the no man's land past the gate of the Zambian customs.

Then, his life changed. In need of good-quality bark to make cylindrical beehives, he followed the course of the Chivombo stream to its source in Angola. He was walking down a sandy path through the forest, mindful to observe the tree trunks as he walked, when he was blown up in the air in a cloud of smoke. He had stepped on a pressure-operated blast mine.

> SAMUZULA: I had gone to the source of the Chivombo stream, looking for bark to cut out a beehive. I had said to myself, "Let me look at the trees on the other side of the 'line' [the international border]." And I crossed the "line" and entered Angola. That's when I stepped on a "bomb" [landmine]. All of a sudden, paa! My leg, my leg. My cousin, who was walking behind me, dragged me to the shade of a tree. I remember noticing dirt all over my body and an intense smell of smoke.
> SÓNIA: Nothing happened to your friend?
> SAMUZULA: No, nothing. I told him, "Come here, help me, come here!" He came and carried me on his back. I asked him to take me to the stream because I felt very thirsty. He scooped a little water with the lid of his plastic canteen and brought it to my lips. He said, "That's enough, too much water will kill you."

It is common knowledge in Chavuma that the border area is heavily mined. Portuguese military forces laid the first landmines in 1970–1971 as a strategy to curtail MPLA infiltration from Zambia, where the MPLA liberation fighters had set up two military bases with the consent of Kenneth Kaunda, then president of Zambia (Pelissier 1974: 99). In the 1980s, FAPLA, the military branch of the Angolan government in independent Angola, planted more landmines in the region in its counterinsurgency operations against UNITA (Samuzala is convinced that he stepped on one of these mines). Beginning in the 1980s, UNITA soldiers too employed "hidden killers," as landmines are often called, reportedly for a different reason: to channel the movement of civilians across the border and tax them in the form of passes and trading fees. In a country so heavily mined as Angola, the risk of stepping on a landmine is high. Angola has one of the highest rates of landmine injuries per capita in the word. In a population of about twenty million, there are approximately 80,000 landmine amputees (ICRC 2008).

Samuzala became injured on a Monday. His cousin hurried back to Chavuma to seek help, and on Wednesday a small party of men finally arrived. They carried Samuzala to the Chivombo clinic, where he received first-aid treatment. The following morning a vehicle from the mission hospital came to collect him. Three days had meanwhile passed, too long to avoid amputation.

The irony of his accident is not lost to Samuzala: he had escaped alive from a military conflict that killed hundreds of thousands of people, only to step on a landmine, a residue of that conflict, while leisurely searching for bark to make a beehive. Being from Moxico, one of the most heavily mined districts in Angola (HRW Arms Project 1997: 29), he knew well that narrow paths are a common site of civilian mine injury. He also knew that antipersonnel landmines, like chemical and biological weapons, fail to distinguish between soldiers and civilians. Yet Samuzala had not let that risk dominate his life. He knew where to find superior bark for his beehives, so he went there. Now, Samuzala felt doomed and literally stuck. He had become a *chitonji*, a disabled person. His days of travel were no more.

In a place where mobility is not only valued and encouraged but constitutes an integral part of the definition of personhood, immobility is tantamount to social death. And in the same way that the experience of mobility transcends the differences among categories of mobility and their underlying causes, the experience of immobility is clearly not reducible to the conditions that caused it—the civil war, aging, or landmines. Samuzala often described himself as an old man. To express his feelings, he sometimes spoke of *mbombolyo*, a heavy word that conveys the sense of being useless and hopeless. Samuzala felt robbed of a crucial dimension of life as an adult. The landmine that took his leg accelerated his life course, turning the travels of adulthood and middle age into the immobility of very old age.

Only the valuing of movement as life itself begins to explain what, to me, came with the jolt of an existential revelation: that, in order to convey the tragedy of amputation, Samuzala invoked not the injustice of what David Birmingham calls "a war by proxy between the United States and the Soviet Union" (2006: 11), a war in which the insignificance of human life sneaks out through the cracks of political demagogy in the form of that most technocratic and indifferent of expressions, "civilian casualties"; nor the anger at the armed men who having not killed on the spot planted landmines that would kill or maim later; nor the anger at a global system that allows for those landmines to be sold for a modicum—but the absolute misery of being turned into an elderly person before due time. Nothing could possibly convey the experience of physical disability and immobility as clearly and completely as old age.

Needless to say, valuing mobility in contrast with physical immobility framed as old age is not in the least archaic or exotic. Certainly, the highly mobile are familiar with both the biological reality of aging and the ontological metaphor of old age, even though great numbers of them nurse the illusion that with cars, cruises, technology, and vitamins they will never be brought to a standstill, not even in old age. Is not old age what we do about it? In this world of mirrors, flashing lights, and dreams, it is refreshing to listen to a man like Richard, a 69-year-old from northeast England: "I don't think I have the energy and I think that some immobility comes with age. You know, I mean I have problems with stairs. I know exactly how to deal with it as far as I can, but in addition to that, you're just not as strong, you're not as fit as you used to be, you can't be, can you?" (Ziegler and Schwanen 2011: 768)

Immobility as Mobility

The Luvale word for being injured, *kulemana*, conveys the feeling of heaviness and of a struggle to walk. By the time we met, though, Samuzala walked with notable ease thanks to a carved pair of heavy crutches. If he needed to travel far, a relative or friend carried him on the back rack of their bicycle. What Samuzala could not do was to carry out the more physically demanding activities typically associated with able-bodied adult men in rural Upper Zambezi: clearing the forest for new cassava fields and cultivating vegetable "gardens" in alluvial soils, setting up fishing camps on the west bank of the Zambezi River in the rainy season, trading dried fish and other commodities in the local, regional, and Copperbelt markets, building and maintaining mud-brick houses, keeping beehives on tree crowns. In a region where walking and traveling are signs of physical strength, maturity, autonomy, and social worth, leg amputation amounts to social death. Samuzala had bravely fled from several situations of immobility in his lifetime; from amputation, however, he could not flee. And yet he discovered other ways to be mobile.

> SÓNIA: Do you remember what thoughts crossed your mind after the accident?
> SAMUZALA: I thought many things. I felt sadness in my heart and I said to myself, "I'll kill myself." Thinking of the difficulties ahead saddened me so much that I just wanted to die. Then, a white person came to comfort me at the mission hospital. That person said, "You are a man, do not think too many things, no. You must pray. God will help you in all your thoughts and give you peace." Later that day, Dr. Burness, the medical doctor who amputated my leg, came to see me. I noticed that he carried a slasher of the type used by the mission workers to cut overgrown vegetation. "Take this slasher and concentrate on

sharpening the blade," he said. When my leg improved, Dr. Burness would drive me to church in his vehicle and drive me back to the hospital after the readings. He told me about God's words and showed me the Bible.

When they took me back to my village, I asked myself, "What will I do?" I thought about this over and over again. One day I thought to myself, "Why don't I become a basket maker like my cousin? I will plait baskets!" So I visited my cousin, the late Saluyambo, who lived nearby. I visited him many times. I sat there and practiced weaving until I learned the skill. I had thought that there was nothing left for me to do, but no, I could still make a living. An older man said to me, "My son, you should make baskets! Difficulties strike without warning. If you have a skill, you and your children will be able to survive." Saluyambo had already grown old (*nazeye lyehi*), so he used to stay at his village plaiting baskets. I learned by sitting there and observing him. One day I said, "Please, let me try." I returned home. Another day I sat there chatting and looking. "Please, you need a break," I told my cousin. I learned basket making by replacing him now and then. Soon I mastered the skill. It took me three months of hard work.

According to Human Rights Watch, the future of amputees in Angola is extremely bleak. As stated in one of their publications on the topic of landmines, the future of most amputees "will consist of being cared for by their families, or attempting to earn a living in one of the few occupations open to them, such as street trading or—for those with education—secretarial or clerical work. The majority, who come from farming backgrounds, are likely to remain a burden on their families for the foreseeable future" (1997: 34). The future of Angolan amputees residing in Chavuma is equally bleak. And yet, much like street trading and secretarial work in urban areas, basket making enabled Samuzala to escape the negative category of "unproductive relative" (HRW Arms Project 1993: 4). Thanks to basket making, Samuzala became a "worker" whose beautifully woven baskets he sells to local clients and exchanges for used clothing with CMML missionaries. He became a "productive relative" who is able to meet the basic needs of his wife and children and earn the respect of others in his community. Samuzala may no longer be able to travel on foot to see the elephants, as the Luvale proverb in epigraph says, but he can weave beautiful baskets with his fingers, baskets that others will travel to see, admire, and obtain.

Writing about the elderly in rural southwest England and Wales, Les Todres and Kathleen Galvin show that the elderly achieve some of the purposes of mobility through technology (the Internet, Skype, webcams, mobile phones) as well as connections with friends, relatives, neighbors, and professional care providers. Movement occurs in different types of space in addition to physical space, making it possible for the immobile to cultivate nonphysical forms of mobility (2012: 61; Ziegler and Schwanen 2011: 760). Although Samuzala has no access to these technologies (I say this at a time when cell phone calls have become as frequent as letter writing in Chavuma), he would certainly not fail to recognize important similarities between Angolan amputees and the elderly abroad (or the elderly in general). Beneath the differences of appearance, cultural outlook, and wealth, both the very old and the amputated strive to devise new forms of mobility through which "the outside world comes in" (Todres and Galvin 2012: 61). From this perspective, modern communication devices and ancient arts such as basket weaving are closer to one another than they appear.

Another powerful way of overcoming one's physical immobility is the act of reminiscing about the past and telling one's life story to friends and visitors, including the anthropologist. Samuzala traveled far and wide as he told me his life story, from his childhood in Luena to the present. Like going on a journey and weaving a basket, storytelling, for Samuzala, defined a line, a movement forward.

And thus it is that walking, storytelling, and weaving are subsumed into one single field of inquiry—line tracing (Ingold 2007: 1). Life is a meshwork of lines. These lines, however, do not go out for a walk on their own, as Ingold claims, borrowing from the artist Paul Klee (Klee 1961: 105, cited in Ingold 2007: 73, 81). Samuzala is the one tracing lines in the process of walking, telling stories, and weaving baskets, the one creating the meshwork we call his life. And Samuzala is neither a "rhizome" nor a "nomad." He is, more simply, and less pretentiously, a Chokwe man who has lived his life as an Angolan citizen and an Angolan refugee at a time of violence and upheaval, a man whose life, like yours and mine, has been lived at the crossroads of mobility and immobility.

I do not think that Samuzala's new lifeline as a basket maker, which he traces back to his encounter with Saluyambo, a gifted basket maker, ever took away his suffering and troubled thoughts. Unable to undo the injury inflicted on him—unable to reverse the steps taken toward the landmine—he continued to suffer alone and with others. Yet his kindness and vivacity showed the world that he found some degree of acceptance and inner peace, some degree of "letting-be-ness."[8] He could not physically flee his condition, but he could devise other ways to be mobile.

Mobility—Immobility

From the viewpoint of high mobility, it may appear that the less mobile have nothing of import to contribute to current debates about mobility in the contemporary world. I hope that Samuzala's life story, as well as my engagement with it from an existential stance, shows that this bipolar view of the world is a figment of positionality, and that, in reality, walkers are in movement as much as flyers (and I do not mean this is in the selective sense that walkers *move* themselves whereas flyers *are moved* by airplanes, and all they see are clouds).

That movement is life itself in the Upper Zambezi becomes clear in Samuzala's life story. Whereas some might emphasize the differences among types of movement, Samuzala stresses what they share as movement. Whereas some might be drawn to the depths of personal and collective suffering at the hands of colonizers and armed guerrillas, Samuzala finds space in his narrative to convey the thrill of adventure and the sweetness of travel encounters. Whereas some might privilege the power of social, political, and economic forces to determine population movements and individual stories, Samuzala highlights those moments when one takes control by acting with one's feet. Movement is an existential cry against immobility. This, to me, is the central message in Samuzala's story, a message that builds a bridge between the Upper Zambezi and the entire world. Being alive is to move—across physical space, across a life journey in storytelling, across the distance between one and others in basket making, Skype, and Facebook.

But Samuzala's story is pregnant with other insights that are directly relevant to current debates about mobility in the contemporary word. In addition to showing that mobility and immobility are relative to one another, Samuzala shows that mobility and immobility are not absolute conditions, with complete immobility being the flip side of pure, unimpeded mobility. We have already seen that, in the case of the elderly and amputees, both of whom are mobile to some degree, it is best to speak of relative immobility. The same can be said of mobility. Dissect mobility down the middle and you will realize that mobility is composed of the same substance as immobility. As a lived reality, mobility includes moments of physical movement and moments of stillness, being best described as relative mobility.

In the Upper Zambezi, all travels, voluntary or involuntary, are perceived and planned as a series of shorter journeys separated by stops to rest and take a breath, savor a hot meal, and chat with friends and relatives. Reflecting this understating of traveling as an alternation between movement and stillness, the Luvale equivalent to the question "Where are you going?" literally translates as "Where will you stop?" To this question, the traveler might answer, "I'll stop at Mr. Makina's home." In long, strenuous journeys through the uninhabited territory of plains and woodlands, travelers will stop at well-known resting camps. In the Luvale language, these camps are known as *vitulilo* (from *kutulila*, to lower one's load). They are always conveniently located near a water source, typically a stream or a waterhole, and they provide good shade. Travelers plan their journeys in terms of *vitulilo*. They might plan to reach the first camp by midday, where they will rest for some time, and then proceed toward the next camp located in the outskirts of the forest, where they will spend the night. Signaling the recent presence of other travelers, many of these camps have makeshift buildings made of branches and long grass, firewood, and remainders of food such as animal bones. In the same way that hikers in the United States may rest and camp at lean-tos, long-distance travelers in the Upper Zambezi depend on their *vitulilo*.

But life happens en route, too. As travelers move across the earth in engagement with other travelers and the environment, they observe the ground on which they walk and the vegetation around them; they listen to the wind blowing and the birds singing; they collect tree fruits for the journey and hunt a hare for dinner; and they engage in conversation with their travel companions as well as other travelers met along the way. These chance encounters provide valuable information. "The sands are too thick down this path," someone might say; "Turn left to avoid a group of soldiers," a second traveler might say. Life happens on the way in the Upper Zambezi and everywhere. A couple I know met in the subway of New York City. Like other commuters, they are in the habit of avoiding the slightest contact with strangers by blatantly gluing their eyes on a written page or blocking their ears with headphones. On that day, though, their eyes met.

It may be the case that travel is always "a liminal space fraught with uncertainty" (1998: 166), as Rasmussen says of the Tuareg of Niger; yet travel is not deprived of dwelling experiences. Conversely, neither is dwelling free of uncertainty and the thrill of adventure, as Georg Simmel reminds us in his thoughts on passion (1965 [1911]). In his later work, Heidegger too moved in this direction by developing the concept of *Gegnet*, or "abiding expanse" (1966).[9] Whereas earlier Heidegger had focused on the germane concepts of dwelling and building as ways of being at peace in a place and caring for one another and one's environment (1993: 361), the concept of *Gegnet* represents his attempt to bring together the notion of dwelling and mobility, opening up the possibility of homecoming within homelessness.[10]

Of late, many scholars have urged us to replace fixity with fluidity, dwelling with mobility, closure with openness. James Clifford (1997) favors routes over roots, Marc Augé diverts our attention from "places" to "non-places"—those sites such as airport lounges, highways, and supermarkets marked by "the fleeting, the temporary and ephemeral" (1995: 78) — and Tim Ingold says in *Being Alive*: "To be . . . is not to be *in* place but to be *along* paths. The path, and not the place, is the primary condition of being, or rather of becoming" (2011: 12). Borrowing from Gilles Deleuze and Félix Guattari (1987), Ingold speaks of "lines of flight" and "lines of becoming," and he sees the tracing of those lines and trails as his "project of restoring life to anthropology" (2011: 14, 83). These radical departures from emplacement are indeed revealing of the history of anthropology and Western thought. But they are sustainable only in print. In daily existence, mobile individuals experience dwelling, and physically immobilized individuals experience movement. As humans, we exist in the crossroads created by the inextricable possibilities of stasis and mobility, a space that sets limits to our existence but also opens up new horizons.

In addition to highlighting the importance of movement outside the technologically advanced wealthier nations, Samuzala's life story also breaks the spell of modernity. It produces this effect not by critically reflecting on modernity in the abstract (Modernity with a capital "M") but by reminding us of truths that we know well but often forget, a common paradox. The first truth pertains to aging. The highly mobile may move faster in some regards, but they too shall not escape the pains and sorrows of relative immobility, if not in the form of forced displacement or amputation, then in the form of that most inescapable of biological happenings, old age.

The second truth concerns the grimmer side of globalized mobility. The highly mobile may treasure their mobility and the many advantages it brings — among them the sense of their distinctiveness from both their own past (the Middle Ages) and the nameless mass of their premodern contemporaries who live in slow motion in developing countries. They may marvel at the beauty of speed, as Filippo Marinetti noted in his Futurist manifest in 1909. But mobility is not without friction, boundaries, and stasis. Sigurd Bergmann asks: "How can an artifact fall to pieces? How can speed turn into rest? How can the freedom of moving turn into the suffering of standstill? How can mobility turn into gridlock?" (2008: 14). If asked how *vindele* (Westerners) have impacted their physical movement in the last one hundred years, residents of the Upper Zambezi will not fail to mention some of the following: the delineation of the international border and the opening of border customs in Chavuma; the forceful relocation of entire villages to colonial settlements in Angola during the liberation war; the tight control of mobility by both sides of the military conflict after independence, including the seclusion of men, women, and children in towns and bush camps; the official refugee settlements in independent

Zambia where large numbers of Angolans were detained for decades; and the devastating effects of landmines on travel and daily life, including possible amputation. Tellingly, to convey their experience of immobility in all these different yet similar situations, people draw on the existential metaphor of entrapment.[11] For them, modernity has meant to a large degree *forced immobility*, an experience that they certainly share with many others throughout the world. Consider the Mozambican women, children, conscripted young men, and the elderly who were forced to remain "in place" within their area of residence throughout the fifteen-year-long Mozambican civil war (Lubkemann 2008); or the case of the growing numbers of illegal immigrants and asylum seekers who find themselves detained in the British Immigration Removal Center (Hall 2012). Following the example of Salazar and Smart (2011: iii), we should seriously ask ourselves what is distinctive about modernity: incessant mobility unimpaired by borders and boundaries, as claimed by modernity enthusiasts, or, to a large degree, the tight control, regulation, and surveillance of mobility in a global system of nation-states.

Not all is negative, though. In the Upper Zambezi, people also associate—indeed welcome—modernity in the form of its commodities, from the soaps and school uniforms introduced during colonialism to more recent goods such as used clothing, cell phones, solar panels, and motorcycles, to name a few. People also value tarred roads, which are now being built by the Chinese. When I visited Chavuma in 2010, eight years after the end of the Angolan civil war and thirteen years after the previous Chavuma subdistrict became a separate district of Zambia, a good-humored Zambian friend told me that now they had a roundabout to funnel the traffic near the market, a clear sign of development. And these are positive developments in the main. I am troubled, however, by the association of modernity with mobile objects on one side and immobile people on the other. Does this not cast a shadow over modernity and the uncritical celebration of mobility?

In a thought-provoking reading of Mia Couto's novel *The Last Flight of the Flamingo* (2004), Andrew Mahistedt explains what he means by the concept of the residual: "The residual exemplifies the contradiction inherent in the dominant narrative of globalization as fluidity, migration, and mobility: movement in some places, or from some places to others, leaves an immobile residue in others" (2013: 461). To his list of amputees, landmines, and bullet holes on standing walls, I add the refugees and the official refugee settlements. As I see it, the material residues of immobility share an aspect of invisibility that enables the empire, as Mahistedt calls the powers that be, to divert attention from them. Examples of such residues are buried landmines, remotely located refugee settlements, and illegal refugees who opt to self-settle in the villages and communities of their host country, blending with the local population, as took place in Chavuma (Silva 2011). Amputees present a problem to the empire because they cannot be hidden away.

But we must not stop here. Critical as it is to acknowledge the place of immobility in the larger project of modernity, we should never reduce the immobilized to their condition of immobility. The process of objectification operates like state violence, by essentializing its target—"effectively extinguishing the person as an individual subject through a process of iconic essentialising that transforms him or her into a mere instance of a more general case: a species, a specimen, a pathology, a class" (Jackson 2002: 78; see also 2005). But the objects of essentializing do not see themselves as objects. In the case of the Angolan refugees, they never saw themselves as *helpless refugees* (Malkki 1996) who have lost everything: loved ones, material possessions, and political rights. True, they lost too much, too rapidly. They also welcomed the help offered by international organizations, and, in order to receive that help, presented themselves as *refugees*. But such calamitous situations only make it the more remarkable that many Angolans in Chavuma explained their flight as Samuzala did in his life story: they fled to Zambia because they refused being trapped in between both sides of the military conflict. Their flight was an act of heroism, not victimage. To offer help to refugees in the process of objectifying them as helpless victims and detaining them in camps is another act of violence perpetrated with impunity. Not surprisingly, some Angolans in Chavuma did not fail to notice the similarities between being forcibly immobilized in the settlements set up by the Portuguese in colonial Angola and being forcibly immobilized in the official refugee settlements set up by UNHCR in independent Zambia. In both cases, the detainees felt trapped and demeaned.

It is against the ever-present danger of reification in all arenas of life—including humanitarian discourses about refugees and scholarly discourses about mobility—that Samuzala's life story, or any life story, becomes a beacon. Whereas others may separate and crystallize, Samuzala, in his narrative of movement, reveals nuance, complexity, overlap, and density. Mobility covers the entire gamut of human action—from the first steps a toddler takes, to visiting relatives, walking to work, hunting, emigrating, and being displaced. In addition to constituting the object of study of the blooming academic field of "mobilities," as several authors note (see Urry 2007: 8–9; and Cresswell 2006: 1), this entire gamut of activities speaks to universal existential themes: life as movement, immobility as entrapment, movement as an act of freedom against immobility, life as a never-ending remaking of the conditions that act upon one. No historical event, however cataclysmic, forces one to become a label. When all else fails, as Jackson puts it, one can act with one's feet; one can hit the road. Existentially speaking, there is much that we share as humans notwithstanding the different social circles that we call our own, and the different paces at which we move.

Notes

1. See, respectively, Aporta 2004: 13; Shubin 2011: 1936; Carling and Akesson 2009; and Wardle 1999.
2. Conversely, fast travelers continue walking on a daily basis, for work and leisure. In fact, as John Urry observes, walking "is still a component of almost all other modes of movement" (2007: 63).
3. This life story is an abbreviation of what was a much longer conversation recorded in Chavuma in August 1999. I thank Samuzala for allowing me to tape record our conversation. I also thank my friend Sapasa, who was present during the recording session, for his willingness to clarify some of Samuzala's historical references and technical terminology. All personal names mentioned in this book chapter are pseudonyms.
4. For information on the Angolan wars, from the liberation struggle in the 1960s to the ceasefire in 2002; see for example Birmingham 2006; Brinkman 2007; Chabal and Vidal 2008; and Marcum 1978.
5. The year of 1966 marked the beginning of the armed conflict against the colonial regime in east Angola. In 1983, UNITA launched a major offensive against MPLA strongholds in the area, gaining control of the entire Alto-Zambeze district located just north of Chavuma. In 1985–1986, MPLA retaliated, and UNITA retreated into the bush. Finally, bitter fighting occurred again toward the end of the war (1998 through early 2002) when the government forces wrested control of important towns from UNITA in the eastern region.
6. Most refugees have meanwhile returned to Angola. As of December 2012, Zambia hosted 23,000 Angolans whose refugee status ended that year. Eligible Angolans are encouraged to apply for permanent residence (UNHCR 2012; 2014).
7. *Aldeamentos* were fortified settlements originally set up by the Portuguese to confine, control, and protect the rural population that they had forcibly relocated. The Portuguese sought in this way to prevent the villagers from supporting the insurgency.
8. Todres and Galvin (2010) similarly draw on Heidegger's concept of "letting-be-ness" (*Gelassenheit*) in their study of the elderly in southwest England and Wales.
9. For a deeper engagement with Heidegger's concept of *Gegnet*, see Mugerauer 2008 and Todres and Galvin 2010.
10. In the same vein, Urry speaks of "[dwelling] through being both at home and away" (2000: 132) and "[dwelling] in various mobilities" (157); James Clifford refers to "dwelling-in-travel" (1997: 2); and Rapport and Dawson address the possibility of being "at home in movement" (1998: 27).

11. Julia Powles reports that the Angolans residing in the official Meheba Refugee Settlement felt "trapped" in the settlement, in part because they were required to seek permission from the Zambian government Refugee Officer to leave the settlement (2005: 5; 2000). See also Hansen 1977: 31–32; and 1990: 31.

References

Aporta, C. 2004. "Routes, Trails and Tracks: Trail Breaking among the Inuit of Igloolik," *Etudes/Inuit/Studies* 28 (2): 9–38.
Arendt, Hannah. 1958. *The Human Condition*. Chicago: Chicago University Press.
Augé, Marc. 1995. *Non-Places: Introduction to an Anthropology of Supermobility*. London: Verso.
Bergmann, Sigurd. 2008. "The Beauty of Speed or the Discovery of Slowness—Why Do We Need to Rethink Mobility?" In *The Ethics of Mobilities: Rethinking Place, Exclusion, Freedom and Environment*, Sigurd Bergmann and Tore Sager (eds.). Hampshire: Ashgate, 13–25.
Birmingham, David. 2006. *Empire in Africa: Angola and Its Neighbors*. Athens: Ohio University Research in International Studies and Ohio University Press.
Brinkman, Inge. 2007. "Angolan Civilians in War Time, 1961–2002." In *Daily Lives of Civilians in Wartime Africa*, John Laban (ed.). Westport, CT: Greenwood Press, 169–194.
Carling, Jørgen, and Lisa Åkesson. 2009. "Mobility at the Heart of a Nation: Patterns and Meanings of Cape Verdean Migration," *International Migration* 47: 123–155.
Chabal, Patrick, and Nuno Vidal (eds.). 2008. *Angola: The Weight of History*. New York: Columbia University Press.
Clifford, James. 1997. *Routes: Travel and Translation in the Late Twentieth Century*. Cambridge, MA: Harvard University Press.
Couto, Mia. 2004. *The Last Flight of the Flamingo* (trans. David Brookshaw). London: Serpent's Tail.
Cresswell, Tim. 2006. *On the Move: Mobility in the Modern Western World*. New York: Routledge.
Deleuze, Gilles, and Félix Guattari. 1987. *A Thousand Plateaus: Capitalism and Schizophrenia*. Minneapolis: University of Minnesota Press.
Durkheim, Emile. 1982. *The Rules of Sociological Method and Selected Texts on Sociology and Its Method*, edited with an introduction by Steven Lukes (trans. W. D. Halls). New York: Free Press.
Erikson, Kirstin. 2003. "Moving Stories: Displacement and Return in the Narrative Production of Yaqui Identity," *Anthropology & Humanism* 28 (2): 139–154.
Hall, Alexandra. 2012. "'These People Could be Anyone': Fear, Contempt (and Empathy) in a British Immigration Removal Centre." In *Emotions and Human Mobility: Ethnographies of Movement*, Maruška Svašek (ed.). London: Routledge, 17–34.
Hansen, Art. 1977. "Once the Running Stops: The Social and Economic Incorporation of Angolan Refugees into Zambian Border Villages." PhD dissertation, Cornell University.
———. 1990. *Refugee Self-Settlement versus Settlement on Government Schemes: The Long-Term Consequences for Security, Integration and Economic Development of Angolan Refugees (1966–1989) in Zambia*. Geneva: United Nations Research Institute.
Heidegger, Martin. 1966. "Conversations on a Country Path." In *Discourse on Thinking* (trans. J. M. Anderson and E. H. Freund). New York: Harper & Row.
———. 1993. "Building, Dwelling, Thinking." In *Basic Writings*, Martin Heidegger (ed.). Routledge: London, 344–363.

Human Rights Watch Arms Project. 1993. *Landmines: A Deadly Legacy*. New York: Human Rights Watch.

———. 1997. *Still Killing: Landmines in Southern Africa*. New York: Human Rights Watch.

Ingold, Tim. 2000. *The Perception of the Environment: Essays on Livelihood, Dwelling and Skill*. London: Routledge.

———. 2007. *Lines: A Brief History*. London: Routledge.

———. 2011. *Being Alive: Essays on Movement, Knowledge and Description*. London: Routledge.

International Committee of the Red Cross (ICRC). 2008. "Angola: Three Decades of Help for Mine Victims. News Release." http://www.icrc.org.

Jackson, Michael. 2002. *The Politics of Storytelling: Violence, Transgression and Intersubjectivity*. Copenhagen: Museum Tusculanum Press.

———. 2005. *Existential Anthropology: Events, Exigencies, and Effects*. New York: Berghahn Books.

———. 2013. *The Wherewithal of Life: Ethics, Migration, and the Question of Well-Being*. Berkeley: The University of California Press.

Klee, Paul. 1961. *Notebooks: The Thinking Eye*, vol. 1, J. Spiller (ed.) (trans. R. Manheim). London: Lund Humphries.

Kuntz, E. F. 1973. "The Refugee in Flight: Kinetic Models and Forms of Displacement," *International Migration Review* 7 (2): 125–146.

Lubkemann, Stephen C. 2008. "Involuntary Immobility: On a Theoretical Invisibility in Forced Migration Studies," *Journal of Refugee Studies* 21 (4): 454–475.

Mahistedt, Andrew. 2013. "Landmines, Language, and Dismemberment: Mia Couto's Imperial Residues," *Textual Practice* 27 (3): 459–478.

Malkki, Liisa. 1992. "National Geographic: The Rooting of Peoples and the Territorialization of National Identity among Scholars and Refugees," *Cultural Anthropology* 7 (1): 24–44.

———. 1996. "Speechless Emissaries: Refugees, Humanitarianism, and Dehistoricization," *Cultural Anthropology* 11 (3): 377–404.

Marcum, John A. 1978. *The Angolan Revolution*, vol. 2: *Exile Politics and Guerrilla Warfare (1962–1976)*. Cambridge, MA: MIT Press.

Marinetti, F. T. 1909. "Manifesto of Futurism," *Le Figaro* (Paris), 20 February. http://www.futurism.org.uk/manifestos/manifesto01.htm.

Mugerauer, R. 2008. *Heidegger and Homecoming: The Leifmotif in the Later Writings*. Toronto: University of Toronto Press.

Pelissier, René. 1974. "La Guerre en Angola Oriental," *Révue Française d'Études Politiques Africaines* 103: 87–109.

Powles, Julia. 2000. "Road 65: A Narrative Ethnography of a Refugee Settlement in Zambia." PhD dissertation, Oxford University.

———. 2005. "A Field-Report: Cazombo." Unpublished typewritten document.

Rapport, Nigel, and Andrew Dawson. 1998. *Perceptions of Home in a World of Movement*. Oxford: Berg.

Rasmussen, Susan J. 1998. "Within the Tent and at the Crossroads: Travel and Gender Identity among the Tuareg of Niger," *Ethos* 26 (2): 153–182.

Salazar, Noel B., and Alan Smart. 2011. "Introduction: Anthropological Takes on (Im)Mobility," *Identities: Global Studies in Culture and Power* 18: i–ix.

Sarró, Ramon. 2007. "La aventura como categoria cultural: Apuntes simmelianos sobre la emigracion subsahariana." Working Papers. Lisbon: Instituto de Ciências Sociais.

Shubin, Sergei. 2011. "Travelling as Being: Understanding Mobility amongst Scottish Gypsy Travellers," *Environment and Planning A* 43: 1930–1947.

Silva, Sónia. 2011. *Along an African Border: Angolan Refugees and Their Divination Baskets*. Philadelphia: University of Pennsylvania Press.

———. 2013a. "Remarks on Similarity in Ritual Classification: Affliction, Divination, and Object Animation," *History of Religions* 53 (2): 151–169.

———. 2013b. "Reification and Fetishism: Processes of Transformation," *Theory, Culture & Society* 30 (1): 79–98.

Simmel, Georg. 1965 [1911]. "The Adventure." In *Georg Simmel: Essays on Sociology, Philosophy and Aesthetics*, K. Wolff (ed.). New York: Harper Torchbooks.

Todres, Les, and Kathleen T. Galvin. 2010. "Dwelling-Mobility: An Existential Theory of Well-Being," *International Journal of Qualitative Studies on Heath and Well-Being* 5: 5444.

———. 2012. "'In the middle of everywhere': A Phenomenological Study of Mobility and Dwelling Amongst Rural Elders," *Phenomenology & Practice* 6 (1): 55–68.

United Nations High Commissioner for Refugees (UNHCR). 2002. "Africa Fact Sheet—June 2002." http://www.unhcr.org.

———. 2012. "Zambia Begins Granting Angolan Refugees Permanent Residency." News Stories 31 December. http://www.unhcr.org/50e162899.html.

———. 2014. "UNHCR Regional Operations Profile—Southern Africa." http://www.unhcr.org.

Urry, John. 2000. *Sociology Beyond Societies*. London: Routledge.

———. 2007. *Mobilities*. Cambridge: Polity Press.

Wardle, Huon. 1999. "Jamaican Adventures: Simmel, Subjectivity and Extraterritoriality in the Caribbean," *The Journal of the Royal Anthropological Institute* 5 (4): 523–539.

Ziegler, F., and T. Schwanen. 2011. "'I like to go out to be energised by different people': An Exploratory Analysis of Mobility and Wellbeing in Later Life," *Aging & Society* 31: 758–781.

Chapter Six

Existential Aporias and the Precariousness of Being

Michael Jackson

In this chapter, I engage the existential themes of contingency and crisis, asking how it is that human beings faced with events they can neither fully comprehend nor control nevertheless struggle to find ways of acting and speaking that effectively connect them with others, thereby rendering life worth living rather than alien and absurd. My narrative covers several generations of a Kuranko family in Sierra Leone and focuses on a former field assistant and close friend, Noah Bokarie Marah, as well as Noah's first-born son, Kaimah, and Kaimah's first-born son, Michael. As I explore lived historicity through individual biographies, I address the "distribution of experience over time as the mark of the historical" (Schwarz Wentzer 2014: 30), and discuss the ways in which personal traits and dilemmas are both preserved and transformed over several generations. Tragic and reflexive elements inevitably enter into this investigation, because, as the ethnographer, I am caught up in the web of relationships that I study, and the ethical and epistemological implications of this dual identity as moral participant and neutral observer must be carefully explicated.

* * *

That our lives confront us with inescapable quandaries and contradictions is a recurring motif in existential thought. We are born into a world we did not choose, and are bound to die. Periodic crises confound our most

---

Notes for this chapter begin on page 176.

cherished beliefs and destroy our best-laid plans. We build viable lives, only to see our handiwork destroyed by war or natural disasters. Though our well-being depends on secure attachments, the course of our lives is punctuated by traumatic separations and losses. Despite the fact that our life stories suggest linearity and progress, our destinies are shaped by contingency and confusion, and meaning eludes our grasp.

Many of these dilemmas do not admit of any resolution, despite the fact that art and wishful thinking suggest otherwise. Why then, do we not succumb to such aporias and double binds? Why live, if everything we live for is perennially compromised or taken from us? Was Camus right to conclude that existence is absurd?

We endure because there is always more than our individual survival that is at stake. Should this cease to be the case, and we have only ourselves to care about, then existence may indeed become absurd, and the question of suicide occlude all other considerations. For better or for worse, however, our lives are interwoven with the lives of significant others, so that the struggle for being is never simply a struggle to be ourselves but to be with others, to be there for them, to find ourselves through them. This is what Maurice Merleau-Ponty meant when he compared the social with the natural world as "a permanent field or dimension of existence." Prior to the process of becoming aware," he wrote, "the social exists obscurely and as a summons" (1962: 362).

A Phone Call from Sierra Leone

It was early evening in Boston when the phone rang. Its unstoppable summons brought me in from the garden where I had been about to water the dogwood saplings I had planted two days earlier.

The voice on the other end of the line was far away, submerged with other voices and interrupted by electromagnetic interference. I pressed the receiver to my ear but could not identify the caller. In exasperation, I shouted down the phone, "Who is it?" but the caller's voice was so badly degraded that I replaced the receiver and walked toward the door. Seconds later, the phone rang again. This time I recognized the voice. It was my friend Sewa Magba Koroma, and he was on the road between Kabala and Makeni in northern Sierra Leone. Despite his voice breaking up, I got the gist of his message. "Daddy" Kaimah had died and Sewa was on his way to Freetown for the funeral.

The interference made it impossible for us to exchange more than a few broken sentences, and I urged Sewa to email me as soon as he reached Freetown. I did not return to the garden. I sat at the dining room table, staring out the window into the trees, and late that night, after another email from Sewa, now in Freetown, I sent my condolences to Kaimah's son Michael, whose forlorn face in the photo Sewa sent from his cell phone reminded me of what Emmanuel Levinas once wrote about the face, "as the most basic mode of responsibility. . . . The face is not in front of me (*en face de moi*) but above me; it is the other before death, looking through and exposing death . . . the face is the other who asks me not to let him die alone, as if to do so were to become an accomplice in his death" (2004: 75).

Not long after Sewa's call, I received an email from Kaimah's cousin Isha who lived in London and had been one of Kaimah's most trusted friends. "It is terribly sad," she wrote. "He was very promising and wanted to achieve his dreams. Let us hope that his dreams will be fulfilled *through* his son." Isha added her thanks to me, "for all your generous support throughout the years."

A few hours after responding to Isha's email, I got a message from Kaimah's sister Jeneba. "I pray he rest in the safe hands of GOD," Jeneba wrote, and she mentioned that, as soon as Kaimah's son's school year ended, she would take him back to Lunsar with her.

Kaimah's Story

I had known Kaimah from the year he was born. His father, Noah, was my research assistant when I first did fieldwork in Sierra Leone, and we became close friends. That I had outlived both Noah (who died in 2002) and Noah's first-born son exacerbated the sense of social injustice that had haunted me for years, for while I had been lucky enough to be born into a society where education and medicine were freely and universally available, and grew up during a period of relative peace, many of my Sierra Leonean peers had failed to realize their dreams, and had suffered the devastation of a civil war. Only days after Kaimah's funeral, I was in Montreal with my wife and daughter to celebrate my son's graduation from McGill. Sitting in the great marquee and listening to the principal of the University extolling the virtues of "knowledge" and "working as one" as keys to "the civilized world's success," I struggled to reconcile these complacent phrases with the grim world in which Kaimah had had to make his way.

In a file in my office I have kept, for eleven years, Kaimah's letters and emails, copies of his academic transcripts and his BEd thesis, essays, poems, and a one-act play. Leafing through this poignant legacy of unfulfilled promise, one of his poems caught my eye. It echoed Isha's comments, and brought back memories of the last time I saw Kaimah in Freetown in 2009. The theme of Kaimah's poem was rebirth. Kaimah had lifted lines from three of my own poems, and built his own around them. Describing the visitors that arrive in the northern town of Kabala every new year's eve to climb the great inselberg that overshadows the town and celebrate the possibility of miraculous transformations, Kaimah draws a contrast between the verdure of the Wara Wara Hills and the "abject poverty" of the town. His poem ends:

> Food, drinks, in no small quantity
> as Kabala boasts the birth of another year,
> previous hopes dashed,
> new promises made.
> Such is life.

When Noah died in 2002, I took Kaimah under my wing and covered the costs of his tertiary education. But after Kaimah's graduation from Njala University in June 2006, I found myself unable to pay for his further education in the United Kingdom or South Africa, and Kaimah reluctantly reenrolled at Njala for an MSci degree in rural development, hoping a second degree would guarantee him employment. Even these fees proved beyond my means, and like many other young West Africans who had allowed themselves to believe that education would give them a bright future,[1] Kaimah came to the realization that without local benefactors, inside connections, and the means to pay bribes he would probably never find employment in Sierra Leone, regardless of how qualified he became.

When I visited him in 2009, Kaimah seemed close to despair. In the darkness of his single room, his clothes hanging from the ceiling above his bed, and surrounded by the books I had sent him over the years, he cut a sorry figure, and I felt guilty that I could not lift his spirits with an offer of material help. As he shared the story of his misfortunes in that candlelit and claustrophobic room, it became clear that he regarded me as his *yigi* ("hope" or "mentor"), his *sabu* ("enabler"), and that he felt both frustrated and humiliated to find himself, at age thirty-eight, still unable to earn a living, or support a wife and family.

"What of your girlfriend who worked in the hospital?" I asked. "Are you still together?"

Aisetta had left him. Kaimah knew from the start of the relationship that it would end this way, because she had a beau before him. This man had gone to London with his family to escape the war. When he returned to Sierra Leone he was able to offer Aisetta security, income, and prospects—so she went back to him. "You can't expect love when you have nothing to give but love," Kaimah said. "Love without money counts for nothing here. You have to have money. Only with children is this any different."

Kaimah then recounted a story that he never shared with his father Noah.

In 1992, when Noah was employed as a trade inspector in Koidu, and Kaimah was a student at the local high school, Kaimah had fallen in love with another student called Fatamata Massaquoi. Fatamata, who was known as Lango, lived with her aunt and uncle in the same compound as Kaimah's family. Not long before the Revolutionary United Front invaded Kono and only a few months after Lango gave birth to their "love-child," the Massaquoi family left Koidu, possibly because of the shame that Lango had brought upon them, possibly because of rumors of an impending rebel invasion. For the next ten years, war destroyed the country. Villages were burned to the ground, thousands killed or maimed, and every scrap of moveable property plundered. Kaimah's family moved, with thousands like them, from one district to another, seeking refuge from the fighting and the atrocities. Despite periodic disruptions to his education, Kaimah passed his O levels in 1994 and sought admission to Fourah Bay

College. Unable to find anyone to help him pay his fees, he completed his A levels and tried again, to no avail. It wasn't until January 2002, when I returned to Sierra Leone, that Kaimah found the mentor he had been seeking and resumed his studies.

During the war years, Kaimah had done everything in his power to locate Lango. But it was only after his graduation in June 2006 that a breakthrough came. "I began having dreams, the same dream over and over again," Kaimah told me

> In these dreams Lango was telling me about our child. In the same dreams, an old man appeared, someone I knew in Koidu town when Lango and I were living there. I was sure these dreams meant that I was soon going to see her again. So one day I went to Koidu with my younger brother, and we found the old man who had appeared in my dreams. I asked him if he remembered Lango, if he knew where she was, and how I could find her. He told me that Lango was dead. She had died in Bo ten years ago. He said she had been seriously ill for some time. So I traveled to Bo next day and found the family. They were where the old man told me they were. I greeted them, and explained who I was, and how much I wanted to see my child. It was very difficult. No one remembered me. No one could identify me. But thanks to God, Lango's aunty Sarah, who Lango lived with when she was in Koidu, happened to be visiting Bo from Moyamba and she identified me and told the rest of the Massaquoi family about my friendship with Lango and about our love child.

Kaimah's son was in the St. Mary's Children's Home in Bo, and after visiting the boy several times, Kaimah petitioned the coordinator of the home to grant him custody, even though he was not married and hadn't raised other children, promising that he would dedicate himself to his son's education, and showing evidence that he had already secured a place for him at the St. Edward's Secondary School in Freetown.

As Kaimah concluded his story, and as if carefully stage-managed for dramatic effect, Kaimah's fourteen-year-old son appeared at the door and I was introduced to Michael Noah Marah—named for me and for Kaimah's late father.

As Michael sat on the bed beside his father, Kaimah proudly showed me his son's school reports. I had a sudden sense of history unfolding before me and tears welled up in my eyes as I recalled how Kaimah's grandfather, Tina Kome Marah, taught himself to read and write while serving with the British in the Cameroons during the First World War (the first Kuranko man to become literate in English), of how Kaimah's father Noah had struggled to complete his education after his elder brother S. B. took him out of high school to help in his political campaigns, of how Noah's mother argued against Noah pursuing studies in New Zealand, fearful that he, like Tina Kome, would throw his life to the winds and "become a child of the white men," and of how, despite Kaimah's years in the wilderness, he was now on the threshold of realizing a dream whose origins lay in his grandfather's conviction that the future lay in a world very different from the world into which he was born.

I asked Michael about his favorite subjects at school. As shy as his father, he spoke little and in whispers. Turning to Kaimah, I assured him I would visit him again when I returned from Firawa, the Kuranko village where I was doing fieldwork. We would discuss the possibility of Kaimah going to the United Kingdom, just as his cousin Sewa had done, and perhaps enrolling for a course of study there. Kaimah said he was ready to give up his MSci studies at Njala, and if I could help pay for his airfare to the United Kingdom, he would find a college course and stay with his cousins until he found his feet.

"But I am concerned about Michael," I said. "What will become of him if you go to England to live?"

"I have thought about that already," Kaimah said. "My sister Jeneba lives close to here, close to Michael's school. She will care for Michael if I go abroad."

Kaimah did not go abroad. He embarked on his studies for an MSci and we lost touch with each other, though I would get regular news of him through Sewa Magba. It was through Sewa that I learned that Kaimah had been hospitalized after suffering some of kind of brain seizure. His health seemed to improve, but he became ill again, with paralysis of his feet. This time he sought treatment from a traditional healer. When this proved unavailing, Jeneba took her brother back to Freetown for orthodox medical treatment. The prognosis was not good. There was some kind of intestinal tract problem, and Kaimah was told that he could die at any time. Ironically, in the last few months of his life he finally secured a job but was told to get his feet cured before he began. He died in Freetown on Tuesday, 21 May 2013.

Life within Life

For phenomenologists, a person's world is inextricably connected with the world of his or her contemporaries and consociates (*Mitwelt*), the global and physical environments (*Umwelt*) of which he or she is a part, and a genealogical stream that includes predecessors and successors. But while Kaimah's life story echoes the stories of thousands of other young Sierra Leoneans, struggling with scarce resources and searching for a life beyond the confines of the world into which they were born, his story remains, in many ways, unique.

But what does it mean to speak of an individual's "own world" (*Eigenwelt*), or to claim that every human life amounts to *more* than can be encompassed by the category terms and causal language that anthropology deploys in order to locate a person within culture, society, or history? How are we to understand the interplay of the "I" and the "we," the singular and the shared?

In his existential biographies of Jean Genet and Gustave Flaubert, Sartre refuses to construe the individual and the group as opposing sui generis phenomena. Rather, his goal is to disclose the subtle ways in which a person is at once shaped by circumstances over which he or she has little control—genetic and cultural inheritance, class, ethnicity, gender, birthright—and yet gives shape to his or her own life. "Personalization in the individual is nothing more than the surpassing and preservation . . . at the core of a project to totalize what the world has made—and continues to make—of us" (1987: 7).

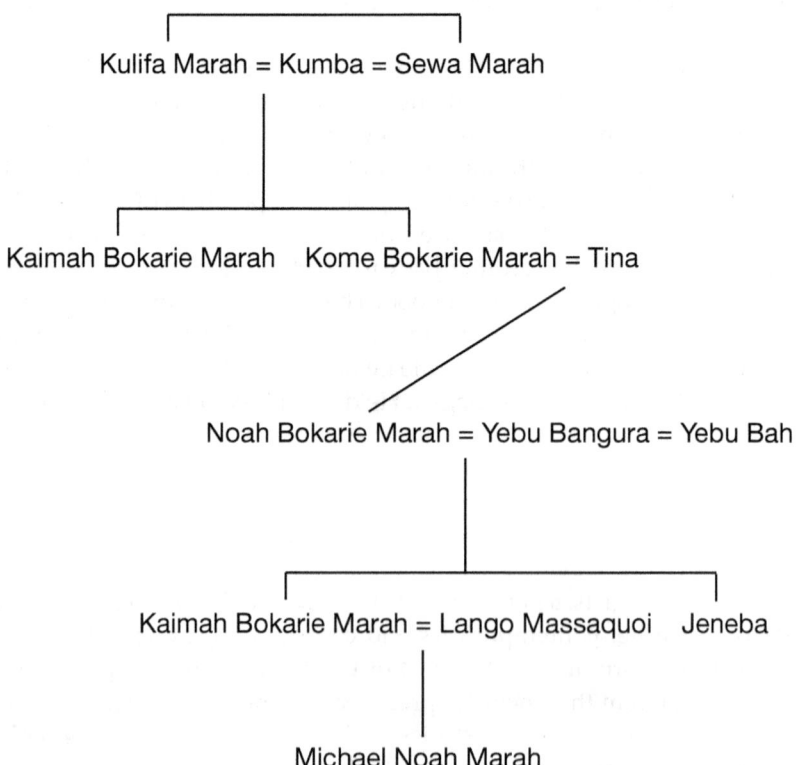

Marah lineage

Let us therefore explore the ways in which Kaimah's life both repeats history and departs from it—the extent to which his life merely instantiates cultural patterns and genealogical precedents, and the extent to which it goes beyond these forms of what Bourdieu refers to as the habitus.

Following Kuranko custom, Noah named his first-born son after his father's elder brother, Kaimah Bockarie Marah, whose father was known as Kulifa ("leopard-slayer"). Kulifa was a formidable warrior, but was betrayed to his enemies by his wife during the Kuranko wars against Samori Turé's mounted horsemen (*sofas*) in the late 1880s, and executed. Kaimah's mother consequently remarried Kulifa's younger brother Sewa, and Kaimah became like a father to his younger brother Kome. Indeed, for as long as he lived, Kome called his elder brother "Daddy"—the sobriquet that passed, in turn, to Noah's first-born.

According to family legend, the circumstances of Kulifa's death led his sons to distrust strangers and women. Although this leitmotif echoes the male chauvinism in Kuranko culture, it was given particular force in this family, and I vividly recall how, when Kaimah was still a toddler, Noah taught his son to be on his guard against everyone, including his own close kin. On one occasion Noah urged Kaimah to jump from a porch into his arms. When Kaimah did so, Noah stepped back and let his son fall, then berated him for not heeding the advice he just been given. "Trust no one. Not even your father."

When I returned to Sierra Leone after the war, and saw how eager Kaimah was to resume his interrupted schooling, Kaimah proudly showed me his school records so that I could write informed letters in support of his application to Njala University where he wanted to study political science, civic administration, and literature. It was a moving moment, for I glimpsed in Kaimah's optimism not only an echo of his father's aspirations, but a replay of Noah's father's success in acquiring literacy when serving with the Sierra Leone Battalion of the West African Frontier Force during the so-called Cameroon War (1914–1915). Indeed, a few days after talking with Kaimah, Noah told me that he wanted his son to reap the reward of his suffering, as if, in Nietzsche's words, the value of a thing often lies not in what one attains with it, but in what one pays for it—what it *costs* us. In undertaking to pay for Kaimah's education I was therefore recognizing the moral credit that Noah and Kaimah had accumulated through many years of hardship, indigence, and upheaval.

The Struggle for Being

If one lives long enough, biography becomes transmuted into history, and one begins to see that critical events in a past generation continue to be felt through the generations that follow. This is as true of blessings as of curses, of nightmares as well as dreams. When Isha wrote to me after Kaimah's death, she commented, "It is . . . sad as he was very promising and wanted to achieve his dreams. Let us hope that his dreams will be fulfilled through his son." But there was a shadow side to this hope, and it had been presaged as long ago as 1907 when Kaimah's grandfather, Kome, enlisted in the West African Frontier Force—a decision that for many of his kinsmen was tantamount to "cutting his mouth off" from his own people. Although Kome's hand was forced by a family crisis,[2] he was judged harshly for "throwing his life away" and becoming "a child of the white men."

After leaving the army in 1918, Kome joined the Court Messenger Force and rose to the rank of sergeant-major. But his ability to read and write, together with his regard for education and his close association with the British, were deeply troubling to many people in his natal chiefdom of Barawa. One year, when the British were short of district officers (DO), "Sergeant-Major"—for this was how people now addressed Kome, his wives included—was appointed acting DO. People called him a black district officer, recognizing his power to collect taxes but unsure if it was compatible with chieftaincy. His children had become white men, some said, meaning that they were receiving an English education. His wives are not Kuranko, said others. If we follow this man our children will never succeed. When Tina Kome made his bid for the Barawa chieftaincy in 1946, following the death of Tenaba Sewa, the then district commissioner, Victor Ffennell-Smith and the Sengbe Paramount chief, Denka Marah, both advocated his election. But Barawa gave him no support, and when he lost the election he rebuked his people, "Ah, you Barawa, I've worked for you and helped you but you do not know it. Perhaps tomorrow, you will."

A generation later, in 1964, Tina Kome's son, Sewa Bockarie ("S. B."), contested the staff of Nieni. Again, Barawa gave no support, and the unforgiving S. B. punished those who had failed his father and failed him in turn, declaring he would thenceforth help his own immediate family in Firawa but not Barawa. "You'll may see an aeroplane fly over Barawa," he declared. "But it will never land here."

There were uncanny echoes of these old resentments in a letter Kaimah emailed me on 8 December 2006, complaining about his uncle S. B.'s reluctance to help him.

> Even when I was promoted to second year [at Njala University], uncle S. B. kept asking me, "Why are you going to college?" His attitude has extended to the entire family. There is always competition among family members, nobody cares about other family and nobody cares about your difficulties in life. The success and achievement of another person is always a threat. When a member

of the family is fortunate to travel abroad, he or she will only help those from his or her biological parents, and even his contact address is kept secret. This is the type of situation our family is operating. This is why, since the death of uncle S. B., no progress has been made. There is no unity among family members, here or abroad. That is why I am so grateful for the generosity you are extending me.

Two years later, as Kaimah and I strolled together along Lumley Beach, the same complaints came to the fore.

Our conversation had begun with me telling Kaimah about my fieldwork in Firawa—how it had prompted me to ponder the question of well-being, and the various things that people imagine will make their lives complete, worthwhile, or at least bearable. I had also been led to wonder, I told Kaimah, to what extent the past—in the form of ancestral custom, war trauma, power struggles, or family feuds—so constrained our present actions that they effectively denied us any future.

"The war is not on people's minds these days," Kaimah said abruptly. "The problem is poverty."

But poverty—as a condition and a concept—was a European invention, reflecting the enlightenment view that human inequality is not the will of God or the ancestors, but the work of man. "People did not complain of poverty forty years ago," I said. "If there was inequality between men and women, rulers and commoners, elders and juniors, it was seen as being in the nature of things. Now it is thought to be the fault of those in power, whose have become wealthy at the expense of others."

"That is true," Kaimah said.

"What interests me," I said, "is that people look to God as much as to the government for a fairer deal. But they do not look for a fairer distribution of wealth; they seem to seek windfalls and benefits solely for themselves."

I mentioned to Kaimah the numerous religious slogans I had seen in the streets of the city. The beaming, chubby-faced preacher, usually depicted with his equally chubby wife, promising everything from a "deeper life" to "miraculous prosperity"—"Jesus the Impossibility Specialist," one flier had read, while another announced "The Year of Supernatural Abundance."

"Most of the ministries are run by Nigerians, or by Sierra Leoneans who have trained in Nigeria," Kaimah said.

> When the war ended and the Nigerian ECOMOG soldiers went home, several of them left the army and returned to Sierra Leone. I knew one retired lieutenant. His name is Ibrahim Godfather. He told me that Sierra Leone was "virgin land," and he began a vehicle spare parts business, though most of the spare

parts are cheap fakes. Many Nigerian traders also came to Sierra Leone, selling medicines that do not work, and passing off counterfeit 100,000 leone bills. As for the pastors and reverends you were talking about, they build mighty churches, able to accommodate two or three thousand people. But let me tell you, Mr. Michael, they are all drug dealers, even my friend Ibrahim Godfather. During their crusades at the National Stadium they smuggle drugs in with the musical instruments they use to entertain the crowds.

"What kind of drugs?"

"Cocaine, brown-brown, anything at all. They distribute it to their agents here who sell it on the street. It's a big problem now. Many young boys and girls are in the habit of taking these drugs as a form of social life and high meditations. But they steal in order to buy the drugs, and many have got mental problems now and are in the Kissy Mental Home."

We were strolling along the narrow dirt path beside the beach road. The mangy grass was littered with plastic, soda cans, cigarette packets, and old shoes. A sordid image of globalization, I thought, knowing that the cocaine in West Africa came from Colombia, destined to be sold on the European market.

I did not want to argue against Kaimah's benighted view of the Nigerian ministries; I was fascinated by his implicit comparison between Pentecostal fervor and drug addiction; and I wanted to understand the source of the vehemence and bitterness behind his words.

"Do you belong to any church?" I asked.

> I am a Muslim. The only Christian churches I trust are the Catholic, Presbyterian, and Methodist churches. The older established ones in Sierra Leone. They help people with clothing, micro-credit, and schooling. They try to improve people's lives. But these new Nigerian ministries are out for their own fame and fortune. They tithe people. They are based solely on making money for themselves. And they are devil worshippers. They practice human sacrifice. You have to give human flesh, human blood, to get fame. And the ministers use human body parts to make medicines to give people more power, more life, better chances. Depending on what you ask for, you have to give to God something of equal value. In many cases this is the life of one of your children. You'll have to sacrifice your child for a chance to go overseas, for prosperity.

My first thought was that Kaimah was feeling uneasy, perhaps even guilty, about leaving his son Michael in Sierra Leone when he went to England to continue his education, though, as it turned out, Kaimah did not pursue this option but stayed in Freetown to take care of Michael. But whatever he did would entail a sacrifice. To migrate would be to place his son's well-being in jeopardy, according to the ominous and unforgiving logic that in return for a favor bestowed by a djinn one must give up the life of a loved one. But to remain in Sierra Leone would be to sacrifice his own dreams of self-improvement.

It was perhaps this double bind that inclined Kaimah to see renunciation as an invitation to the demonic, and to speak of the Charismatic and Pentecostal ministries as an "underworld" whose "evil works" were done clandestinely. "They perform cleansing ceremonies at night in the hills, rivers or sea. Sometimes in the forest. They use lime, black soap, red candles, kola nuts, alligator pepper, perfumes, and Surrine [a kind of baby oil] from Nigeria. The black soap, lime, and water are common among The Burning Bush churches and the Allajobie Churches. They wear white, with a red robe, and walk bare footed with a bell on their hands, preaching the word of God and at the same time predicting events that will befall the land. And they instruct people in the sacrifices they have to make in order to avert problems in the future."

"What kind of problems do people bring to them?"

"Many women who are barren go to them. Women who cannot find husbands. People who are not prospering. People who want to block someone else's chances of progress. People seeking political office or employment. People who want control and command over others."

We had reached the end of the beach. So focused had I been on Kaimah's account of Freetown's occult economy that I was startled to see that the ocean was pouring ashore, tongues of salt water licking the white sand, as innocent as ever.

"How far to the bread shop?" I asked.

"It's not far now. Are you tired? Do you want to wait here while I go on to Lumley and buy the bread?"

"I'm fine, Kaimah. But let's rest a little. I want to take some notes so that I can remember all the details of what you are telling me?"

When we walked on, I asked whether these new religious practices were essentially different from the old practices of Muslim alphas and mori-men.

"It's all the same," Kaimah said. "It is all based on sacrifice. Like in the gospel of Luke. 'To whomsoever much is given, of him shall be much required.'"

"'And to whom men have committed much, of him they will ask the more,'" I added.

Kaimah was not amused:

> To get a better opportunity in life, you have to offer money. Sometimes you have to offer your child. Sometimes you have to pay up front; sometimes you pay only if the work is successful. We Africans are of the conviction that all of

these supernaturals have an element of truth. They are not strange to us. Most alphas or pastors have snakes or devils or evil spirits to whom they pledge their loyalty in order to get fame and fortune. This is why they do their work at night, in the sea, hills, or forest. We Africans find it hard to succeed because so many people here are full of envy, grudges, and jealousy, always trying to block your progress in life. You are trying to achieve something, but other people with evil intentions are fighting to block your progress and ambitions. It is very common in polygamous households where every woman is fighting for her own son or daughter to achieve fame. Some go the extra mile and visit alphas or mori-men, looking for a way of spoiling the chances of their cowives' children.

"Was this an issue in your family?"

"My father's second wife never liked me. Even now she makes things difficult for me. The very day you left Freetown for Kabala, she came to my house and said that Ibrahim [Kaimah's "half-brother"] had phoned her from London. He said that you were going to help me go to London and continue my studies. She asked me if this was true. She sees me as a threat, because I am better educated than Ibrahim. This is why I never confide my plans to anyone. You never know what people might do to spoil your plans. I don't say a word about what I am planning to do, except to my friends. Friends you can trust, but not family."

We had reached the Fula bread shop, and I bought several sticks of bread and a bunch of bananas.

Walking along the eroded edge of the road back to the beach, I asked Kaimah if he believed all the things he had told me about the increasing use of lethal medicines and illicit drugs, the human sacrifices, the Nigerian crime networks, the corrupt churches.

Kaimah immediately recalled an incident in his early childhood. He had traveled with his parents to his mother's natal village in Temneland. On their first night in the village, Kaimah fell ill. He was so weak he could not even get out of bed. After much discussion, it was decided that Kaimah was bewitched. A local woman with shape-shifting powers had transformed herself into a night owl. She had perched on the roof of the house where Kaimah was sleeping, and consumed his blood. But on the second night, the villagers caught the owl and beat it to death. The witch, now weakened and seriously ill, confessed to her crime and explained how she had assumed the form of an owl in order to attack Kaimah. Perhaps she bore some grudge toward Kaimah's mother, Yebu. Her exact motive was never known, for she died soon after confessing.

Kaimah's second story was hearsay. A certain man with powers was able to appropriate his wife's genitalia and pregnant belly. Leaving his own sleeping body at night, he would then move around the village as a pregnant man. One morning, just before first light, he found himself unable to reenter his own body. He was discovered, struggling and writhing, with the swollen belly and genitalia of a pregnant woman. He died soon after. As for his wife, she woke that same morning no longer pregnant.

"These things are strange," Kaimah said.

I did not comment. For me it was not a matter of *what* had occurred, but *how* it was interpreted. There is no mystery in the oneiric experience of journeying to other places, of flying, of bizarre encounters and metamorphoses. Nor is it mysterious that human beings should nurse resentments, or bear malice toward a kinsman or neighbor. But where some anthropologists might be inclined to see misfortune as the fall-out of historical events or global socioeconomic forces, Kaimah suspected foul play, conspiracy, and greed—in a word, witchcraft. Having explored the phenomenon of "witchcraft" in the course of my ethnographic work in Kuranko villages over many years,[3] I found it easy to see parallels between Kaimah's "persecution narrative"[4] and the combination of factors that usually precede witchcraft confession. First, are the enervating and demoralizing effects of a prolonged and seemingly incurable illness that leads a person to ask the unanswerable question, "Why me, why now, why no cure or respite?" Second, is a history of vexed intrafamilial relationships (in Kaima's case the rivalry between sons of the same father but different mothers [*fadenye*] who find themselves competing for scarce spiritual and material resources). That a person imagines himself or herself to be "bewitched" should be explained in terms of the social situation in which he finds himself and the existential distress he is suffering, and not simply in terms of the cultural beliefs he or she has internalized. These beliefs exist in potentia, and not every individual will invoke them in the same way, though they afford some kind of understanding of a person's extreme suffering.

What led Kaima to set such store by beliefs that others took less personally? And whence arose his allusions to siblings trying to impede his progress, spoil his chances, and deprive him of the blessings or bounty he had sought through higher education and hard work? Was there any truth to these assertions or were they also fantasies, born of his frustrations in getting a job, in improving his situation, in finding the wherewithal to marry?

At one point, Kaimah touched on the vexed issue of his uncle S. B.'s legacy. It was rumored in the family that when S. B. passed away, a considerable amount of money was left in trust, but that Sewa's widow Rose or one of S. B.'s most favored children had contrived to prevent this legacy being equitably distributed. Kaimah was convinced that this was the case. It was, as he put it, another sinister example of how people will "go the extra mile" in securing a scarce resource for themselves and disinheriting anyone they disliked or considered to be "distant kin."

As we passed the grey concrete shell of a new beachfront hotel under construction, Kaimah said it was being built with money earned overseas by the famous Sierra Leonean footballer Mohamed Kallon. Kallon had been signed recently by AEK Athens, but earlier contracts with French and Saudi professional clubs had made him a lot of money. "But he's the younger brother," Kaimah said, "and his older brothers have squandered much of his wealth. Fortunately, this hotel is in the hands of a private contractor. It is a fixed asset, so he can protect it from the vultures."

What truth there was in Kaimah's story I did not know. But like his other stories, it gave me glimpses into what it feels like to be marginalized, to be "cut out" —as his father Noah often said of himself, comparing his desperate situation to that of his elder brother S. B. There is historical, even contemporary, evidence of human sacrifice and the use of human body parts in producing empowering magical medicines.[5] But the force of these grim images mostly derives not from empirical evidence but from their metaphorical weight. As Derek Hughes puts it, human sacrifice is "a metonym for all transactions in which life is the currency" (cited in Kermode 2008: 11). In existential terms, material scarcity translates into a sense of being socially *without*—outside the pale, lacking the recognition that one's life has the same worth, the same potentiality, as any other life, and lacking the luxury of ever being able to take for granted that the life-energy one has today will be sufficient to see one through tomorrow. It is this constant anxiety that the scarce resource of life itself will be drained from you, sapped by the ill will or negligence of others, or from underhand dealings of which one can never be aware. One is gradually worn down by the lack of any reciprocity between what one reasonably expects from one's environment, the energy one expends in improving one's chances of "progress," and the corrupt and corrosive forces that deny you any advantage. One is sometimes driven to countermeasures, simply to survive—seizing the symbolic capital, the wherewithal for life, that has been unfairly withheld. And in this dialectic, images of eating give objective form to an inchoate sense of being deprived (one's life stolen or overwhelmed by another) or of being reempowered (literally through getting one's own back).[6] It is a dog-eat-dog world. Either one's life energies are consumed by others, or increased through the acquisition of consumer goods—from imported commodities to symbolic substances such as the blood of others—that effectively transform one's external world into an *inner* world of strength, personal solidity, and vital power. It is this experience of empowerment through the ingestion of life-energy that underpins the social institution of exogamy (guaranteeing the life of a lineage by incorporating child-bearing women into it), finds expression in cosmologies that assume that the social order can avoid entropy by tapping into and domesticating the "wild" powers of the bush, feeds the notion of economic increase through migration and "development," and generates images and fantasies of human sacrifice (in which the flagging powers of the old are reinvigorated by eating the vital organs of young victims). But the line between actual and imaginary strategies is never clearly drawn, and the *logic* of human sacrifice never *necessarily* entails the *practice* of human sacrifice. Nor, for that matter, do people necessarily turn to the occult when deprived of real avenues for self-realization. Indeed, I was often impressed by how faithfully Kaimah stuck to a secular agenda, despite his embrace of Islam, his belief in witchcraft, and his stories about the machinations of his kinsmen. For him, the gospel of prosperity, the talk of righteous riches and of health and wealth was hollow; he had placed his faith in education, and in going abroad to widen his horizons.

"You should talk to Sewa," I said. "He will tell you that the streets of London are not paved with gold *or* knowledge, but with a lot of human misery. You should know what you are getting into, exchanging Sierra Leone for England."

"I know it will be hard," Kaimah said. "But it will be worth it."

"Yes," I said. "It will be worth it." For hadn't I once left my own homeland with exactly the same dreams? And had anyone tried to dissuade me from my course with talk of expatriates returning home with empty hands, ending up in a local mental asylum, exhausted by the cumulative impact of family intrigues, malicious gossip, endless demands, and envious criticism—would this have held me back?

Nevertheless, I had misgivings about the destiny I was visiting upon Kaimah by helping him go to London. Although Kaimah had painted a somber picture of African sociality as claustrophobic and depleting, it seemed to me that the ebullience, laughter, and energy generated in face-to-face relations with others was precisely what compensated people for the lack of work, the lack of money, even the lack of food on one's table. But who was I to romanticize a lifeworld that so many saw as an obstacle to their self-realization?

That evening, walking alone on Lumley beach, my thoughts turned to well-being as the possession of existential power. To some extent, this power lies within, manifest in the conviction that one has what it takes to endure one's lot, survive a setback, improve one's fortune, or turn one's life around. But existential potency is equally contingent on one's relationships with others, and on what the world affords one as opportunity or possibility. These entwined motifs of internal and external potentialities are central to Kuranko notions of well-being. Empowerment comes from a combination of innate giftedness, acquired social skills, inherited status, luck, ancestral favor, and powerful connections. Although money, migration, education, and development are now fetishized as avenues to well-being, a viable life depends on commanding as many resources as one can legitimately locate and exploit. It is not that God, the ancestors, and djinn have ceased to be sources of earthly well-being; rather, that blessedness now depends on other factors as well—though the same reasoning governs attitudes to the new as to the old. Just as sheep, goats, cows, rice flour, and kola are ritually given to the ancestors and to God, so now, in the new churches, money is prayed over, blessed, and purified in the hope that it will, once given, pay dividends or protect the giver from predatory strangers. However, occult economies do not generate wealth. They magically redistribute what already exists. This is why the gains from occult practices are always mixed blessings. One person's windfall entails another person's loss. And those who are blessed must pay a price for any improvement in their fortunes—the death of a loved one, the alienation of close kin, or the loss of the lifeworld that shaped their identity.

A week after Kaimah's death, I received a second email from Kaimah's sister Jeneba that confirmed many of the suspicions that Kaimah had confided to me in Freetown four years before. "I am sure u know that me and daddy r from the same mother and father, and we r only two, all the rest r just the same dad, now that he is gone I am all alone, but I have Michael, so I want to see the best for him, so that his daddy will be happy where ever he is." As for her half-siblings, "I don't trust them any more," Jeneba wrote, suggesting that clandestine malice had been responsible for Kaimah's illness and death. She invited me to review Facebook photos of him, as if these were evidence of the kind of wasting diseases associated with witchcraft and sorcery. "If u go through my pictures u will see him. I know what I am talking about, and b4 he died he told Michael not to go to the family house any more."

Jeneba's dark comments reminded me of the critical role one's mother plays in Kuranko society in mediating relations between her children and their patrilineal ancestors. Should her behavior toward her husband be less than dutiful and obedient, the blessings of her husband's ancestors will be withheld from her children. Should she die, her children are left defenseless, for ancestral blessings will now flow to the children of her cowives. But this cultural explanation for why fortune and misfortune are unequally distributed may be seen as a rationalization of the *psychological* effects of being motherless. Kaimah was a small boy when his mother

Yebu died. His sense of abandonment and his loss of ontological security translated easily into a sense of being cursed, for without the blessings that accrue to a child through his or her mother's behavior, a person is effectively bereft of the spiritual resources that will enable him or her to survive illness and show fortitude in the face of adversity. In other words, one's capacity to act in the world is contingent on the inner confidence that comes from being loved.

Theoretically, one's destiny is a combination of ancestral blessings *and* hard work, though patience and forbearance are equally important, since one never knows when good fortune will come one's way or diligence pay off. Undoubtedly, Kaimah's traumatic loss of his mother in early childhood made him more than ordinarily susceptible to the hardships that would subsequently dog his life—his father's and father's brother's inability to support him, the impact of the civil war, the death of Lango, the desertion of his girlfriend Aisetta, unemployment. Each new setback seemed to compound Kaimah's difficulties and increase his despair. Even gifts could turn poisonous, so that when I told Kaimah that I could no longer pay him a monthly stipend because my own children's education had to take priority, he may have experienced this blow as a replay of the discriminations he had suffered as an orphan child. At the same time, the successes of his close cousins and half-siblings were seen as personal slights, or read as signs that scarce resources were being secretly siphoned off, benefiting them at his expense.

Coda

When we attempt to explain how a person comes to be himself or herself and not someone else—we typically have recourse to notions of nature or nurture, though nowadays it is becoming more common to speak of an interplay between genetic and epigenetic factors. Unfortunately, these approaches to ontogenesis are both based on notions of predetermination, and endeavor to show how genetic and environmental factors combine and permute in constituting an individual human being. Thus, Kaimah's life course might be accounted for in terms of a series of external determinants—the death of his mother, Yebu, bouts of tuberculosis in early childhood, the civil war, endemic poverty, inadequate education, social discrimination, the impossibility of finding work, and a medical system that proved inadequate when he fell gravely ill. But in emphasizing these circumstances over which Kaimah had no control, we risk ignoring his intentions, his will, and his inner resources—particularly in fulfilling his commitment to his son, while pursuing his own dreams of higher education.

Existential anthropology assigns to our capacity to act responsively to the world and to project ourselves into it the same determinative power that orthodox social science assigns to culture, class, gender, and history. One's humanity depends on being able to act (or to feel that one can act) on one's world, even under circumstances in which one is overwhelmingly acted upon (or feels that one is acted upon) *by* the world. Before any coherent account is rendered, any meaning is proposed, any explanation offered, or belief embraced, there exists an ontologically "primitive" imperative to act in some way or other in response to the actions of others or the world at large—to be a who rather than merely a what. It is this responsiveness (which is not necessarily responsible), whether protest or acquiescence, that defines the difference between being an object and becoming a subject.

In a recent study of monozygotic ("genetically identical"[7]) twins who shared the same childhood environments for the first eighteen years of their lives, it was found that despite initial similarities, the outcome of these lives were very different. In explaining these differences, Professor Tim Spector, head of twin research at King's College, London, invoked environmental changes that alter the behavior of genes, i.e., epigenetic factors.[8] But while this insight helps us understand some of the *causes* of variations in disease susceptibility in identical twins, it does not explain the *reasons* why two individual personalities should become so different. Are we justified in speaking of an existential imperative—a causa sui—that motivates a person to identify with some people and not with others, regardless of how genetically or socially "close" they are? In the case of Kaimah, why did he, like so many other young men, *not* identify with the rebel cause, but identify against them? And was this act a consequence of a disposition already in place or a genuinely rational or ethical choice?

One problem with the notion of choice is that it is impossible to know whether an act is based on reasoned reflection or is the inevitable expression of an unconscious predisposition. This is why I prefer to speak of acting rather than choosing, for actions both embody habitual responses and involve new initiatives. Even when we think we know someone well, we are often surprised by the way he or she responds to a novel situation.

There are echoes here of Sartre's view of existence as a dialectic of constituted-constituting, whereby something new constantly emerges from what is already established, culturally or psychologically. But is it not in the nature of things for the "new" to make its appearance belatedly or in a form that is unfamiliar. A tragedy that befell a single Kuranko family in a remote region of northeast Sierra Leone 130 years ago transformed the destiny of a lineage and continues to have repercussions in the present. But whether the past visits upon us tragedies or quandaries, we can never know how these will play out. There are times when nothing seems to be happening, nothing is getting resolved, when we are stuck, as the saying goes, between a rock and a hard place.

What was Kaimah to do, when faced with the possibility of abandoning Michael in Freetown in order to further his own education in the United Kingdom? If he remained in Sierra Leone he risked losing the final vestige of that sense of acting to create one's own future that defines what we call hope. He would succumb to the depressing sense of being under assault on all sides from people seeking his downfall, by authority figures turning their backs on him, by his own growing sense of futility and despair. But to go to England would be to risk becoming a nobody, a dependent, struggling against a different set of odds, and possibly beset by guilt at having abandoned his son.

In Camus's *Myth of Sisyphus* we find the glimmerings of an answer. It lies in the difference between being oblivious to the absurdity of our condition and becoming lucidly aware of it. It is in Sisyphus's clear knowledge that his task is interminable that it becomes *his* task and no one else's. The great stone ceases to be a curse placed upon him by the Gods; it is a human burden that *he* takes up, and in doing so he becomes more than the rock, his life belongs to him, and he "silences all the idols" (1955: 98).

A Kuranko adage echoes this train of thought: *Dunia toge ma dunia; a toge le a dununia*, literally "the name of the world is not world; its name is load." The adage exploits oxymoron and pun (*dunia*, "world," and *dununia*, "load," are near homophones), to imply that the world is like a head-load, the weight of which depends on how one chooses to carry it. You can bear up under it, or allow it to bear down upon you. You can accept or resist, but you cannot escape the fact that the weight of the world *has to be borne*.

There is another way in which Kuranko reasoning addresses the preciousness of life, and that is by prioritizing life itself or the life of a lineage over the life of any one person, giving genealogical continuity precedence over individual longevity. By contrast, we in the West have come to expect world-changing accomplishments from individual actors. We like to think that we make history, rather than that history makes us or, more accurately, that we *participate* in history so that historical experience "is never purely individual, but intrinsically social" (Schwartz Wentzer 2014: 37). By extolling the life of an individual, we can easily forget that potentialities require many generations to be realized and that what appears to be the work of one person is the product of myriad interactions with significant others. In Michael, the issues that beset the lives of his father, grandfather, and great grandfather may be finally resolved, but the chances are that new issues will emerge that will, in turn, require more than a single lifetime to be addressed.

But as I write, these rationalizations provide little comfort. Kaimah lived at a time when young men no longer accept the rule of tradition, the stoic virtues of boundless patience and forbearance. Yet Kaimah was never so immobilized or dispirited that he turned to stone. He pushed the boulder uphill every day not only because he found a way of making the stone his own; he did so because he assumed this burden on behalf of another, and because his son's future depended on what Kaimah did in here and now. He therefore exemplified what Merleau-Ponty wrote of "our relationship to the social," which is, "like our relationship to the world, deeper than any express perception or any judgement," and implies a "dual being, where the other is for me no longer a mere bit of behavior in my transcendental field, not I in his; we are collaborators for each other in consummate reciprocity. Our perspectives merge into each other, and we co-exist through a common world" (1962: 362, 354).

That this holds true of my relationship to significant others in Sierra Leone as well as to those who actually inhabit that country is what gives social anthropology a meaning for me that goes beyond the limits of an academic discipline and assigns the social an existential value that is *there* before any specific social, historical, or discursive formation is in place, and outstrips any intellectual understanding.

Notes

1. There is a widespread belief in the affluent West that education creates jobs and is, therefore, a key to social development in poor societies. In fact, education tends to create and entrench inequality in such societies, partly because schooling for all is unaffordable or unavailable (even if the state committed all its resources to education), partly because the demand for jobs far exceeds the employment options that are open to young graduates. Indeed, it was the frustrations and resentments of educated and unemployed youth that were significant driving forces behind the Revolutionary United Front and the civil war.
2. For a detailed account of the circumstances under which Tina Kome left home to enlist in 1906, see Jackson 1986: 49–51.
3. Jackson 1975: 387–403.
4. Girard 1986: 22.

5. Law 1985: 53–87.
6. What is foregrounded in one culture will be backgrounded in another, but psychological analogues of a cultural trait will be found universally. In a compelling study of "concretized metaphors' in the discourse of anorexics, Finn Skårderud (2007) shows that images of voiding, emptying, vomiting, and purging convey a desire to escape an oppressive external circumstance that allows no freedom of direct negotiation, shifting a weight, lightening a burden, restoring a sense of firmness, security stability, and control that had not been experienced before.
7. Robin McKie, "Why do identical twins end up having such different lives?" http://www.guardian.co.uk/science/2013/jun/02/twins-identical-genes-different-health-study?INTCMP=SRCH.
8. "The cells in a multicellular organism have nominally identical DNA sequences ... yet maintain different terminal phenotypes. This nongenetic cellular memory, which records developmental and environmental cues ... is the basis of epi- (above) — genetics" (Riddihough and Zahn 2010: 611).

References

Camus, Albert. 1955. *The Myth of Sisyphus* (trans. Justin O'Brien). London: Hamish Hamilton.
Girard, René. 1986. *The Scapegoat* (trans. Yvonne Freccero). Baltimore, MD: Johns Hopkins University Press.
Hughes, Derek. 2007. *Culture and Sacrifice: Ritual Death in Literature and Opera*. Cambridge: Cambridge University Press.
Jackson, Michael. 1975. "Structure and Event: Witchcraft Confession Among the Kuranko," *Man* 10 (3): 387–403.
———. 1986. *Barawa and the Ways Birds Fly in the Sky*. Washington, DC: Smithsonian Institution Press.
Kermode, Frank. 2008. "Offered to the Gods," *London Review of Books* 30 (1): 11.
Law, Robin. 1985. "Human Sacrifice in Pre-Colonial West Africa," *African Affairs* 84 (334): 53–87.
Levinas, Emmanuel. 2004. "Ethics of the Infinite." In *Debates in Continental Philosophy: Conversations with Contemporary Thinkers*, Richard Kearney (ed.). New York: Fordham University Press, 65–84
Merleau-Ponty, Maurice. 1962. *Phenomenology of Perception* (trans. Colin Smith). London: Routledge and Kegan Paul.
Riddihough, Guy, and Zahn, Laura M. 2010. "What is Epigenetics?" *Science*, 29 October, 611.
Sartre, Jean-Paul. 1987. *The Family Idiot: Gustave Flaubert 1821–1857* (trans. Carol Cosman). Chicago: University of Chicago Press.
Skårderud, Finn. 2007. "Eating One's Words, Part 1: 'Concretised Metaphors' and Reflective Function in Anorexia Nervosa—An Interview Study," *European Eating Disorders Review* 15: 163–174.
Schwarz Wentzer, Thomas. 2014. "'I have seen Königsberg Burning': Philosophical Anthropology and the Responsiveness of Historical Experience," *Anthropological Theory* 14 (1): 27–48.

Chapter Seven

Existence, Minimality, and Believing

Albert Piette

In this chapter—which resembles a play in three acts—I begin by defining the goals of my existential anthropology: to observe human beings, to meticulously analyze experiential moments and presences, and to follow, describe, and compare individuals in a succession of moments and situations over time. My focus is the individual existent and *anthropos* in general, rather than cultures, societies, groups, and activities. In my case, existential anthropology is an anthropology *tout court*, not a social or cultural anthropology. I give particular analytical attention to presence-absence, the mixture of activity and passivity of human beings, and what I call the "minor mode of reality." I illustrate this theme with examples of religious believing. Acts of believing are described as hesitant moments followed by various shifts into other activities, and entailing irony, doubt, or detachment. But this mode of minimal being is everywhere, in every situation of everyday life. I wonder about the evolutionary beginnings of this attitude that is so typically human. I suggest a narrative of the origin, an existential prehistory from the graves of *Homo sapiens* and *Homo neanderthalis*.

* * *

Just as a philosopher might wonder if all philosophy is not the philosophy of existence, an anthropologist might ask if all anthropology is not an anthropology of existence. Historians of philosophy would reply that, for a long time, this discipline was a debate about essences and categories,

---

Notes for this chapter begin on page 210.

far removed from the reality of the real-life experience of existence. Anthropologists could themselves also surmise that their discipline has its own "essences," that is to say themes and perspectives that allow them to sidestep existence: societies, cultures, social issues, representations, structures, but also, more recently, activities, actions, and even nonhumans.

In anthropology, especially in France, the impact of structuralist thought hindered the development of an existential anthropology, so virulent was its contempt for the "me," which it deemed only suitable for a "shopgirl's philosophy" (Lévi-Strauss 1961: 62). Isn't the (unfortunate) genius of anthropology, in all of its still-current manifestations, that it misunderstood, dissolved, and forgot individuals in their most unique characteristic, the fact of existing?

And what if there were only one and the same answer to the two following questions: What is anthropology? What is existential anthropology? Anthropology would or should be the observation and description of the existence of human beings, of each human being in his or her individual singularity as he or she goes about living, being here-and-now, and continuing, each coming from various situations and moving toward other situations. Beyond a merely empirical exercise, existential anthropology would constitute "the analysis of what constitutes existence," what Heidegger called "existentiality," with a view to discovering the general characteristics of the human way of existing (1996: 10). But how is this to be done?

In the process of constructing an object, science works with necessary filters and methodological selections. Would humans as they exist be a relevant scientific theme? Would linking existence to time, continuity, and finiteness be a way of approaching this theme? If we proceed in this way, existential anthropology would consist in observing individuals at moment t, as they come from elsewhere and as they continue toward other situations until they die. Existence is not the total human being as a sum of social, psychological, and cultural characteristics; rather, existence denotes the fact of existing, of being-in-the-world. Does this mean that the anthropology of existence incorporates this dimension of mortality into every field study? It is, in any case, on the horizon, more or less explicit, more or less implicit in human existence, which constantly produces apparitions and disappearances, presences and absences, engagements and disengagements, consciousness and unconsciousness.

From this perspective, I believe it would be appropriate for anthropology to effect a methodological shift: turning away from observations (often called ethnographies) focused on sets of specific situations and interactions (linked to an activity or event) and giving preference to detailed observations of separate individuals in their continuity from situation to situation—a method I have called phenomenography.[1] The individual thus becomes the focus of the observation process. Moreover, a good number of details are needed in order to make comparisons between ways of existing, engaging, and being conscious. This point most certainly implies criticism of the social sciences and particularly of social or cultural anthropology, since existential anthropology would challenge any "collectivist" methodology, focused on shared social and cultural characteristics. During a moment of presence, to exclusively note what constitutes the singularity of the culture, action, or activity in progress means missing the characteristics of individual presence, in which culture and action are only a more or less thin or dense stratum of what I would call the individual's volume of being.

Anthropology has to reach the point at which it is possible to say that human existence can be an empirical object in social science. Using methods and words, concepts and descriptions, it has to explain what these empirical units are like, as they are and where they are, as they exist and continue to exist. What is it like to be human? This would be the fundamental question for existential anthropology. It would constitute a proposal for founding or refounding anthropology, which has been too philosophical or sociocultural, and has almost never been sufficiently anthropological, which is to say descriptive of human beings existing.

From this perspective, existential anthropology is an invitation to focus on situated beings, existences in a situation, and allow oneself to be surprised by the fact that they exist. What is this human being really like, what does he really feel, what does he really perceive, how does he really interact? And what will he be like a few moments later? How does he engage with this or that idea, value, or representation? How does he believe in it? It is important to start with the numerical unit—this one, that one and to follow it as long as possible, and to keep it present even during the final writing. The individual is a numerical unit either aware or unaware of a self, continuing, changing, or not changing in terms of his various qualities or properties. He is a concrete unit attesting to itself, feeling, uniquely experiencing emotions, adversities, acts, words, and constituting an aggregate of actual and potential experiences, also with permanent properties and a system of predispositions and tendencies. By phenomenographing presence, attention is shifted onto the whole volume of being, not just the visibly acting or interacting stratum. In the continuity of his presences and his actions, what the here-and-now individual is doing and saying constitutes a partial, visible actualization in a volume of being that is also composed of other strata—actual, irrelevant elements that leave visible but unnoticed traces and have no consequences; potential elements with more or less visible, sensed, and perceived traces in the scene, always ready to act and produce action, traces left by experiences, events that are more or less recent or remote, skills, abilities, various predispositions such as sociocultural predispositions; virtual elements not made explicit or conscious, such as reasons for being there and doing this or that.

Let's not delude ourselves: the map is not the territory! And yet, the ideal methodology would be to film every person on earth. The ideal methodology—certainly impossible for many reasons—would be a continuous film of the entire life of every person on earth, with his or her own explanation of the captured sequences. All other methodologies would be second best, with some falling below minimum requirements. Ideally at minimum: one human being for a few consecutive hours, a whole day, a week; several selected human beings observed from a few hours to several weeks, repeated at regular intervals. We should place infants at the heart of this research. Every anthropologist should have his own baby to observe and follow continuously for several years! This approach would be continual, involving observations of the continuity of existence, as well as constrasting and comparing diverse continuities according to selected criteria such as age, cultural or social setting, and psychological orientation.

Faced with the great diversity of philosophical theories, I am always struck by their incompatibility, which generates debates that are difficult to resolve. Associated with different anthropologies, each of them probably contains its share of truth. But I often get the impression that they are not true for all individuals, and even that they are all true for the same individual but at different moments. I am convinced that what the philosophies of existence have taught us is, on the one hand, to focus on existence, therefore on the individual, but also, on the other hand, to slide the underlying anthropologies toward certain philosophers (Jaspers, Husserl, or Heidegger, Kierkegaard, Sartre, or Levinas) as combinable tools that can be used to describe all of the modes, modulations, and modalizations of individuals as empirical units. Existence is that of an individual[2] whose successive moments will justify sometimes emphasizing self-becoming, the resolute consciousness that faces up to things, sometimes emphasizing communication with others and power in extreme situations, and sometimes emphasizing theories concerning the solitary, desperate human with no ties to anything, who has become a stranger in the world, theories of human being as he develops in a community, or in the process of feeling conscious and of either becoming or not becoming "free."[3] Researchers who dare to grasp individuals in the continuity of moments and situations will bring much order to the endless controversies (which establish themselves by taking advantage of the methodological spinelessness of the social sciences) between sociological and philosophical paradigms. This relates to a proposition of Wittgenstein: "A main cause of philosophical disease—a one-sided diet: one nourishes one's thinking with only one kind of example" (Wittgenstein 1953: fr. 593). This position is linked to my dissatisfaction with sociological theories, whether Durkheim's, Bourdieu's, or Garfinkel's, because every theory is only relevant to a certain moment, a certain place, for a certain individual, but not more. Life circumstances prove all theories right, but never all at the same time. This implies observing and taking account of the continuity of the individual's existence, instead of a certain activity, a certain state, in a certain location, at a certain moment.

Existential anthropology would produce bridge-descriptions. These would be anthropologically compatible bridges to other descriptions realized on different scales, some larger-scale (those of sociology), some smaller-scale (with psychology, cognitive science, even neuroscience). Between existence as an effect of trajectories and utterances, ontological realities as a collective system of representations and cultural expressions, and cognitivism that omits experience, there is room for an anthropology of existences. Therefore, an anthropology that is existential aims to observe individuals, their existence, and to understand *anthropos* in general, through comparisons with other living species, in particular with nonhuman primates. That is what a project of existential anthropology would be. Based on meticulous descriptions and comparisons between existences and presence modalities, the objective of an existential anthropology would also be to find new "existentials," to use Heidegger's terminology, that is to say general characteristics of the human act of existing. This would be one of the most ambitious goals of existential anthropology.

In this chapter, I analyze only the presence-absence or that which I have designated the "minor mode." It is undoubtedly an existential. My chapter consists of three acts. The first presents this universal characteristic of *Homo sapiens*: the mixture of major mode and minor mode, of presence and absence, of activity and passivity. The second act illustrates this human mode of being with examples of religious believing. The third act searches for a genealogy of this characteristic. I find this genealogy in a hypothesis about the evolutionary origins of the capacity of believing and accepting religious statements. This would have triggered a difference between *Homo sapiens* and *Homo neanderthalis*. Thus, believing is a good laboratory for the study of human minimality. At the end of these three acts, perhaps the human enigma of presence-absence will be resolved.

Act 1: Minor Mode and Reposity

When I look at people in their successive moments, trivial presences often appear that become catalysts for decisions, or generators of various consequences. These presences sometimes remain inconsequential, and often allow themselves to be infiltrated by empty moments, secondary gestures, or wandering thoughts. A moment of human presence is usually made up of a large number of details—that is to say things that are as unimportant to the people who effect them as they are to their fellow participants in a situation or to outside observers. The reality of action is, on the one hand, a body in the process of moving, accompanied by sideways glances and peripheral gestures, and on the other hand a state of mind that often has little to do with the action in progress. All of these details make up the minor mode, which is neither a general action, nor a particular type of activity (Piette 1992; 1996). It constitutes a specific modality by which an individual is necessarily present in the space and time where two or more people find themselves co-present. The minor mode widens the field of details to be described and considered. It is useful for describing the real, concrete person, and for getting the clearest possible view of his or her constant variations of intensity. From a theoretical perspective, it is certainly also useful for considering anthropological difference. Details are constant leitmotifs in the social sciences, as well as in ethnographic activity. But with the minor mode it is a matter of considering the detail qua detail, as something unimportant, whereas the usual semantic co-optation of the social sciences masks, overlooks, or loses the status of small things by linking them to attributes that are different from those of a detail.

Unimportant details

My first fieldwork on festive rituals in Belgium led me to discover, with the help of a very large number of photographs, this ever-present aspect of people in a situation that I call the minor mode of reality. Let us first note that it constitutes a "lesser" way of performing actions, without the introduction of this "less" constituting a new attribute or having supplementary effects on the situation, and also without changing the act in question, which unfolds with its socially expected meanings. The minor mode is a way of being present in one's action that releases a human being from the action without disengaging him or her. It neither adds nor removes a layer of meaning from the performed action. In the performance of human actions, the minor mode is constant in varying doses, whatever these actions may be. It is a fact that does not attract attention. It even counts among its characteristics, manifesting itself in forms that are lesser in relation to the expected action, forms that are involuntary and unnoticed, singular and particular, and do not lead the situation's other participants to share in them.

This "less" in the action partly consists of the presence of other layers of action and attention in the present volume of being. But why "less"? One reason is that these layers present themselves in a lesser manner relative to the expected meaning of the principal action. In this case, direct observation of the action consists in separating the expected—that which is relevant in this action—from physical, gestural, and cognitive signs that attest to the presence of that which is irrelevant in the action. Another reason is that the action, as it is encompassed within a set of heterogeneous details, has a characteristic dampening effect on the ways of being that are present in the situation. This minor modality constitutes a way of being in the world; it is even specific to the *Sapiens* species through our ability to not see and do directly, head-on, exclusively, totally, and to introduce, to varying degrees, a layer, a loosening stratum. I will explore this later.

One form of minor mode therefore resides in gestures and thoughts that are different and simultaneous in relation to those that are expected in the action, that are not relevant, that are not noticed or barely noticed, that are thus tolerated, and that do not imply an active, willful, strategic approach by the person executing them. In any situation in the life of society, people do what is appropriate but they also look left and right, seem to become detached, come back, and then once again release themselves from the scene. They are somewhat distracted, absent, thinking about other things. From this we can conclude that people are skilled at doing two things at once: managing the collective aspect necessarily implied by the interaction in which they are participating, and managing their own singularity through gestures, movements, and thoughts that are specific to each of them. They introduce the individual detail against a backdrop of coordination.[4]

The individual details present a few characteristics: they are inherent in a human being's participation in an action, they cannot be shared by others without a lapse into irrelevance, they are contained within limits beyond which they cannot pass without the risk of engendering an inopportune situation. They have no relevant effect on the interaction in progress or on a subsequent description, but are tolerated by the interactants, who implicitly dissociate them from any fault. The presence of these minor gestures does not invite one to think about the succession of different actions, but rather about the simultaneity between the action that is appropriate to the situation and the residues of other actions. In a situation, human presence would seem inconceivable and impossible without this variable dose of small details. Its agreeableness depends on them.

Is it necessary to point out that many observations and descriptions are formulated as if the world operated only in the major mode or, put differently, only with individuals who were connected to only one stratum in terms of their mode of presence? The appropriate one, but also inversely the one that is inappropriate. A descriptive improvement can be achieved by recognizing the presence of this minor mode.

Focusing on the minor mode enables attention to be drawn to one way (the human way) of looking, perceiving, and being attentive—that is to say, "being in the world." Much of the minor mode resides in the following few traits. First there is the human mode of perception, which is most often parsimonious and light in everyday situations, not involving an active, nervous, or alert exploration of an object's characteristics and thus enabling its trigger effect to be blunted. Also, in various situations, people are usually surrounded by many things that are "there," things that they might see but not really observe—the minimal, even imprecise perception of these things does not entail any action. People also associate an object with various meanings or purposes, and when they use it in a situation, they may associate it with a representation that is now secondary to that from which it was previously perceived. Thus people perceive with a system of open blinders that enable them to see a prominent object without eliminating awareness of what is all around them, maintaining a kind of backdrop from which things become visible as unimportant details. People are able to be distracted without losing sight of the main object of their attention, continuing their main activity without becoming detached, without losing their concentration. Finally, they live in the world, from which things they perceive appear with a certain continuity from situation to situation, without involving the abrupt replacement of one perception by another, against a backdrop of relative stability, without the need to control and far from a state of readiness. Wandering thoughts are possible, straying far from the activity underway, thoughts concerning the past, the future, or other things. These thoughts may also become critical in relation to the present act, as if it made one sense one's restriction, a problem, weariness, a habit, and may give rise to a doubt or an inner conflict. They then cause one to leave the minor mode.

If a retailer is someone who deals in small quantities or bits and pieces, can ethnographers be compared with retailers? It seems to me that they too often deliver sets in bulk. Summarizing observed situations, selecting one aspect of the individual that they consider relevant to the activity, paring the individual's existence down to a single activity—these are big, anti-realistic faults that can be avoided by focusing on the minor mode. The task I assign to phenomenography is precisely to deliver in pieces. This is what is implied by its focus on individuals that are separate but of course always situated. Phenomenography tracks human beings' inner gaps, and attempts to penetrate presences in their details. Among some of the remains of the social sciences, human beings have a curious presence that it is possible to place under the anthropological zoom lens.

Activity and passivity

The minor mode can still teach us something about the human way of existing, by displacing the meaning of "less." It does not just concern secondary layers of presence, as I have just said, but the whole presence in the action, in which light distraction is but one element. I have proposed the term "reposity"[5] to more closely capture the natural attitude of human beings, with four characteristic elements describing the part repose plays, and their respective opposites (Piette 2009; 2011).

On the basis of habits, previous experiences, and mental scenarios, cognitive economy enables people to forego verifying that they have all the information and skills necessary for performing an action. Not only does cognitive economy correspond to the routinized application of sequences of actions without reference to an instruction, it also facilitates the process of social interaction, by virtue of each partner's material supports and stable identities. The opposite of cognitive economy is the work of evaluating, strategizing, justifying, and scheming, all of which direct attention—sometimes obsessively—to specific fragments of reality. Docility corresponds to the possibility of preserving the present supports, rules and values, the existing signs and points of reference (as opposed to the intention or desire to change them), and the avoidance of the cognitive, emotional, or moral tension that results from the ordeal of change. Fluidity corresponds to the possibility of linking opposite or contradictory information or modes of reasoning in the same situation, or in situations that closely follow one another. It illustrates the human ability to let go immediately, to accept inconsistency, and to shift from situation to situation. The opposite is inflexibility. Finally there is distraction, which corresponds to the cognitive ability to attribute to a being, object, or event the status of a detail (without importance), to reduce it to an element of distraction without compromising the minimal attention required in the situation. It is the state of concentration or intransigence that is the opposite of distraction.

I think these concepts can be useful in dissecting instants of individual existence. In human presence, the proportioning of work and repose, of activity and passivity—indissociable from one another—is of course different for each person in a shared situation. It is important to emphasize this mixture. According to "the degree of our attention to life," "now nearer to action, now further removed from it," this interweaving of modes of presence produces "diverse tones of mental life" (Bergson 2004: xiv). And over a set of successive activities, depending on what they are, a specific individual will pass through variations of proportion between work and repose. When people are very active, they remain "carried" by the interlinking of moments and the presence of points of reference and other supports. There is no active dimension (evaluating, changing, losing, scheming) that is not accompanied by at least one of the other constitutive dimensions of "repose."

Supports and repose combine to generate different modes of presence. Tranquility develops from a mode that is perceptive or even infra-perceptive of reference points and spatiotemporal signs, against a quite stable backdrop, sometimes experienced as such, with the possibility that unimportant details might emerge. In a familiar situation, some points of reference and signs are new, or at least different, and others are found to be lacking relative to previous situations, though the difference is still absorbed in the economical mode, against a backdrop that is still well anchored. It is when the at least partial disintegration of this backdrop is sensed—with the imposed or created absence of certain supports—that weariness arises and reduces the possibility of distractions. There follows an attentive, concentrated tension of (re)construction, judgment, and evaluation. Then, it is as if the backdrop were withdrawn, giving way to the nearly exclusive prominence of this or that fragment of attention. It appears to me that it is essential to perceive the constant, tangled play of these modes of presence in terms of the mobility of supports that either remain, go away, or are recreated. Even though one or two supports are lacking, others remain. At the height of conflict, alienation, anxiety, and rupture, people can and must find forms of repose, and find them in order to continue, to survive. When cognitive economy gives way to the struggling determination of the senses, or docility gives way to instability, or fluidity to rigidity, or distraction to intransigence, tiredness can only be either isolated, in which case it is quickly absorbed, or diffuse, in which case it is still permeated in different doses by various rules, points of reference, or signs supporting the situation. These different forms of support and repose, as well as their respective opposites, constitute a descriptive framework for understanding and representing the movement of the sequences of human actions in situations that link from one to the next, between repose and work, between tiredness and tranquility, between tension and familiarity.

What does a person do when he or she is with others in a so-called collective action at a given moment? A lot may be accomplished, but most of the time not much is actually done: one is simply there, doing what is necessary, though without much mental or physical effort, out of habit, with economical perception varying according to the situation at hand. Most human actions develop in a situation without requiring more than this minimal integration behavior from the people who are there. These are expected behaviors whose obviousness reflects previous commitments, intentions, or decisions. At the same time, indeed most of the time, these behaviors go without saying, also reflecting prior situations, as we have just seen. Highly visible externally, the stratum of minimal integration behavior often intrudes little upon the immediate presence experienced by any person. It is executed all the more lightly insofar as the corresponding actions are routine, linked to known rules, to co-present objects or resource-persons.

But in addition to this stratum, as I have pointed out, human presence also includes remains, a volume of remains. In fact, taking a good look at minimal integration behavior in a single situation, no two behaviors are ever really alike. There are, of course, different styles and social tendencies surrounding the same gesture, but more importantly, in parallel with the execution of the behavior, there are remains that are thus characterized because they do not jeopardize the minimum integration behavior. These are gestures peripheral to the expected action, thoughts heterogeneous to it, the absence of an inner state in relation to gestures that are simply conformist. But they are also personalized and sometimes emotional evocations, stemming from what is being done or said, or isolated feelings that an experience is unfulfilling, or even an impression of constraint or a brief critical doubt about what is happening. Whereas their integration behavior is highly visible to everyone, remains are often invisible to other individuals; in any case they are not interpreted as a sign of anything. On the other hand, expected behaviors can be (though not always) less present in inner experiences than remains, which are sometimes strongly autoperceived and felt (at least some of them) in the course of the action, but not enough to jeopardize the successful unfolding of the situation.

Collective life in a given situation also involves, therefore, a suspension of the search for these requirements, and an acceptance of the undecidability of what other people think.[6] In each case there is a shared minimum and a varying volume of remains, which are more or less indistinct for the others, and are viewed as irrelevant. The situation's participants achieve minimal integration behavior through the reciprocal establishment of visibility. The presence of remains is also shared but in an invisible way, at least without being recognized or hardly being recognized, and their contents are different for each person though not made explicit to all. Thus, integration behavior is minimal, and the remains are minimal as well, since they do not produce any change and are not experienced as differences between people. Minimality is very much a crucial principle of sociological operation. It enables a large volume of remains to exist alongside the gestural and mental minimum of social presence.

The subject of the social sciences in general most often concerns minimal integration behavior, and focuses on certain remains that are precursors of change in a course of events, such as doing something under the effect of restriction, in critical doubt, with a present strategic aim. A phenomenography of the remains stratum implies not isolating the shared minimum of modes of presence and treating it as if it were the sole, maximal volume of presence, but also analyzing the volume of mental and gestural remains that exists alongside the shared social minimum. An instance of successful coordination requires suspending all requirements beyond the completion of a minimal substratum that is itself accomplished minimally, with perceptional and cognitive economy through habits and routines, in lightened co-presence with objects and resource-persons, against a background of rules and norms that are both general and nonetheless virtually present, as well as against the background of a still-possible "ordeal" and of the existence of intense engagements that are more or less remote in time and space. There is also another minimum that, through successive presence in instants, makes it possible to keep living when confronted with a dreadful situation, when a near tragic event fills people's whole situation and presence. Continuity, from instant to instant, situation to situation, is achieved through the extraordinary conjunction of the tragic—dominant—anchored and almost fixed—and these more or less "secondarily" present remains that can forge links between moments and situations and so keep a person going. The effect of continuity is directly linked to the availability, next to the human presence, of nearly inexhaustible, constantly revitalizing supports. They are made up of reference points, signs and rules, as I have pointed out. They are people or objects, spatiotemporal indicators, in the foreground or as a backdrop to the situation. There are therefore several types of minimum:

- the social minimum, that is to say the execution of what is expected in a situation with several people against a backdrop of rules, laws and habits;

- the minimum of human presence, in which cognitive engagement can be very economical and inner engagement can be unnecessary;
- the minimum of remains, those that stay on the sideline and do not get overwhelmed by more or less total types of situations (dreadful ones in particular), those very remains that link together the continuity of existence.

Humans possess a special skill for modalizing their presence by constantly injecting nuances, by creating mixtures of being, by fluidly shifting between modes and situations, and also by establishing degrees of consequence that make people, their activities, and their spaces appear more or less important. By living with gods, institutions, and animals, people create new supports for themselves—supports for repose—giving themselves an even better chance of living in the minor mode. As if we in fact had a strong sign of their specificity, humans inject this modal characteristic into the lives of their close day-to-day companions—let's call them parahumans since they exist alongside us—who, with their own ability to minimize, make it all the easier for the humans to relax when they are at their side. The human being who personifies animals or humanizes machines bestows upon them a "pliable ontology." As a minimal being, he is so specifically minimal that his minimality permeates the being of parahumans, such as dogs, whose own minor-mode expressions were shown by Marion Vicart (2014), through the imitation of humans and/or the tranquillization of their lives at their sides. The existence of parahuman companions therefore proceeds through the minimization of their modes of presence, achieved to different degrees in each of them. One constant characteristic of institutions, gods, domestic animals, social groups, etc., consists in their restrictive, negative presence, dare I say, in the minor mode. The potential pressure of their active side (which is obviously real; I do not intend to claim it does not exist) is thus counterbalanced by various restrictive modes of existence. The omnipresent god is also invisible, often faded, and even raises doubts about his existence. Political institutions such as states are very structuring but are particularly virtual. Groups, which are also structuring, are particularly irregular and polymorphous. The social (that is to say social predispositions), which can be real and active, is particularly potentialized and often implicit. Domestic animals, which are interactive, are contingent, passive, and often neutralized in everyday situations. Humans seem to understand their anthropological specificity—minimality—in the world of the living because they externalize and accentuate it in parahumans' existence and through different ways of being co-present with them.

What is the source of collective life? In each situation, co-presence develops around three essential elements.

- the continuity of present beings: that of humans who have their own reasons for being there, with their skills and abilities, in accordance with a variable number of past situations; that of parahumans, particularly that of prominent objects in the scene in question, themselves deriving from a long continuity;
- the minimality of the person who, in the situation, employs most of his necessary skills and abilities more or less automatically, disregarding questions about the origins of the continuity of each participant, whether human or nonhuman;
- the virtuality of a set of parahuman entities, which are there without really being there, like collective beings that, in their own way, are present in this or that situation object.

Continuity, minimality, virtuality: could these be key elements that make it unnecessary to seek other principles to explain social life? At any rate, the obviousness of presence and co-presence defined in this way seems to me essential in this life together. It would be a worthwhile challenge to try redescribing the world and its scenes by determining the minimal portion of actions and presences they require, as well as the part played by the infiltration of irrelevant details and the minor mode. In an obvious way, this kind of perspective reintroduces the modalities of adherence and engagement by which people relate to representations, to systems of collective representations—sometimes called ontologies—those adherence modalities too often set aside in that "ontological turn" we discussed in the introduction to this book.

Act 2: Believing, a Laboratory of the Minimality

Now let us try to observe some figures of the minimality in everyday situations. The experience of believing offers a starting point for such an analysis. In the social sciences of religion, the temptation to overinterpret jeopardizes the description and analysis of beliefs, or more specifically modes of believing. Religious beliefs are often treated as synonymous with homogeneous, shared cultural representations, as if adherence, acceptance, and the mode of belief were self-evident.

Numerous examples taken from diverse cultural contexts illustrate the minor mode of beliefs. Half-believing, believing contradictory things, believing while being skeptical, floating between wonder and credulity, being able to change "programs of truth," hesitating or remaining indifferent when facing the choice between truth or fiction: this is the multiplicity of attitudes and modalities of belief that Paul Veyne (1988) highlighted in his analysis of Greek myths.

It is therefore a matter of setting aside the usual image of people adhering to beliefs either in conformity to or in spite of those instituted by society, being conscious and logical within themselves, always being serious in the actions they perform, and therefore always being overinterpreted in relation to events they most often experience simply and mundanely. The point is not to replace this with the image of unbelieving, unconscious, inconsistent people who lack serious action, but rather that of people who believe without believing (Mair 2012).

The work involved in a large-scale ethnographic study and the notion of culture are such that individual differences risk being disregarded—overshadowed by the cultural representations thus collated. Matching an individual's beliefs with representations that are public, pervasive, or orthodoxly organized, and linking these to the coherence of a singular cultural entity distracts attention from concrete behaviors and actions. This is not only to ignore individual variations but also to assume that individuals have full access to entirely transparent representations.

An approach focused on particular variations and individual expressions is needed if one is to get closer to modes of belief and moments of believing. This exercise must be read as a consideration, a sort of dissection of "what goes on" when people are believing. It aims to present theoretical reference points with a view to establishing an anthropology of hesitant and fragmentary modalities of belief. The examples provided are mainly drawn from my study in Catholic parishes of France (Piette 1999). Close observation and personal interviews enabled me to obtain the data that follows. I shall go into individual details of acts of believing, at different levels. A set of characteristics shall appear. It would be important to make other phenomenographic explorations in different religious universes and to compare them.

Belief statements

"Jesus is alive." "The spirit of the Lord is present among us." These are the kind of statements one usually hears in Catholic religious ceremonies. They have at least three characteristics (Boyer 1994). They contradict individuals' intuitive expectations and ordinary anticipations, such as when they attribute the quality "alive" to a person who is known to be dead.

They are composed of notions or concepts that have a certain complexity for those who utter them—the "believers" themselves—and are vague in meaning (such as the notion of spirit, the idea of presence, and many others), making them sources of doubtful interpretations and persistent controversies. Finally, they do not imply—again, for the "believers" themselves—a necessary link to other statements or behaviors that would seem to follow from them logically and directly. Would any Catholic asserting Christ's "real presence" be prepared to search for physical traces of this? Dan Sperber uses the term "semi-propositional" to describe the contents of a mental representation that is incompletely established (1985). The believer does not fully pursue the propositional logic by which a representation identifies one and only one proposition. Since it opens an array of interpretations that might clarify this content (without there being any single "right" interpretation), semi-propositional representations allow a kind of loosening in the face of vague contents that are not taken literally (ibid.: 71–73). The individual does not receive this semi-propositional content as a fact but as a representation that involves a certain mental vagueness that does not prevent him from having confidence in both the authority that issues the statement and the orthodoxy of its representation.

Every act of believing is linked to some cognitive vagueness. From the remarkable mind map (which can be interpreted as a set of semi-propositional representations) of an octogenarian subscribing to the idea of the immortality of the soul but wishing to delay Heaven as long as possible, while at the same time desiring to live on in the memory of his descendants, while at the same time asking that his loved ones place a valued object in his final resting place and that they not forget to look after his grave, Paul Veyne extracts the gist: "one believes in Heaven, one is afraid of being a corpse, one feels one's future death will be a kind of sleep, one does not want to be neglected or forgotten like a dog" (Veyne 1992: 249). According to Veyne, "only the first of these four modalities is influenced by religious beliefs; but, even in a population that believes in the Resurrection, the three other experiences persist." He explains: "It would be a mistake to believe that religion is coextensive to culture; some attitudes to the beyond vary according to beliefs, but only some; faith in personal immortality did not prevent Christians from also wanting to survive in their descendants" (ibid.: 247–249). Someone slips a few photos into a coffin just before it is closed. He knows that the corpse will not be able to use these objects but he offers them anyway. At the moment of the gesture, it is impossible to mentally strengthen this act of believing without at the same time summoning one's critical knowledge. The individual prefers to keep his semi-propositional representations below the level of consciousness;

this is the minimal internalization that makes it possible to manage incompatibilities in this case.

Telling ones' beliefs

Responding to the researcher by saying, "Yes, I believe that Jesus Christ is the son of God," does not amount to "being in the middle of believing." It is the conveying of an "opinion" or "piece of information" — in this case about one's own religious ideas. It appears that the phrase itself can constitute a bad model for conceiving of belief: it is based on the association of "precise verbal expression to convictions that lack the hard edges verbalization endows them with" (Dennett 1987: 21). But at the same time, the positive answer clearly shows that the interviewee thinks various realities (God, the resurrection) really exist. Believing is not just playing along for the duration of a book or film. It is also retaining the thought after the religious celebration is over, and possibly expressing it to the anthropologist.

The responses and comments that the believer offers the anthropologist do not make the meaning of his beliefs clear. Rather, these constitute a set of supplemental remarks in a specific type of situation. Their distinctive features must therefore be identified. They will help us understand the management of religious statements in actuality. With this in mind, I have questioned Catholics about the idea of resurrection, not to get them to give me the key to their beliefs, but to discover the modalities by which they link together belief statements. The interview imposes a certain bias since they are asked for "information" on life after death and the resurrection. It is up to them to respond and make a series of statements. What do we find? The responses revolve around the idea of a spiritual life after earthly life, and this possibility is presented as a "mystery" that is capable of uniting the spirits of all people and creating a world of "peace and light." Spiritual life is described as a state of "love to the highest degree": it is to live "in God's love." The foundations of the possibility of this spiritual life are the qualities of God: "he is infinitely powerful and he will offer us something unexpected"; "he is someone good fighting to destroy evil. This absence of evil is impossible in this world. There is a future for humanity outside of our way of thinking and our space"; "I have strong faith in the goodness of a God who creates, and real happiness means penetrating beyond death"; "God loves people to the point that he can do all."

The terms used to suggest this spiritual life (love, peace, happiness) are polysemic and somewhat vague. Most often, there is an explicit refusal to imagine and describe what lies beyond death: "I'm not trying to imagine it. You shouldn't try to find it in a human model"; "I don't really have a conception." Based on their certainty that "another" world exists, its qualities can be a matter of indifference: "maybe it's bad, but I don't care"; "I admit it's not something I'm worried about."

When respondents give more precise information about this other world, one of the recurring characteristics of their mode of expression is the presence of mental restrictions that modalize and even deny the described quality: "The resurrection of Christ means something, but I don't understand it"; "I think there's something there, maybe"; "I believe in the communion of saints. But no one ever said anything about it." In fact, modalizing has just as much of an impact on the metaphorical interpretation of the other world as it does on the literal interpretation. It is as if both interpretations could not be pursued to their conclusion. Thus, the metaphorical version is sometimes strongly expressed in a way that would appear to deny postmortem resurrection: "The resurrection means that dead people are still around, even today; it's that I'm talking about them. What we experienced together left traces that still affect me. The resurrection means that the link existing between us is stronger than death." But this sort of interpretation comes to a halt as soon as it runs up against "trust in God," and the respondent recognizes the inadequacy of words to explain it: "We have no images to describe it. It's a bit like if a blind person had to describe the world. But I believe that those who have passed away will be in a position to explain it to us." So there is "something."

It is important to stress that mental restrictions also affect the literalist interpretation that Catholics use to express the idea of the resurrection of the body and of being reunited with loved ones in a specific place. Several types of modalization can be identified:

- Incomprehension, or at least the professed inability to know: "It's an open question. Christ said nothing explicit on the subject. I'm no intellectual myself"; "on the resurrection scenario, nothing can be said"; "Personally, I've never delved into those questions. I had seminary friends who did, but they all let it drop"; "I don't understand."
- Doubt tinged with hope: "It think there's something, maybe. I hope so."
- Irony usually expressed through laughter, in response to the request for a description of the resurrection, particularly in relation to being personally reunited with loved ones.
- The rejection of one's own past belief: "I used to believe in the physical resurrection, but now I'm less categorical."
- The appeal to theological knowledge: "In Jewish anthropology, the resurrection of the flesh does not mean the revival of the dead."

There are also denials—sometimes adamant—of the literalist interpretation of the resurrection: "That's one part of the credo I'm skeptical about. I don't believe in the resurrection in the flesh"; "The way it works isn't that bones are taken out to put a guy back together. Heaven can't be conceived in terms of astrophysics"; "I struggle against the idea that the resurrection is a revival of corpses." At most, these literalist images can be pedagogical means of reassurance: "One of our children became very distressed about death. He was completely reassured the night I told him that there is a place where we all find each other, and that existing links are not broken. You know, the hackneyed image."

But these denials, like the metaphorical interpretation and the literalist version, are not pursued to their conclusion because they are positively re-modalized in connection with ideas of love and spiritual happiness, which make it possible to reconnect to the hope of reuniting with loved ones and maintaining interpersonal bonds after death. We are therefore seeing a process of distinguishing between what life after death can and cannot be. These are the most frequent statements: "There can be no resurrection without the communion of saints. I often wonder how I'll find my father. I can't imagine him without his caresses, the look in his eye. He expressed so many things through caresses with the backs of his fingernails. I believe I'll find him. Not his fingernails but his heart and his tenderness"; "I don't think we'll be any different, except for our bodies"; "People's faults will be gone. I think that with my husband, I'll no longer have a husband-wife relationship, but we'll still have a special bond"; "God placed within us relationships and connections that make us who we are. He's not going to demolish what he put into us. So we'll rediscover these connections after death. We won't find ourselves sitting together side-by-side, with reassembled families and people who recognize each other. The relationship will have a more spiritual form, love will really be the essential thing"; "The resurrection doesn't mean leaving the tomb; I don't see billions of people resuscitated with their bodies but I believe there will be a dimension that goes beyond myself, my abilities. It is something exceptional within God's love, with all other people. There is no loss of humanity. We will all be there"; "I'm sure I'll find them; I won't recognize them but I'll see them through the resurrected Christ. My faith makes me believe that there is something eternal in everyone"; "I know I'm destined to exist in God. It's so amazing that those dearest to us can never be absent. That's the highest degree of love. But I don't know if our loved ones will see us. Christ wasn't recognized."

These are various modalities used by Catholics when they speak about death and the resurrection—that is, how they deal with a set of signifiers (containers) about which there is no strict agreement on the corresponding signifieds (or contents):

- the maintenance of the division between a material world and a spiritual world whose possible existence one believes in;
- irony in relation to the idea that there is no guaranteed content, and that most people seek content or keep content in their heads;
- the rejection of the notion of revived bodies;
- taking the question seriously, while expressing regret about the uncertainty of answers;
- dual language, which involves speaking in one way with some people, another way with others (at a public meeting: "no, the resurrection is not the revival of dead people," behind the scenes [it was a dinner]: "I can't do away with the image of Christ leaving the tomb," then making fun of himself for this admitted contradiction; also the dual language of irony [or dismissiveness] behind the scenes and liturgical assertions in public);
- the institutional authority of the priest, sometimes applied in liturgies, sometimes reasserted during discussions (as opposed to self-disqualifying attitudes);
- the simultaneous assertion, on the one hand, that representations have limitations when applied to transcendent and inexpressible realities and, on the other hand, that these are a pedagogical necessity;
- the logic of uncertainty, that is, a dialectical logic that expresses, according to different modalities, the life and nonlife of the dead (it isn't material but it's real; it's not about physically finding the people we've loved, but it's ...);
- the idea that the answer to questions about contents is not important, the implication being that the religious lies elsewhere.

Believers seem to be torn between literalist discourse of the kind that institutional discourse never really escapes—and which in any case retains ambiguity (with such notions as "real presence" or "transubstantiation")—and their desire to be in God's presence. On the one hand, there is "belief" in this materiality of resurrected life that they do not want to believe in, but at the same time they give the impression that they don't dare not believe in it, or at least that they believe that they believe in the beyond. On the other hand, there is love, the simple desire to love, to express it and to be in the presence of the loved person, perhaps in hope of "something" more. Hence the almost infinite mental restrictions and successive denials when they are questioned—what Bruno Latour aptly called the "floundering" of people getting tangled in contradictions, denials, and denials of denials (2013).

Metaphorical sentences are literally false. Believing cannot consist in approaching religious statements as metaphors that are literally false. Of course, believers do not perceive these statements as literally and completely true, but they do not consider them literally false either. This is their extraordinary specificity. The act of believing is part of this uncertain oscillation: "It's not literal, so is it a metaphor? No. But neither can it really be literal, without consequently being a metaphor." Believers perceive religious statements as neither realistic, associated with a reference and a precise reality, nor as unrealistic, without any referential counterpart. They are not one, not the other, not both; they are nothing exclusively. Believing consists in referring to religious statements, while thinking or feeling that they are not metaphorical expressions, yet not really accepting the literality of their contents. This oscillation, hesitation, and mental interspace are fascinating. They make up the act of believing. This does not mean that there are not occasional moments when believers make more distinct stops at doubt or certainty, when they keep their acceptance or their modulation in their background thoughts, as we will see. To believe is to enter into this oscillation.

This is a crucial point. As we will be discovering, the rules governing the links between belief statements show that every answer given is part of a constantly rebounding movement, in the course of which each statement gives way to the next while constituting a critical axis relative to the previous one. This is what happens situationally: a movement of reversal and perpetual hesitation between various conceptions of the resurrection of the dead: it's literal, no it's not literal, it's symbolic; no it's not symbolic, it's more than that; no it's not literal, but it's . . . , and so on. This proceeds according to a movement that asserts, that denies, that questions the relevance of one point of view or another, or unites them in their complementarity. And it seems to be continually tested by a problem to resolve. Because how is one to state that rather paradoxical proposition, "Jesus, son of God, dead and alive," which would be hard for anyone to understand, other than through this game of reversals, hesitations, and juxtapositions between contradictory points of view?

Acts of believing

There are other situations in which semi-propositional statements are spoken, recited, or chanted. In religious ceremonies, many assertions like

"Jesus lives" are made, often in association with declarations of love or fidelity, or with expressions of praise. They are devices for establishing co-presence with the absent, who is made present in the statement through the aforesaid declaration or through every entity (object, icon, holy bread) that represents the addressed being (Piette 1999; Finch 2009). Just as internal dialogue is a way of preserving the presence of an absent person, prayer or declarations of love are specific modalities for remaining in the presence of the divine being.

According to this perspective, semi-propositional statements constitute possible points of departure—within a specific spatial-temporal situation—in a process of emotional evocation that activates the presence of the absent being according to various modalities. We know that no ritual necessarily implies, by virtue of its performance, a mental attitude that corresponds with it perfectly, and implies even less an unproblematic adherence to any explicit or implicit meaning of the rite. Bourdieu often states that rituals are performed because "that's what is done" or "it has to be done" and one has no choice but to do it, without needing to know what the rituals mean (1992 [1981]: 18). But if, like Bourdieu, one moves the act of believing away from mental representations in order to make it a product of infra-verbal and infra-conscious dispositions, this leaves no room for analyzing forms of adherence and the experience of human beings in the process of believing, or more specifically the believers' modes of interactional presence. This co-presence of humans and gods, inserted into a particular context, according to specific circumstances, and mediated by objects, can take on different expressions. It can also appear outside of collective contexts. In any case it is a temporary meeting between a prevailing semi-propositional representation and an emotional disposition or intellectual process proper to the individual who is present in the situation. I would say that this momentary encounter is a state of belief, more specifically an act of believing. Here is a nonexhaustive list of modalities of the act of believing:

- Addressing the divine being. A man and woman are in front of a closed chapel containing a Virgin Mary; the man removes his hat; they both mumble a few prayers for two or three minutes before leaving. Here there would be a "state of body" to borrow Bourdieu's term, a "bodily hexis" and a "linguistic habitus" in a way that would seem self-evident, but I would add that it is only a temporary state. They are in the middle of believing.
- Personal presence. Alone yet alongside other worshipers during a ceremony, a young man weeps during the story of the Last Supper

and the transformation of bread and wine into the body and blood of Christ. The semi-propositional content of the priest's statement invites this individual, according to his own interpretation and his personal evocation, to experience "transubstantiation." He is in the middle of truly believing that Jesus is present.

- Perception and vision. This is the individual who, in a particular state of grace, sees the divine being (Jesus or the Virgin Mary), which he can describe according to particular traits. This individual believes that the divinity really exists. Triggered by a particular emotional process, this "vision" is not independent of the content of prevailing semi-propositional representations.
- Link to an emotion. A human being, convinced that the "final judgment" does not exist, but conscious of having made a serious mistake, is haunted by fear of his fate to the point of asking a religious authority for forgiveness. Another, alone in a house in which a dead person lies, associates the slightest nocturnal sound with a manifestation of the dead person in a particular form. Even if he is convinced that ghosts do not exist, this type of emotional reaction, connected with latent semi-propositional content ("ghosts exist"), constitutes a state of belief, though certainly an ephemeral one. In these cases, the individuals believe X anyway.
- Inevitable gesture. A person who, as mentioned above, slips personal mementos like photographs into a coffin before it is closed, to accompany the deceased. There is tension between the unshakeable need to preserve a connection with the deceased by means of the object, and awareness of the pointlessness of this gesture (and he does not want this awareness to become too vivid). The person does not really believe X.
- Positive mental connection. The operation usually takes place outside of the actual ritual. It enables the individual to mentally construct, from latent representations, the image of a situation that he either hopes for (being reunited with his parents after death) or fears (the burning of his body in hell). This type of connection can be associated with a deciphering of everyday events, in which the believer finds communicative "signs."

Shifts

A believer's everyday life is no doubt structured by a dynamic between all of these synchronizations between himself and the divinity. Someone who truly believes with regularity will probably frequently produce positive mental connections, as will someone who believes X is real. But it will also sometimes happen that this person believes X anyway, or that he does not really believe X. Phenomenographic methods are important for these explorations.

When observing these everyday lives, attention is necessarily drawn to an element that I consider crucial: the principle of shifting from the moment when the individual enters into a state of belief (in which he "performs" his ephemeral act of believing) to the collapse of this state due to ordinary distractions and wandering thoughts, even skepticism and irony. This is what Paul Veyne calls "quotidian mediocrity": "[it] is precisely the result of this plurality, which in some states of neurotic scrupulosity is sensed as hypocrisy. We move endlessly from one program to another the way we change channels on the radio, but we do it without realizing it" (1988: 16). From a 100 percent possibility, there is a quick drop to 5 percent or 0 percent. Indifferent to inherent contradiction, the belief makes this flexibility all the easier, without in any way compromising the individual's sincerity.

One point should be stressed. Analysis of this everyday life reveals that these statements are not affected by subsequent empirical refutations or by the absence of practical consequences. As Paul Veyne says, those who can positively connect with the semi-propositional content that places gods in the heavens would be astounded to see them in the sky, and it would be completely ridiculous if they hoped to see gods from the window of a plane. If a believer, having seen Jesus appear before him, went out in search of empirical evidence of the appearance, he would be abandoning the state of belief or act of believing. He would even be taking a positivist approach, as if he were incapable of imagining a world beyond the objective one. And if a human being goes to his family tomb to introduce his newborn to deceased family members, does he really believe that they will be able to see the baby? "No," he would later say to someone who asked him about it. "But maybe a little," at the moment of the act, which is brief and cannot be fully thought through to its conclusion. Does the human being know whether or not he believes? "Lethargic indifference," Veyne replies (ibid.: 27), reminding us that people know very well what they should keep below the level of consciousness. These are instances of "eschatological inconsistency." They say a lot, not just about the relationships between belief statements (particularly about the beyond) and the incompletely pursued logical and/or practical consequences of the act of believing, but also about the relationship between specific behaviors and their corresponding mental attitudes. And none of this pertains to any sort of weak faith.

Personal encounters with the divine being or positive mental connections can lead from one to another and back again. In the course of a person's day, they are only limited, ephemeral moments. But the shifts away from these states of belief also have their own modalities, which can shed light on Veyne's remarks. Let us look at a few of them.

(1) The most common is no doubt detachment between the state or act of belief and other situations into which the person can shift—what could be called the severance principle. At church, a person who has a mental inspiration or positive mental connection about the semi-propositional content according to which Jesus Christ was resurrected forgets this content on Monday morning or even a few minutes later.

(2) A completely different context: when people read their horoscope (the appetite for optimistic information about the future or fear of an unfavorable situation constitutes an ephemeral act of adherence to semi-propositional content). One possible reaction, stimulated by a minimal amount of critical thinking, is skepticism and even an ironic wink of the eye, right after reading the statement in question. As we have seen, for believers, this sort of irony and skepticism are just as likely to generate ironic or doubtful attitudes about the idea of being reunited with loved ones (Pelkmans 2013).

(3) Hesitation associated with distraction or indifference is another modality, this time the management of the co-presence of adherence and critical distance. A believer at church listening to the priest's words, looking at others standing and leaning, hesitates, dramatizes the ritual gesture, attempts to get into "sync," thinking that he has to get into it like the others. Can we not relate this situation to the state of "pluralistic ignorance" in which participants can find themselves during a ceremony: each, based on his own attitude—on his not entirely satisfying act of believing—keeping quiet about his spiritual dissatisfaction, simulating an optimal experience (in the characteristic way of getting caught up in the situation), thinking others are experiencing the moment perfectly and genuinely. All of these people, also thinking they are alone in lacking a relationship with God, can produce the same narrative of a successful experience and go along with the crowd, each of them thinking he was the only one pretending, and so on (Stark and Bainbridge 1985: 272–273)

(4) At a higher level of consciousness than in the previous situations, the object of the act of believing (for example expecting the arrival of extraterrestrial beings) runs up against reality (they did not come, it was not realized). In this case the act of believing can, in other situations, alter into a firm conviction that is asserted, detailed, dogmatized, and made the subject of a demand for respect.

(5) Searching for proof is another way of effecting a shift from the state of belief to another situation. Depending on various mental attitudes, it consists in searching for traces of a UFO landing, taking photos of the sky that could

confirm the appearance of the divine being, developing physical theories to demonstrate the reality of what people report in accounts of near-death experiences. It can also quite simply be a matter of reading the history of the life of Jesus or visiting landmarks in the holy land. These proofs do not just concern the credibility of witnesses, they are also about demonstrating the authenticity of testimony content, employing experimental approaches that are sometimes complex.

(6) The very isolated moment of the state of belief is reflected in an array of everyday behaviors, attitudes, and rules for living, for example in charitable acts. These behaviors, directly attributable to the intensity of a past act of believing or indirectly associated with an interest in one or another semi-propositional representation, kept at the back of the mind, can also demonstrate a skill for deciphering signs in life's small events.

(7) The rhetorical use of the divine metaphor can take on different forms. It is used ironically, without any real comparison to the religious referent, such as when journalists or fans comment on the exploits of a football player. In new age groups, divine appellations ("cosmic energy," "universal spirit") can be used as relevant metaphors, not so much for their underlying truth as for the dynamism, security, and meaning they can bring. But this is just as possible with religious beliefs[7].

An existential theory of ordinary religion

No one says that Alice, who went to Wonderland, exists. The believer says that God exists. This statement points to all of the specificity of divine beings and belief. In a way, if there were nothing but religions with various messages and gestures directed at God, one would almost be tempted to categories gods as fictional characters. But unlike the latter, God continues to "exist" and be present in various ways before and after the ritual, before and after the reading of a story. On the subject of divinities, people are quite capable of saying in all seriousness that they exist. Believing is not just playing along, doing the "done thing" during a ceremony; it is also a matter of attributing a nonfictional status to the divinity outside of the ceremony. This is a first "little more." But there is another, because underlying all social validations, transmission rationales, and personal accounts, belief constitutes a private and mental experience. Believing means doing it and a little more. A strong characteristic of belief resides precisely in this "a little more," several levels of which make up belief and particularly the believer: the reality, outside of the human world, of existences that are not confirmed and not confirmable; moments of co-presence with these entities—a co-presence that is sensed or simply automatized; isolated moments of acceptance felt at the thought of these existences, or proclaimed acceptance; the day-to-day dynamics of this acceptance and co-presence. This "a little more" is crucial: actual sensed and felt moments of acceptance, their micro-quotidian occurrence, their mental experience in real life. The act of believing as a moment of acceptance is this extra, and it is hard to reach. Social sciences risk overlooking it, dissolving this moment into rituals, representations, statements, or social rationales. But this is the risk that an existential anthropology of belief must avoid. At certain moments, individuals who trust the orthodoxy of the church can genuinely believe in the resurrection of Jesus. They can have positive mental connections with this semi-propositional content. At other moments they can be ironic about their attitude, or search for a historical proof of the resurrection of Jesus, or hesitate about how their belief should be formulated between metaphor and literality. After a critical process, they might retain only the main core of church dogmas and only believe in the existence of God by means of positive mental connections. They may also either believe anyway that Jesus was resurrected, or not really believe it. A religious statement can also become a kind of floating idea disconnected from the church's authority. With this idea, he may believe X anyway, perhaps really believing and also metaphorically adapting its formulation when speaking about it. In different cases, it can also resonate in various ways through actions and interpretations of everyday events.

The difficulty of a phenomenography of acts of believing arises from the fact that one is always trying to capture the subtle complexity that results from the interweaving of statements of belief, different modalities used for approving them (really believing, not believing, believing anyway), and forms of shifting (into distraction, skepticism, irony, the search for proof, detachment).

I would like to draw attention to the impact of negation in order to understand the reality of religion. Passing in front of a positive pole, a believer is immediately driven to a negative pole according to a process of oscillation marked by back-and-forth movements and hesitation. Is the person acting as if there is a visible, tangible divine being before him? But he does not see the divinity and cannot touch him; it is even pointed out to him that the mediation is not really God, only a trace to which he should not become attached, and he is told that he must keep searching. Will our individual then start thinking that there is "nothing at all," nothing real, only spectacle and fiction? But this fiction itself comes with the message that it is not really a fiction and that the divine being is represented by a diverse array of signs. Religious activity thus finds itself in a permanent in-between state. People, like gods, can only exist there on the move, in oscillation, in a state of minimality. This is what an existential exploration of French Catholic beliefs and acts of believing enabled me to see.

Act 3: The Genealogy of a Mode of Existing

I have illustrated the minimal mode of existing in religious believing. We know human beings are (almost) always like that—minimal, hesitant, accepting the contradictions, passive, docile, not really lucid in the everyday life, although to different degrees. Why are humans like this? I hypothesize that this minimality is specific to *Homo sapiens* and was absent in Neanderthals, another species of *Homo*. Here arises what I consider the quintessential anthropological enigma: "Despite these afflictions, man wants to be happy, and only wants to be happy, and cannot help wanting to be happy. But how shall he go about it? The best thing would be to make himself immortal, but as he cannot do that, so he has decided to stop himself thinking about it." This is what Pascal wrote (Pascal 1997: 37). What happened?[8] What has caused people exist as they do, in their characteristic absence-presence, traversing a state of anxiety but as light as ever? How can a person exist, attached to his or her own life, to the details of his or her singularity and that of a few others, a singularity that is no more than a detail considering the reality of the more or less remote disappearance of the universe, a disappearance that no one is really unaware of? Let us attempt both a speculative and empirical account of this existential prehistory.[9] In my hypothesis, we will again confront the act of believing, especially in its possible impact on the human mode of existing.

According to evolutionary psychology,[10] the cognitive hybridity stage consists in mixing information and/or activities from different spheres. To put it briefly, the functioning of the brain became more pliable, separating into modules linked to separate categories of activity and information— an advantage that Neanderthals did not enjoy. The still-debated data on Neanderthals most significantly indicates that they had different sites for each activity: a hunting place, a butchery site, a cutting-up area. These were different scenarios that did not intersect: meat would be cut somewhere near the hunting site and then transported, or the animal would be transported directly to the habitat to be processed on-site. Accordingly, archaeological discoveries of tools seem to confirm that Neanderthals separated activities into different small spaces,[11] whereas *Homo sapiens* was at this time developing multiple conjunctions between spheres of activity: sharpened bones or stones for marking a social affiliation using a natural or technical element, tools made of ivory or stone, statuettes mixing the body parts of humans and animals, the organization of the habitat on a central site where various technical and social exchange activities could be take place, or at least the setting up of specialized areas for work, after which workers returned to the camp in order to favor social contacts. This cognitive hybridity is also evident in the production of contradictory statements, expressing, for example, an equivalence between the living and the dead, implying that the dead were alive.

The act of believing is an acceptance that attributes an existence to certain entities or to entities referred to in statements. "The dead alive! What if it's true?" occasionally becomes plausible, according to varying degrees of acceptance, and is probably associated with a set of rules and prohibitions in relation to the new entity. What is at play in this mechanism, generated by an unbelievable proposition that reflects a moment of belief? It is not just an occasional thought that "it is thus true," an acceptance of this or that slightly "bizarre" statement, it is also—and this is crucial, as we have seen above—an acceptance of not having a clear understanding of what is implied and evoked by the contents of this proposition and the whole world it reflects, not thinking too much about it, suspending one's critical sense and therefore preserving a kind of cognitive loosening (Sperber 1985).[12] This is the cognitive fluidity stage.

The moment that lies at the root of belief as a mental act is decisive. Neanderthals certainly had their graves, with protected skeletons, intentionally separated skulls, and stone or limestone slabs placed on the body. What more is there in the graves of *Homo sapiens*, who were contemporary with them, and even preceded them? There are numerous interpretations of animal bones as offerings to the dead, despite the fact that researchers have repeatedly called for caution.[13] But recent, highly technical studies of various objects discovered in Neanderthal graves have raised new doubts about most of these interpretations, reducing the number of "positive" or indisputable facts nearly to zero (Soressi and d'Errico 2007; d'Errico 2009). Etched and pierced bones discovered in several Neanderthal graves have developed these marks as a result of natural processes. Regular incisions found on stones are not the work of humans, and pollens that some have linked to litters of flowers were transported by animals.[14] And although one or another offering had to have been recognized as such in Neanderthal graves, they may have had only a sentimental value, and not involved the idea of a gift to a still-living dead person.

For our purposes, the unquestionable presence of an offering, for example about 90,000 years ago in Qafzeh (*Homo sapiens* graves), raises the possibility (not the certainty) of fluidity as a new cognitive operation. The offer of an object to the dead did not imply acting as if the dead person were still the person who had been known in life, momentarily activating a kind of respect, and it did not mean giving the dead a presence in the realm of the living through a sign of its body—Neanderthals were able to do that.[15] It was more about representing the dead person as the still-living recipient of a gift. In that case, the dead person was no longer present as a dead person in the sense of a former living person, but as still alive. Living where? It would of course be premature to think that this constitutes a representation of another world, toward which death was a passageway. But the offering of specific objects at least suggests that it was no longer only a matter of acting as if the dead were still alive, but rather of thinking that the objects were being given to a dead person as a revived person. It therefore meant acting as if he were once again alive, starting a new life "elsewhere." It is thus that the power of language made of arbitrary, combinable signs is reintroduced. By disconnecting signs from that which was perceived there and then, language made it possible to create a world detached from concrete situations and speak about unrealistic and unbelievable things that did not necessarily exist.

By making the suggestion "What if it were real!" was our individual not able to enjoy feelings of well-being, comfort, reassurance, and relief in face of a real absence (Clément 2006)? From this point of view, it is not difficult to imagine how this act of believing could have a positive, selective effect on the evolutionary process. By individually imagining that other world or invoking it in a ritual setting, "living" it, imagining it repeatedly and regularly: this is the cognitive process of believing. It consists in accepting an incredible statement: "the dead person is still alive." It is to believe in an imagined, described world, and doing so according to various types of acceptance: believing X a little, believing X anyway, wanting to believe that the person is still there while knowing that he is not, etc. A new state of mind would appear to be emerging: the cognitive loosening linked to the attitude of not pushing certainty all the way, of accepting uncertainty. There are three components to the cognitive mechanism that gives rise to a moment of belief, as highlighted by Dan Sperber (1985): an ability to mentally simulate another reality disconnected from ordinary life situations, another world that would be possible if the "living dead" proposition were true; the possibility of thinking even occasionally that something is really true, mentally accepting this or that element of this new simulated world; a resolution not to have a clear understanding of what is implied and evoked by the contents of this proposition and of the whole world it reflects, not to think too much about it, to suspend one's critical sensibilities and therefore remain in a kind of cognitive vagueness.[16]

Thus contradictions within religious statements do not generate a dissonant effect that must be reduced, but rather a cognitive loosening that indicates the suspension of various things: certain logical conjunction constraints (but not all, as Pascal Boyer has shown); practical conjunction constraints; questions about the visibility of the divinity, about his specific intentions; answers to the question of his existence; the demand for a total agreement that one knows is not possible because of different individual representations. I think, as we have just seen, that a tolerance of cognitive vagueness arises from the relationship of credulity toward religious statements and is able to extend to other day-to-day activities. This is crucial. Allowing for the possibility of creating unconfirmed and unconfirmable things is to believe. This can generate tension, but by virtue of the beneficial effect of the believed idea, it can also generate loosening and significant advantages in social life: compromise, tolerance, acceptance, distance, looking the other way.[17]

Conversely, could one not assume that Neanderthals went out of their way to filter plausible information, and trusted only a few expert individuals whose competence had been proven, rather than people who wanted to dominate by force (Coubray 2012). This form of rigidity could have generated problems in cases where verifications revealed failures to meet expectations. Was it difficult for them when they did not practice "epistemic vigilance," for example when they could not evaluate the source of a piece of information? Was it difficult to practice "trust," particularly in cases where it was impossible to evaluate sources and when the communication chain was too long? Did they have problems practicing social consensus? As we know, children are susceptible to the choice of the majority; would Neanderthals have been uncomfortable with "conformism" if verifications were not possible? Could they have considered ideas shared by the majority as "superior"? I am inclined to think so, and to think that it was later, as I have shown, that things eased up, with the minor mode enabling humans to accept the presence of beings and information that were external and contradictory, but did not disturb the activity in progress, while also accepting the constant shifting of meaning, without requiring a solution, an agreement, closure, as well as the erection of separators, sometimes very tight ones, around a situation or event, outside of which behaviors and thoughts seemed inconsequential, as if forgotten. This mode of conscience that veils, that does not make you see things head-on, that reduces the acuteness of presence seems not so much to be something that accompanies immediate perception, the representation of images or the unconscious performance of habitual actions, but rather accompanies the underuse of the superior type of thought linked with consciousness of the self and of time.[18]

Human minimality became all the more possible ten or fifteen millennia ago as social life became more and more structured by the material marking of social roles, which gave them more stability, and also by a sedentary life surrounded by fields and herds. But minimality was also all the more necessary because this new sedentarization, entailing a social life that was more intense and therefore more conflictual, needed to be balanced on a foundation of stable (but arbitrary) norms and rules, which were increasingly appealed to and became more and more visible as they were committed to diverse media. These humans knew they belonged to a specific group and sometimes lived as such but rarely gave any thought to this fact. In these situations, it was a matter of behaving "as if," while well aware that reality was more than could be assumed or pretended. Basically, what *Homo sapiens* started to learn was to not be maximal—that is to say, to introduce layers of shock absorbers into consequential actions and situations. One can imagine how these new characteristics would have gradually affected neuronal operation, as well as modes of attention and perception, for example by increasing their lability and fluidity, simply by not being in lockstep with them because the new characteristics were intrinsically labile. The minor mode would thus be more than compatible with neuronal and attentional processes. If this was the case, cognitive tiredness would be even more likely in other species of *Homo*, like Neanderthals, with little or no minor mode. It is as if the acceptance of contradictions released this minor mode and gave humans the possibility of strong adaptive advantages, in how they expended energy and in their creative potential. Minimality established itself as a tendency retained by evolution, extending to other human activities. The minor mode resulted from a tendency selected by evolution insofar as it was advantageous in relationships, as a shock absorber and relaxer under the pressure of situations and significant confrontation.

Accounts of the history of life and evolution are only retrospective selections of events, based on various sets of assumptions. The account I have presented does not escape this limitation. It is obviously very difficult to make an objective selection that guarantees relations of cause and effect. But, as Guillaume Lecointre (2009) points out, it is important that the account not hinder a proper understanding of evolution. Can the account I have just presented help clarify what I consider one of the major anthropological questions: How do *Homo sapiens* exist in the world, and by contrast how did Neanderthals exist?

Homo sapiens became quotidian and Neanderthals never really were; they were "thrown-toward-death," as Heidegger would say, without any way to escape! They are a drastic illustration of the "misery" of the human condition, and we are the quotidian species. Just as it has been said that life dazzles children, I would say that *Homo sapiens* continued to exist by becoming dazzled compared with Neanderthals. The minor mode, that "unthought" of anthropology, certainly is a major characteristic of human existence. By giving detailed attention to the existences, existential anthropology also says something about anthropological differences.

Notes

This text has been translated by Matthew Cunningham. I thank the Centre for Ethnology and Comparative Sociology (CNRS—University of Paris-Nanterre) for its subsidy. Many thanks also to Michael Jackson for his editorial assistance with this chapter.

1. With a very different meaning and methodology, phenomenography is sometimes characterized by the educational sciences as research (through interviews) on forms of categorization. See Gloria Dall'Alba and Biörn Hasselgren (1996).
2. Thus Nigel Rapport's anthropology, which targets individual existences, seems to be to be too directly associated with a Nietzschean philosophy. Because when are concrete, living humans really Nietzschean? Sometimes. Only from time to time (Rapport 2003).
3. Hence the importance of Heidegger's theory of existentials, as long as they are flattened, without being organized into hierarchies such as propriety-impropriety, authenticity-inauthenticity.
4. One of the central ideas in the work of Michael Jackson is also the tension between the sociocentric dimension and the egocentric dimension. See for example Jackson 2013.
5. In French, the term *"reposité"* simultaneously indicates the idea of repose and the idea of counting on something.
6. It is particularly in the religious "field" that hesitation, the constant transfer from situation to situation, as well as minor modes of believing appeared to me to be central. See Piette 2003.
7. Therefore it does not seem relevant to me to separate systems of representations (or of interactions), sometimes called "ontologies," from modalities of believing and adhesion.
8. From this perspective, the question of the minor mode of monkeys and apes seems to me to be a beautiful theme for observation: signs of absence during an activity, not responding and being indifferent to an appearance, doing two things at once like making a tool and scratching, thinking about another situation during an activity. Out of all of these, what can monkeys and apes do? Wandering thoughts? Do they have them? A side activity during another principal activity? If they have an ability to be indifferent, when does it arise? After a more or less brief look of vigilance?
9. Let us indicate that social anthropologists' interest in the question of origins is more and more rare. See Barnard 2012.

10. On this point, the work of Steven Mithen is conclusive. See *The Prehistory of Mind* (1996). However I prefer the term "hybridity" to designate this operation of mixture and conjunction. See also Mithen 2009 and Carruthers 2002.
11. See also Tattersall 1998: 135ff.; and the very critical interpretation of Gargett 1999.
12. It is worth mentioning the point of view of Pascal Boyer, who, when he presents the characteristics of religions (existing separately in other areas of activity) does not mention vague modes of adherence. See Boyer and Bergstrom 2008. It should also be noted that the cognitive anthropology tradition often shows little interest in the link with archaeological and prehistoric data.
13. See also the new synthesis of Paul Pettitt (2011a; 2011b).
14. About this point, see the debated hypothesis of Jeffey D. Sommer (1999).
15. The reader can find information and comments (and also a more exhaustive bibliography) about the evolution (from the apes to *Homo sapiens*) of the attitudes toward the dead in Piette (2013).
16. From this perspective I should emphasize that the discovery of a certain offering does not necessarily imply a belief as a mental act, like an act that expresses acceptance. This assumes a counterintuitive statement that itself assumes the possibility of mixing pieces of different information, something that Neanderthal man would have lacked, for example in his organization of space. Moreover, were modular hypotheses were decisively refuted (which is not the case today), this would not rule out the preservation of the hypothesis of the nonbelieving Neanderthal. And ultimately, admitting that Neanderthals believed does not refute the idea that they did not sufficiently minor their existence, as *Homo sapiens* did. Then where would their minorization come from? From a better implementation of the act of believing, especially its cognitive effects, from the creation of more sociological points of reference, etc. For me, the most important question is this: was the act of believing, as a specific cognitive act, through its strong implementation in *Homo sapiens*, able to generate a way of being which we know is so specific to humans? What are we to think of this scenario, if it is true and also if it is not entirely true? See also Wynn and Coolidge 2004 and Coolidge and Wynn 2009.
17. This is the hypothesis I have developed: see Piette 2013.
18. It is meaningful to notice that Robin Dunbar does not see indices of religious beliefs in Neanderthals' graves. He links religion to a collective and coercive aspect, which would not be present in Neanderthals' lives. According to him, the absence of this coercive aspect would have been a key element in Neanderthals' extinction, contrary to *Homo sapiens*. On the opposite, I link the impact of the religious statements (specific to *Homo sapiens*) not to this coercive aspect but to an effect of cognitive loosening, the absence of which would have been determining in Neanderthal's extinction. See Dunbar 2004.

References

Barnard, Alan. 2012. *Genesis of Symbolic Thought*. Cambridge: Cambridge University Press.
Bergson, Henri. 2004. *Matter and Memory* (trans. Nancy Margaret Paul and Scott Palmer). New York: Dover Publications.
Bourdieu, Pierre. 1990. *The Logic of Practice* (trans. Richard Nice). Cambridge: Polity Press.
Boyer, Pascal. 1994. *The Naturalness of Religious Ideas: A Cognitive Theory of Religion*. Berkeley and Los Angeles: University of California Press.
Boyer, Pascal, and Brian Bergstrom. 2008. "Evolutionary Perspectives on Religion," *Annual Review of Anthropology* 37: 111–130.

Carruthers, Peter. 2002. "The Cognitive Functions of Language," *Brain and Behavioral Sciences* 25: 657–726.
Clément, Fabrice. 2006. *Les Mécanismes de la Crédulité*. Geneva: Droz.
Coolidge, Fred L., and Tom Wynn. 2009. *The Rise of Homo Sapiens: The Evolution of Modern Thinking*. Oxford: Wiley-Blackwell.
Coubray, Anne. 2012. "Vers une naturalisation des croyances religieuses." In *L'Expérience Religieuse. Approches Empiriques. Enjeux philosophiques*, Anthony Feneuil (ed.). Paris: Beauchesne, 241–262.
d'Errico, Francesco. 2009. "The Archaeology of Early Religious Practices: a Plea for a Hypothesis-Testing Approach." In *Becoming Human*, Colin Renfrew and Iain Morley (eds.). Cambridge: Cambridge University Press, 104–122.
Dall'Alba, Gloria, and Biörn Hasselgren (eds.). 1996. *Reflections of Phenomenography: Toward a Methodology?* Goteborg: Goteborg Studies in Educational Sciences.
Dennett, Daniel D. 1987. *The Intentional Stance*. Cambridge, MA: The MIT Press.
Dunbar, Robin. 2004. *The Human Story: A New History of Mankind's Evolution*. London: Faber and Faber.
Finch, Martha L. 2009. *Dissenting Bodies: Corporealites in Early New England*. New York: Columbia University Press.
Gargett, Robert I. 1999. "Middle Paleolithic Burial is Not a Dead Issue," *Journal of Human Evolution* 37: 27–90.
Heidegger, Martin. 1996. *Being and Time* (trans. Joan Stambaugh). Albany: State University of New York Press.
Jackson, Michael. 2013. *Lifeworlds: Essays in Existential Anthropology*. Chicago: University of Chicago Press.
Latour, Bruno. 2013. *Rejoicing: Or the Torments of Religious Speech* (trans. Julie Rose). Cambridge: Polity Press.
Lecointre, Guillaume. 2009. "Récit de l'histoire de la vie ou de l'utilisation du récit." In *Les Mondes Darwiniens. L'Evolution de l'Evolution*, Thomas Heams et al. (eds.). Paris: Syllepse.
Lévi-Strauss, Claude. 1961. *Tristes Tropiques* (trans. John Russell). New York: Criterion Books.
Lewis-Williams, David. 2009. "Of People and Pictures: the Nexus of Upper Palaeolithic Religion, Social Discrimination, and Art." In *Becoming Human*, Colin Renfrew and Iain Morley (eds.). Cambridge: Cambridge University Press, 135–158.
Mair, Jon. 2012. "Cultures of Belief," *Anthropological Theory* 12 (4): 448–466.
Mithen, Steven. 1996. *The Prehistory of Mind*. London: Thames and Hudson.
———. 2009. "Out of the Mind: Material Culture and the Supernatural." In *Becoming Human*, Colin Renfrew and Iain Morley (eds.). Cambridge: Cambridge University Press, pp. 123–134.
Pascal, Blaise. 1995. *Pensées* (trans. A. J. Krailsheimer). London: Penguin Books.
Pelkmans, Mathijs (ed.). 2013. *Ethnographies of Doubt, Faith and Uncertainty in Contemporary Societies*. London: I.B. Tauris.
Pettitt, Paul. 2011a. *The Paleolithic Origins of Human Burials*. London: Routledge.
———. 2011b. "The Living as Symbols, the Dead as Symbols." In *Homo Symbolicus: The Dawn of Language, Imagination and Spirituality*, Christopher S. Henshilwood and Francesco d'Errico (eds.). Amsterdam: John Benjamins Publishing.
Piette, Albert. 1992. *Le mode mineur de la réalité. Paradoxes et photographies en anthropologie*. Leuven: Peeters.
———. 1996. *Ethnographie de l'action. L'observation des détails*. Paris: Métailié.
———. 1999. *La religion de près. L'activité religieuse en train de se faire*. Paris: Metailie.
———. 2009. *Anthropologie existentiale*. Paris: Pétra.
———. 2011. *Fondements à une anthropologie des hommes*. Paris: Hermann.

———. 2013. *L'origine des croyances*. Paris: Berg International.
Rapport, Nigel. 2003. *I Am Dynamite: An Alternative Anthropology of Power*. London and New York: Routledge.
Sommer, Jeffey D. 1999. "The Shanidar IV 'Flower Burial': A Reevaluation of Neanderthal Burial Ritual," *Cambridge Archaeological Journal* 9 (1): 127–129.
Soressi, Marie, and Francesco d'Errico. 2007. "Pigments, gravures, parures: Les comportements symboliques controversés des Néandertaliens." In *Les Néandertaliens. Biologie et Cultures*, Bernard Vandermeersch and Bruno Maureille (eds.). Paris: Editions du Comité des travaux historiques et scientifiques, 297–309.
Sperber, Dan. 1985. *On Anthropological Knowledge*. Cambridge: Cambridge University Press; Paris: Editions de la Maison des Sciences de l'Homme.
Stark, Rodney, and William S. Bainbridge. 1985. *The Future of Religion*. Berkeley: University of California Press.
Tattersall, Ian. 1998. *Becoming Human: Evolution and Human Uniqueness*. New York: Harcourt Brace & Company.
Veyne, Paul. 1988. *Did the Greeks Believe in the Myths?* (trans. Paula Wissing). Chicago: University of Chicago Press.
———. 1992. *Bread and Circuses* (trans. Oswyn Murray and Brian Pearce). London: Penguin Books.
Vicart, Marion. 2014. *Des chiens auprès des hommes. Quand l'anthropologue observe aussi l'animal*. Paris: Petra, 2014.
Wittgenstein, Ludwig. 1953. *Philosophical Investigations* (trans. Elizabeth Anscombe). Oxford: Basil Blackwell.
Wynn, Tom, and Fred L. Coolidge. 2004. "The Expert Neanderthal Mind," *Journal of Human Evolution* 46: 467–487.

Chapter Eight

Considering Human Existence
An Existential Reading of Michael Jackson and Albert Piette

Laurent Denizeau

How is it possible to approach the philosophical question of existence in an anthropological manner—that is, by observing and describing moments of being and modes of human experience along lines suggested by existential anthropology? Pursuing this question requires a certain distance from traditional sociocultural paradigms. In discussing Michael Jackson's and Albert Piette's bodies of work, I offer an understanding of existential anthropology as a literary though nonfictional description of life as lived. I argue that existential anthropology is based less on theoretical foundations than on an epistemological project and posture. Its project is to describe moments of being. Its epistemological posture may be characterized by a withdrawal from the level of cultural representation in anthropological understanding and an engagement with the relation of a human being to the world, which is fundamentally equivocal.

* * *

Human existence can be regarded as the terra incognita of anthropological thought. Paradoxically, the anthropologist seems to speak more about society and culture in their various forms (social relations, interactions, identities, representations, the imaginary, and so on) than about human existence *in itself*. So much so that we refer to ourselves as *social and cultural* anthropologists, to insist on the fact that we study man quite aside

---

Notes for this chapter begin on page 235.

from his bodily characteristics (physical anthropology) or origins (prehistorical anthropology). Is anthropology only social and cultural because man himself is only a social and cultural being? The theme of existence would appear to belong more to the realm of philosophy than anthropology. And yet existential anthropology cannot be reduced to merely an anthropology that is inspired by philosophical existentialism. Can we not approach the question of existence in an anthropological manner, i.e. by observing and describing existence, studying man in each one of his instants of life? Considering this question inevitably requires a certain distance from traditional sociocultural paradigms, which may not actually be very helpful in understanding people's real lives. The question also leads to another, more personal, one: Why does it often seem that writers of fiction describe human existence better than anthropologists do, when anthropology is defined as the science of man? While writers of fiction can describe, with great literary finesse, moments of life that did not really occur, ethnographical writing sticks as close as it possibly can to the actual life of the people concerned. But the latter often loses the textured nuances that literary writing can give to these instances of life. Perhaps it is because literary writing is more attentive to describing inner feelings, from which anthropology, like other sciences, feels it must keep a respectable distance. So could we not consider existential anthropology as a literary, yet *nonfictional*, description of these genuine moments of life? What drives me in anthropology personally is its fundamental aim of thinking about man and grounding this thinking in concrete existence, with fieldwork acting as the meeting point between these two. The meeting point I discuss in this chapter is that of Jackson's and Piette's bodies of work, and also some of their main sources of inspiration, notably Virginia Woolf and Martin Heidegger. Other anthropologists may invoke existential anthropology without, however, inscribing their work in a theoretical or methodological perspective. Existential anthropology is thus seen as a way of emphasizing the empirical over the theoretical, or an extension of existential philosophy. By contrast, the challenge of this book is to justify theoretically and empirically—as Jackson and Piette invite us to do—an existential anthropology.

This chapter discusses different ways of understanding what constitutes existential anthropology for Jackson and Piette. It is a reading and not a comparative study of their work, which would be too great a task for the scope of this chapter. Within this reading, I have found sources of inspiration for my own response to the central question of the present book: What is existential anthropology? This reading has led me to consider existential anthropology in light of the question, or wish, to write about being in a way that goes beyond the traditional notion of fieldwork to encompass the existence of the anthropologist himself, which is implicitly present in the anthropology practiced by both Jackson and Piette. I invite the two anthropologists to compare and contrast a certain number of their approaches to existential anthropology, and occasionally take the liberty of joining in the discussion myself. The authors invite us to take several journeys, often in very different directions, but always from the same starting point: to move away from social and cultural anthropology when these frameworks involve abstractions that lose touch with actual human experience. By this we seek to bring a system that operates in the shadows, as it were, into the clear light of day. In response, the two anthropologists make a similar call to action: to return to actual human experience— through situations described in narrative form for Jackson, and through varying degrees of presence, which are described in terms of modes, for Piette. The aim of existential anthropology, as I understand it from the works of these two anthropologists, does not limit itself to describing the representations concealed within observed actions, but rather attempts to say something about the human condition. It is not so much a matter of revealing structures of meaning than considering human existence. From this epistemological challenge, the authors go on to develop markedly different understandings as to the place that is best adapted to observation of the human condition. Being-in-the-world is being with others ("interest") for Michael Jackson, which leads him to consider intersubjectivity as the central notion of existential anthropology. For Albert Piette, however, man is more than the sum of his relations, and this leads Piette to focus his attention on the human being at his most fundamental numerical entity, namely the individual. From there, Piette considers existential anthropology as an "anthropography" concerned with man as a being characterized by "minimal" forms of attention. I then use this reading of the two writers to offer an understanding of existential anthropology not so much as a theoretical model with postulates than as a way of approaching the timeless question of human existence.

From a Social and Cultural Anthropology to an Anthropology of Human Existence

The writings of Michael Jackson and Albert Piette both address the same epistemological challenge, namely the attempt to free anthropology from paradigms of society and culture that focus only on totality. Social and cultural anthropology attend to intellectual subjects before moving on to consider the complexity of human experience. The fundamentals of contemporary anthropology invite us to consider humanity by using a system of classification. In this way, human beings can be classified in terms of culture, group, or social class, and so on, just as observed *facts* are considered as intrinsically religious, social, etc.—independently of the people who *perform* those acts—according to the definitions the anthropologist calls upon to support his interpretations. The danger here is to confuse the theoretical model (for example, what is considered a religious fact often refers to the notion of the rite as a way of enacting a belief system or social form) with the observed reality (the experience of belief that cannot be reduced to religious representation). The aim of this theoretical reconstruction of the observed is to go beyond a simple description of the situation to arrive at a description of a whole (a culture, a social organization, ritual activity, a belief system), of which any particular situation is just one reflection. This global perspective on a given situation—which attempts to go beyond singularity—aims to consider not a particular situation but a system. The attention of the anthropologist is turned exclusively to these systems and not on people in their concrete existence.

This perspective tries to make it possible to think of the whole *as such*, and also to employ holistic thinking, as if it were possible to exhaust the complexities of actual life as it actually manifests itself in a given situation. However, this is done at the expense of simplifying it, even making it into a caricature or archetype whereby human existence disappears behind the sociocultural model it incarnates (implied in the terms of role, actor, and especially *habitus*). In this way, for Michael Jackson, subjectivity is absorbed into a transcendent vision of the social: subjects are actors who play roles, carry out their commitments, follow rules, perform rituals, and internalize beliefs (2013: 4). Their experience of the world can be deduced from collective representations. Subjectivity—in other words, human experience—disappears behind the objectivity of a systemic thinking that is capable of illuminating any particular situation by transcending individuality.

So the anthropologist does not describe what happens in reality but rather a logical, balanced model that allows for a more coherent description. Placing what is observed into this "sociocultural perspective," to use the Albert Piette's expression, is another step toward the abstraction of human experience, airbrushing out the paradoxes, ambiguities, and contradictions inherent in any situation that are not intrinsically significant but carry differing meanings depending on the individuals involved. The theoretical model quickly becomes quite detached from the human realities that it was meant to describe. In this gap between the reality and the concepts used to describe it, we can see the desire, common to many human sciences, to reveal the hidden forces that shape our lives—cultural or social structures, or indeed both, as expressed in the notion of *habitus*. Of course, certain anthropological movements have been more attentive to actual experience, particularly phenomenological anthropology, ethnomethodology, ethnopsychiatry, and the anthropology of conflict and crisis. However the temptation remains to gloss over individual experience with layers of sociocultural structures.

In this way, the singular in experience all too often gives way to the typical, the larger whole that the anthropologist tries to bring to light. Albert Piette, however, has taken a particular interest in the status of detail in anthropology. He points out that, when returning from fieldwork, the anthropologist retains only the significant ethnographic details from the sum of his field notes, only the details that he deems worthy of the status of cultural representation. But there remain the "leftovers": details that are not directly meaningful with regard to the representative picture. Observation in anthropology is thus an overarching view, where details serve to shed light on the overall meaning. Details are not meaningful in their singularity, experienced in the here and now. The temptation here is to present an idealized, perfectly coherent social whole, only focusing on those details which are fully significant with regard to this vision. The anthropologist only considers ethnographical details as instances of a generalized frame of meaning that transcends the observed situation. The anthropologist looks for ethnographical details that may bring to light underlying social or cultural structures. What interests him in a person's behavior is what that behavior says about the sociocultural category of that person, or the system of representation being played out. This structural reduction illustrates man's nature as belonging. The individual becomes a product of his culture. Detail is only valued inasmuch as it reveals the different structures that characterize human life.

Situation and Presence

For Michael Jackson as for Albert Piette, the aim of an existential anthropology is to lay the foundations of a radically empirical anthropology, a human science that does not limit itself to social and cultural characteristics. In this way, man can become a subject of study in his concrete existence, i.e., in situations, and not only in social and cultural dimensions. For this reason, Jackson prefers to emphasize "lifeworld" over "worldview." It is a means of getting closer to existence as it is actually lived in concrete situations, and not simply trying to formulate the transcendent meanings as suggested by actions. And yet Piette and Jackson do not have quite the same approach. Whereas Jackson takes a linear approach to accounts of situations, presenting first one situation and then the next, Albert Piette insists rather on the "layering" of situations, where one ongoing situation can hold within it several other concomitant situations, which together make up the full picture of an individual's experience in any given moment, and which the anthropologist needs to be careful to observe. What an existential approach can bring to anthropology is to show that a situation is not to be understood in itself alone, but rather as part of an ongoing life experience, a complex and ambivalent presence in the world.

As an alternative to what they consider the tendency to abstract from observations and make sociocultural generalizations, thereby losing touch with empirical reality, Jackson and Piette propose different approaches. Michael Jackson uses a register of writing that comes close to storytelling, where the anthropologist is the narrator of situations in which he is a character, situations where he listens to and responds to others recounting their own existence. This storytelling reveals interrelated journeys through life and this leads Jackson, contrary to Piette, to regard intersubjectivity as a core concept. Jackson presents situations that are always, to some extent, unique, and the aim is not to try to demonstrate coherence with the cultural significations of the society in which they occur, but rather to give a voice to subjects who are simply doing what they can to get through what are often very difficult circumstances. By this means, Jackson demonstrates the importance of negotiation in the social life of the people he presents, and the limitations in attempting to find one sole meaning in any situation. Meanings are plural, and multiple interpretations can be equally valid (see "The course of an event" in *Existential Anthropology*). So the full meaning of an event for a group cannot be understood outside the recounting of that event, which implies a relativity of interpretations (the Rashomon effect) according to the life experiences of those involved. At the same time, Jackson's writing gives equal weight to emotions and thoughts, demonstrating how inseparable they are in any life story.

For Albert Piette, the aim of existential anthropology is to differentiate anthropology from sociology and ethnology, by taking the human being, independent of his social relations (sociology) and cultural representations (ethnology), as its subject. He bases his anthropology on a genuine methodology of detail, which involves retaining all the details, even the seemingly insignificant ones, in the construction of the anthropological interpretation. Those details may say nothing about society or culture as a whole but are nevertheless revealing as regards to a situation as it is experienced. In this way, the aim is not to describe actions that are directly significant with regard to a system of representations but to observe the concrete behavior of real people, which is not always coherent with cultural representations and can even reveal a certain distance from the meaning of the situation and actions. As opposed to Jackson, Piette focuses less on a particular situation (which actually becomes very difficult to isolate, given that every situation is directly connected to others) than on modes of presence. To do so, the anthropologist must pay attention not so much to a single situation but to a particular experience, i.e., not to focus on a group, and even less on an activity, but to follow an individual through the series of situations he experiences, as if following an ethnographical trail. How is this person present to this situation? Over and above these modes of presence in the particular situations observed by the anthropologist, what are the characteristics of human presence to the world? To answer, Piette employs a comparative methodology of modes of presence, between beings that can be considered as prior to humans, notably primates (the great apes, *Homo erectus*, *Homo neanderthalensis*) and beings that are essentially nonhuman (dogs, the dead, gods, collective entities, robots). The human way of being in the world has evolved gradually. Piette's aim is to identify what constitutes a specifically human mode of presence, and then situate its appearance in the history of human evolution (2009).

To clarify his own idea of existential thinking, Michael Jackson takes inspiration from the descriptions found in the novels of Virginia Woolf and her focus on "moments of being": "Though this is fiction, and concerned with the flux and subtle shadings of lived experience, it succeeds in giving us a vivid sense of what is at stake at any moment of being, and in introducing us to some of the ways in which existential-phenomenological thought has theorized the question of being" (2005: xiii). For Jackson, though it is impossible to fully apprehend the complexity of existence through analytical reason alone, it is possible to describe these "moments of being" and thereby come closer to understanding important existential experiences for a person (xxv). For Woolf, these "moments of being" refer to passing or commonplace instants that have no particular intrinsic depth of meaning, but which take on a greater existential significance by their suggestive power to one character in particular. For Woolf, the moment of being is not just any moment; it is one that comes to be seen as an event. And yet even though the moment is considered as an event, it is a singular event that first and foremost occurs as an inner experience of a certain character. It is in this way that the moment of being is memorable, as opposed to the countless moments of nonbeing that fill ordinary life, "a kind of nondescript cotton wool" (Woolf 1985: 70). Although they are events, these particular moments do not emerge from extraordinary circumstances; they may be produced by actions that are in appearance quite innocuous. It is thus not the action that defines a moment of being, but rather its inner resonance within the character. These fleeting moments carry a revelatory force for the person concerned. They serve as a window into the character's very being, and enable the writer to describe that character's deepest feelings. In Woolf's writing they call for a descriptive style that does not simply provide mere inventory of what happens, but also puts into words the experience of the people to whom these things are happening. Woolf's aspiration here is very close to that of existential anthropology: facts do not have an inherent meaning of their own. Meaning is provided only by our presence to these facts. Anthropologists give neat descriptions of facts, practices, organizations, and structures without attempting to describe presence, life, existence, or human nature (a reviled concept in social and cultural anthropology). For to do so would involve giving up the attempt to impose definitions on social facts, i.e., to place limitations on those facts. It would also mean giving up trying to think in terms of totality, and accepting that human being cannot be reduced to any theoretical model. This means coming to terms with the fact that any anthropological description must be—at least partially—incomplete. What is noteworthy for the existential anthropologist is Woolf's intention to describe modulations in being that are not connected to the meaning of the action taking place, and to find in these moments of being a possibility to free ethnography from the norms and interpretations of the situation, and describe life as it actually reveals itself—as being in action. This description of situations as "moments of being" requires a literary finesse that is attentive to, and can be suggestive of, atmosphere, auras, and states of mind. It does not limit itself to situational descriptions, categorizations, definitions, drawing boundaries, or a partial selection of actions and words.

    Albert Piette also draws inspiration from Woolf's "moments of being" to propose a writing of human existence that he calls phenomenographical (2009). These moments of being can lead the anthropologist to consider his observation as a description of modes of presence: each person has his own "moment of being"—a density that Piette calls a "volume of being," and leads to a different understanding of the relationship between space and time in an ethnographic description. There is no unity of space and time but rather a simultaneity of varied happenings that favor this play of modulations of presence within an individual. To observe these modalities of presence is to observe the different modes of perception—fluctuations in attention, variations of intensity, the intermingling of situations within the same external flow of action, seen from the perspectives of each different person involved. Piette sees photography as especially valuable in phenomenography. Photography allows different postures to stand out, and allows us to see a hierarchy of different gestures and movements, some of which add to the action and others that are peripheral to it. Although photography, like film, does not allow an interruption to the usual flow of perception, it too can be of use in obtaining a phenomenographical perception that uses the methodology of the cognitive sciences to observe states of mind through the observation of movements. This methodology is particularly useful in picking up on subliminal actions. The challenge for Piette is to go beyond phenomenology, which lays too much emphasis on action as a result of consciousness. In the methodology he proposes, observation must be completed by additional explanation of the actions, given by the individual concerned. In this way the individual, with the help of the researcher, can elucidate his way of being present at the time—which can sometimes come as a surprise to the individual himself. As the explanation unfolds, the researcher and the individual discover the full details of the experience. Phenomenography is not against self-referential writing. Writing about one's own experience is sometimes the only way to fully apprehend the emotions that are in play. Piette has put this into practice especially in his work on the experience of belief. In phenomenographical writing, it is thus not so much a particular situation or the relation to others or even an observed activity that is to be described, but rather a unique existence in its modulations between different existential states. It is a question of "observing what makes a man, alone and among others, what he perceives and feels when he is alone and when he is with others, in the continuous undulation of his life" (2011: 99, author's translation). The description is of an individual in situ. It refuses to let the action take precedence over the subject's way of being present to this action. In phenomenography, situation and action become secondary. Rather than attempting to observe a collective reality, phenomenography focuses its attention on certain moments of being of a particular individual. If there is one fact that retains the attention of the phenomenographer, it is the simple fact of being (Piette speaks in this way of an anthropology of presence, which is not always being present to the action taking place now). It is resolutely independent of any intention, or indeed anything that takes us away from this state of being, and which would try to make a human into a rational subject, a purely social being who acts in relation to the meaning, not of the situation but of the interactions he experiences.

Observing the Human Condition

The goal of existential anthropology is thus not to speculate about the human condition—this task more properly belongs to philosophy—but to actually observe it, thus placing its considerations on existence on a firm empirical footing; to observe the human condition through these moments of being which in themselves constitute events of presence. The attempt to bring the focus of anthropology onto actual human beings has led Albert Piette to study more closely the philosophy of Heidegger and his central concept of *Dasein*, which rests on a fundamental ontology in order to describe the particularity of being a man: "This being which we ourselves in each case are and which includes inquiry among the possibilities of its being we formulate terminologically as Da-sein" (1996: 6). According to Heidegger, the philosophical approach to beings has always considered the question of Being as self-explanatory. What distinguishes man from other beings is his capacity to understand himself in his state of being, in the very act of existing. Thus Man is not characterized by the cogito: it is Being that is the question for beings. Considering this question, Heidegger invites us to consider the existential ontological phenomenon that characterizes a being thrown into the world without explanation. The *Dasein* (Being) is thus fundamentally incomplete, as he is waiting for something: "In Da-sein there is inevitably a constant 'fragmentariness' which finds its end in death" (1996: 225). It is from its temporal dimension of being-in-the-world that Heidegger attempts to deduce the ontological structures of *Dasein*. Being as "being-toward-death" naturally has a particular relationship with its existence, which it questions. The essential characteristic of *Dasein* resides in its understanding of itself as mortal. Heidegger gives the title *Being and Time* to his treatise on *Dasein*, to emphasize the temporal essence of being. This dimension of ending, and the awareness of that ending, seems to be relatively absent from current anthropology in its social and cultural understanding of man. And yet it is this very dimension of experience that distinguishes man from other beings, this experience of his own ending. Man exists, as confronted with his awareness of death.

This philosophical approach adds a further dimension to the literary endeavor of Virginia Woolf: to describe moments of being in passing instants of life. A being that exists is a being that is traveling toward death. A being can thus only be understood in its instantaneity of being, a being in situ, in the consciousness that he has of himself, but also in the modalities that allow him to continue to be. We can see glimpses of this last point in Michael Jackson's work, with its recurring theme of the struggle for life within limits. This term is used to refer to different forms of struggle for human existence, and covers the various means that human beings use to continue being in this world, in their social environment. It is a term to understand the resilience of the human being in the multitude of situations that attempt to deny it existence. It thus enables us to understand existential anthropology as an anthropology of existential events that testify to this fundamental struggle for life.

The theme of vulnerability, and the consciousness of this vulnerability as part and parcel of the human condition, is therefore a fundamental theme of any anthropology that claims to be existential and, for Jackson, attempts to reveal the processes by which human beings manage, *despite circumstances*, to maintain their freedom within the fatality of events. He insists on the very human obstinacy to refuse to consider one's life as ruled by forces beyond one's control, which one can neither comprehend nor influence. Even though this might seem to be an illusory project, Jackson insists on this human need to feel that one partly determines one's own destiny. This struggle can be seen as striving to maintain balance between being acted upon and being the agent of one's own life (2005: 182.). Jackson here joins with Sartre in his attempts to conceive of human freedom in the face to the fatality of existence.

An anthropology of events is thus for Michael Jackson an anthropology of difficult life events that disclose this struggle for a life worth living. Confronting and surmounting adverse events, as unique as they each are, are common to all humanity. For Jackson, this intersection between the unique, as found in these singular existential life events, and the universal, as instances of the common human condition, is the very core of existential anthropological thinking. The aim of anthropology is thus an exploration of the human condition, and not simply of culture. In these instants, there is a tension between the universally shared human condition and the moment as uniquely experienced by one individual. For Jackson, the theme of the human condition is a way of transcending the traditional dichotomy of the universal and the particular. The central challenge of existential anthropology thus emerges as the link between the particular (events) and the universal (human condition). Although being-in-the-world is inevitably expressed symbolically, the question of being itself is always universal and can serve as a starting point to explore the human condition (2005: xii) and blaze what Jackson, echoing Heidegger, calls "paths toward a clearing."

Heideggerian *Dasein* also contains this link between the universality of being and the uniqueness of actual beings. The expression "being human" designates singularity (a human being as a numerical entity) and, in parallel, a mode of being that is common to all humans. With the notion of *Dasein*, Heidegger is able to speak at the same time of man and of Man. In the context of existential anthropology, it is in "moments of being" as instances of existence—*ekstasis*—that a unique situation can be seen to hold a wider significance. If we wish to find the universal within being, it is necessarily in singularity that we must search for it. In this approach, the singular retains its uniqueness and refuses conceptual abstraction and systemic thinking, while still managing to say something about universal humanity. We are once again reminded of the literary efforts of Virginia Woolf. The moment of being is the instant a situation expands to reveal to the writer the depth and breadth of inner human experience. The existential event, for Woolf, is a moment when being and the world are born simultaneously. The event in its most-subjective (most-inner) facets becomes universal. In these moments of being, existential anthropology finds its phenomenomogical inspiration: life and the world are not two juxtaposed things. The world is only comprehensible through a particular life, through its immediate world. *The* world is only understood through *a* world. Being can only be understood through *a* being.

Individuality or Intersubjectivity?

To focus on existence implies, therefore, a focus on *an* existence, if we wish to avoid the snare of intellectual abstraction. Existence does not exist outside of a concrete existence, just as there is no life outside of what is lived. Albert Piette and Michael Jackson both see eye to eye on this point, but they then go on to develop the idea in very different directions. A being is very much tied into an *inter-est* for Michael Jackson, who would like us to use intersubjectivity as a foundation for further thought on the matter. And yet for Albert Piette, thinking must begin with the being in itself, i.e., in a situation, as an individual, and not as the mirror of its relations.

For Jackson, a being is always a subject in relation with other subjects, be they persons, abstract ideas, or things. Reality is relational. However, by this intersubjectivity, we must not think of the subject as a product of her culture, but rather of culture as the product of interaction, thus opening up a way of thinking of oneself through this "being-together." Jackson insists, however, that relational being never completely occludes a sense of singular being; "I" and "we" modalities of existence are mutually arising. While Jackson seeks to explore the existential and phenomenological implications of Levi-Strauss's conception of anthropology as a "general theory of relationships" (1963: 95), he is equally mindful of the fact that existence is always apprehended in both personal and interpersonal terms.

At certain moments and in certain contexts, a person experiences himself or herself as "being a part of" the world; at other moments or in other contexts, he or she feels "apart from the world" (2012: 2). The analytical challenge is to transcend the subjective-objective (or individual-society) dichotomy in order to arrive at a phenomenological perspective in which the subjective and the objective are not competing *epistemologies* but terms that capture alternating forms of *experience*. Hence the reliance on first-hand accounts in which subjects describe, in their own vernacular idioms, their experience of the world. The objective, like the subjective, cannot be thought of a priori, "but seen phenomenologically as words with which we mark moments or modalities of experience that reflect the various potentialities that are realized or foregrounded in the course of interactions between persons and persons, persons and things, or persons and beliefs" (2013: 261–262).

Experience, which is inseparable from the recounting of that experience, always happens within a context of relations, both intrapsychic and intersubjective. Both these fields of relationship are dynamic, not static. The struggle for life finds its place both in the mind and in the world. And objects, abstraction, and other persons are implicated in both these fields of relationship. Indeed, people themselves can also be treated as objects (2013: 5–6). Moreover, what defines the existential field for Jackson is the relation between the world we are born into and the world we act upon (1998: 28). In this way, we focus on the endless negotiations that take place, within the mind and with others, to secure and sustain one's own life as well as the lifeworld one shares with significant others. The notion of intersubjectivity highlights the fact that others are an integral part of one's being, while retaining the perception of oneself as an autonomous subject. Jackson indicates, again echoing Virginia Woolf's moments of being, that intersubjectivity is also a relation between different psyches, in other words social interactions cannot be understood without taking into account the states of mind of the subjects involved in those interactions (2013: 5–6).

Albert Piette takes a radically different approach. In his view, the concern of anthropology is not relations (which would bring it too close to the field of sociology) but rather human beings in their singularity, i.e., empirically, as individuals (2011). Piette points out that for anthropologists, the identity of man is always rooted in the collective. This comes from the certainty of the existence of a social structure, with its own laws and symbolical significations. By insisting on the connected nature of the individual, all sociological, ethnological, or anthropological speculations cannot help but consider individuals as merely parts of the collective: the individual is always involved in some social play based on a common agreement as to the outcome of the action. In this way the individual is never considered as such, but always through the prism of relations, which is constantly referred to and yet rarely questioned. Piette warns against this tendency toward "all-encompassing relations" that leads to the relation itself, rather than the human being, becoming the subject of anthropology. What is important for Piette is to emphasize not what is between human beings but to consider the human being in himself. For Piette, making constant reference to relations can lead us to downplay or even disregard the existence of individual singularity. In this way, man ends up reduced to the sum of his relations. The anthropological and anthropographical projects that Piette defends attempt to consider the human being in his fundamental and numerical singularity, i.e., as an individual, and not through the light of theoretical reconstructions that transform him into a social agent. This presupposes that we do not reduce the individual to a mere role, and also that we do not regard a moment of presence as a way of establishing a social link. Phenomenography allows us to get closer to the individual and to see him as a "volume of being" engaged in relations, but also disengaged from these relations, as his modalities and intensity of engagement are always variable, revealing a play between presence and absence to the situation. For Piette, it is a question of understanding the modalities not only of engagement but also of disengagement from the action taking place, the individual existing in a situation but also before and after, through the nuances and changes in his presence.

This by no means amounts to a denial of the intersubjective dimension of existence; Albert Piette speaks of "co-presence" (2011: 137) rather than intersubjectivity or interaction, to insist on the fact that his anthropology focuses on the subjects currently present, rather than links and relations. Living together is not so much interaction—which presupposes that the players exchange messages in order to construct action together, so necessarily locked into a game of interpretation, playing their role as best they can—but being present side by side. The term "interaction" implies full identification with behavioral codes to accomplish common action. The word has connotations of strategy, consciousness, and consensus, which support the image of man as rational subject. Presence or co-presence, however, imply an individual who is not only a rational subject, acting according to the interplay between his own perceived meanings. Co-presence retains the possibility of minor modes within one common action. The term takes into account as much engagement in the situation as disengagement, with a resulting gap, or conflict, between the different meanings experienced and acted upon.

Can man be understood not independently but above and beyond his relational dimension? The epistemological challenge that Albert Piette presents is to go beyond this relational and cultural reading of human experience. And in this way, he aims also to reaffirm anthropology: not as sociology, and not as ethnology (2011). The existential project of observing human existence at its most fundamental level implies a return to situations themselves, aside from what they might represent at a social and cultural level. For Piette this requires a methodological approach of focusing on the primary numerical entity of existence (the human being), which should not be mistaken for considering this being as an independent numerical entity. The human being is defined by her symbolic activities, an extension of meaning that is necessarily shared, and which forms culture (the key term in so-called social and cultural anthropology, as a reminder that these two are inseparable). Existential anthropology does not intend to denigrate or deny this approach, but states its own intellectual mission as distinct. It strives to focus not on human production but, on a more primary level, the human being herself in her modalities of presence in the world. Relations are thus no longer considered as a prerequisite for human experience, but rather as one aspect of an observed situation, whereby the human understands herself through her reflected image, through her relations to others. What then is this experience? Being is being *with*. There is indeed a shared experience, that of experiencing this world together, but we also share a certain solitude—that of facing death. Existential anthropology, contrary to social and cultural anthropology, does not take this shared experience as its starting point, even though it may indeed take it into consideration along the way. In this way, for existential anthropology, the social link is secondary to, but certainly not excluded from, human experience.

Man at a Distance from Himself

In developing an "anthropography" of human beings, Albert Piette considers what he calls a *minimal* approach to the world as being what is quintessentially human (2009). In this way, a person is never fully involved in the given meaning of the situation he is experiencing, totally attentive to what is going on before him. A person is always partially present to the situation, but simultaneously elsewhere, in what remains of other situations in his mind. Thus human experience does not take place in one unity of space and time, but rather in spaces and times which succeed one another and indeed continue to resonate in any given moment.

These modulations constitute the movement of human life. Each situation contains within itself reminders—traces, echoes—of other situations, which together make up the "density of being" (*volume d'être*) of an individual. Each situation contains within itself much more than would appear at first glance. In this way, a situation cannot be understood by and of itself, independent of the individual who experiences it. These remainders serve to defuse somewhat the power and intensity of a situation: the situation does not have a total hold, and its meaning is not all-encompassing. Our humanity expresses itself in these remainders of presence, in this capacity for distraction and thus distance from the direct meanings that are so central to theories of action. What Albert Piette calls the "minor mode" (1992)—which began as a methodological tool in anthropology, to give center stage to seemingly unimportant details—has become the central theme of Piette's anthropological project. Piette sees anthropology as relating not to social and cultural representations, which disincarnate and abstract from human experience, but to our specifically human way of being present in a situation. The minor mode reveals a human being who is never completely involved in the semantic implications of his effort, but instead is constantly experiencing moments when this search for meaning is suspended, when the subject is sidetracked from the logic of meaning. The phenomenon of belief is a perfect illustration (2003). The person is divided between engagement in the statements of meaning, and a detachment from them. Divided between action and simple presence, what characterizes human beings is their capacity for partial engagement in a situation ("mental rest," to use Piette's image). In any situation, however intense, human beings have a unique capacity to insert detachment, distance, even lightness. The direct meaning of a given situation is weakened by this distance. As opposed to animals, that can be seen to be in a state of constant vigilance, ready to give full meaning to whatever arises in the situation, man has a relaxed attention. Minimality in human beings is seen as a capacity to be sidetracked from the sense of immediate necessity that governs other beings that are fully focused on the direct meaning of the action.

The Heideggerian problem of awareness of one's eventual end is suspended in this minimality of human presence in the world. It is precisely this minimality that, in fact, makes the world human, i.e., a place where people can live. *Dasein* is being-here for only for a limited time; it is a being toward death. And *Dasein* is conceived as the consciousness of this being toward death. To sidestep this, one represents death "as an indeterminate something which first has to show up from somewhere, but which right now is *not yet objectively present* for oneself, and is thus no threat"

(Heidegger 1996: 234). The existential quality of the minor mode is that it allows one to be simultaneously in a mode of being-toward-death, (engaged in meaning), that is in itself unbearable or impossible to live with (one cannot "go on living" with this idea) *and* a mode of being-here, that suspends this anxiety of extinction (disengaged from meaning) and creates a space for being in the here and now. His capacity for mental detachment allows man to continue living despite his awareness of his own ending. The paradoxical dynamic of the minor mode reveals the human being as never *fully* absorbed by direct meaning, *totally* present in the action, but on the contrary a *minimal* being.

When the anthropologist studies ritual activity, he observes behaviors that are significant within a system of representations. But to see the ritual as the performance of meanings given to the world does not take into account what is actually experienced. In the ritual, it is less a matter of understanding what is said, than letting oneself be "taken up." Being "taken up" involves setting aside the given registers of meanings, and opening oneself to the experience of meaning, in other words the force of living the experience itself. Being "taken up" can also be seen as one form of existential thinking. As well as the different levels of meaning in the ritual, the anthropologist will focus less on the representations behind the ritual than on the experience of a particular ritual, with its successes and failures, its high points where everyone is "into it" and its low points. This perspective brings out details that may be at odds with the stated principles of the ritual—yawns, signs of flagging interest, or asides that stand in contrast to the solemnity of the ritual. These details, which are often unremarked because they tell us nothing about the meaning of the ritual, are extremely revealing in terms of human experience. When the anthropologist points out these lateral behaviors on the part of those involved in a ritual, the response is unanimous: "That's only human!" In other words, these actions are not worthy of too much attention; they are a result of our human weakness, which is far less significant than the ritual itself. The originality of Albert Piette's work is to give anthropological credence to this "only human." What is human are precisely these details that attract nobody's attention—not even, paradoxically enough, that of the anthropologist—even though they are highly revealing of our lived humanity.

This disengagement from the direct meaning of situations opens up a different way of thinking—that of minimality rather than totality. Although logical reasoning is a highly valued way of thinking, it turns out to be rather ill adapted to describing our modes of presence to the world. Michael Jackson calls for caution in putting too much stock in rational thought in human sciences, as this may lead us to pass over much of the complexity of the world, "our sense of the *variety* of ways in which human beings create viable lives—emotional, bodily, magical, metaphorical, anthropomorphic, practical and narrative" (2005: xxviii). The subject that emerges here is markedly different from the rational subject found in theories of action: "Most human action is unreflective, which is to say we do not necessarily form any conscious idea of our intentions before we act. . . . Conceptualization, reflection, and representation tend to follow *from* our actions; they are seldom scripts or scores that precede it" (2013: 24–25). Ambiguity characterizes this way of being, with its multiple modes of experience, its changing moods and emotions, its fugitive thoughts, and its constantly changing self-states. Existential anthropology is an exercise in breaking down barriers: far from being an attempt to list all the meanings of a given situation and to reduce being to representations in action, it opens up a situation to a way of thinking that does not try to confine it within the limits of rational thought. Minimality is a way of thinking incompleteness, and also uncertainty. We no longer wish to explain situations (by situating them on the register of social mechanisms), nor even understand them (by situating them on the register of social semantics) but rather to describe the human being: to describe as accurately as possible what is experienced, including (and especially) its strangeness, its ambiguity, its fundamental unfathomableness—in other words, its humanity. Although ambiguity may endanger the credibility of a theoretical system, it is inherent to human experience that is, situationally speaking, never completely one thing or another, but rather a tension between logical systems, or perhaps, one might say, between contradictory forces.

The Anthropological Enigma

Within this framework of minimality, the questions raised do not necessarily call for answers, but rather a writing of being. Existentially, it is a matter of formulating the anthropological question par excellence: What is this "I am" that implies that man is perhaps the only living being capable of formulating a consciousness of his own death? Heidegger asks what is being, and begins with the metaphysical question initially posed by Gottfried Leibniz, "Why is there something, rather than nothing?" We quickly become aware of the impossibility of answering such a question. We must rather let the echo of the question resonate through the anthropological problem, and remain there, in the background, as it invites us to rediscover the utterly astonishing fact that things "are," rather than "are not." To ask the question of being in order to rediscover this marvel or astonishment of being might be considered a prerequisite of existential anthropology. It is a matter of retaining this astonishment at being and not being that, as Heidegger noted, is often take for granted in philosophy.

Infants provide a perfect illustration of the existential project, as Piette suggests in his chapter in this volume. While anthropology has devoted a good deal of attention to the final moments of life, it does not seem to have spent much time studying infants, outside of the sociocultural practices that aim to integrate them into a group. Psychology has taken more interest in the topic. And yet there is much to say about this subject from an anthropological point of view. My greatest personal insight into the subject matter of existential anthropology has come since the birth of my own daughter. For where else would the enigma of being be more perceptible than the arrival into the world of a newborn child? A birth is experienced as the emergence of a being, which, while finding immediate warmth in the loving acceptance of its parents, is at the same time slightly estranged from them as they consider this *new being*, profoundly their own yet mysteriously different. How can the social and cultural anthropologist come to terms with this enigma? How can we consider the mode of being of a baby? The baby is presence, being in its fundamental state, i.e., outside of the strategies presupposed by social relations, or the interplays of meaning that belong to one's own culture. The baby is not yet the rational subject of theories of action. In the anthropology of newborns, there are no social and cultural meanings surrounding the activities of babies for which we can propose and compare different interpretations. The presence of a baby is not interpretable in the terms of theories of action because a baby is not able to apprehend the world, to read within it a prism of representations, or situate itself within the interplay of meanings of situations in which it participates. It is even less in action than in contemplation: it is not in an accustomed relation to things, but rather in a relation of strangeness toward situations, which it is discovering for the first time. We see the world in itself as it already is, a "volume of being," to use Piette's expression, that is not reducible to a social and cultural model of existence or a world of representations, since the baby is not yet in representation but in the presentation of this world that unfolds before it in the first months of its life. The anthropologist who wishes to follow a baby as his subject cannot interview that subject to gain information on the significations of observed activities. She can only observe behaviors that escape the intentionality of the player of the social game. In the end, she is only able to observe existentially, i.e. observe that being itself, and its modalities of being in the world, describing the frequency of its cries, the variations in its facial expressions, its twists and turns, what sustains its attention, what frightens it, what it sees, what it does not see, the surprise with which it notices its own hands, hears music for the first time, and so on. She could also imagine, in light of these details, what the baby is experiencing internally. The way in which, little by little, the world is born for it, the way in which it experiences these instants of life. As we have already seen, existential anthropology is an anthropology of human presence, of "moments of being."

Astonishment, or marveling, is a fundamental posture of thought. It implies bringing strangeness into the familiar, and uncertainty into that which is taken for granted. The question of being does not call for a response but a movement. It is about considering the (human) being as an enigma, as the primary enigma, which requires a certain intellectual position: not to act *as if* we could find the answer, as if we could actually know, but instead to give center stage in our thinking to this astonishment at being. This posture takes as its epistemological foundation the acceptance that the questions raised by thinking about a particular being call neither for explanation nor reassuring elucidation, but rather a vitality: one must let oneself be surprised and carried away by this astonishment at being. There is something poetic in this posture toward being. Heidegger speaks of marveling before the fact that there is something and not nothing. And yet the anthropological project is not one of poetry—although poetry can of course have its place in the life and thought of an anthropologist, as Michael Jackson himself has shown—though it calls for a poetical posture before this enigma of being that one is trying to describe at the same time that one is endeavoring to preserve its enigmatic nature. One strives, as it were, to write simultaneously of the necessity and the impossibility of thinking. To write of oneself, faced with this enigma. To my mind, what the existential project has in common with poetry is its resolve to maintain a contemplative posture that aims to release us from the grasp of the very desire to grasp. This posture presupposes a certain distance from any particular state of being, in order to marvel at the being itself. The contemplative distance one maintains does not back away from being but from action. It is less a matter of working on a question than letting a question work on oneself. To this end, the contemplative posture is a bringing of attention toward being itself. We are, and this escapes us. Thinking about this being that escapes us is, in my view, the aim of existential thought. Piette's phenomenography is the writing of this confrontation with the enigma of being.

This feeling of the incompleteness of thought is at the heart of existential thinking. Existential thinking is markedly less self-assured than rational thought. An illustration of this existential attitude is that of thinking about death. Death, the recurring theme of much human thought—above all philosophical—is characterized by its ungraspability, its unreachability, as if it by its very nature escapes all thought and thinking. Thinking about death from an anthropological point of view is not to give meaning to death (which would seem more the role of theology), but to think of oneself faced with this insoluble mystery. Behind the many cultural significations of death lies one sole necessity: that of speaking about the unspeakable, thinking the unthinkable of existence. It is less a question of anthropology than one of bringing our full attention to this human experience of that which escapes us, i.e., the mystery of existence. We cannot in all honesty speak in great detail about such mysteries as God, life, and death, but we can however think about the impact of such mysteries on us. The existential imperative is to think of such human experiences as concretely as possible, taking into account not only the beliefs that are generated by our confrontation with death (religion), but the instances of a person shaken to his very being, his desperation when faced with death, his impossibility to conceive or elaborate, his paradoxical beliefs, his ambiguity. Existential thinking accepts this gap, these contradictory statements, just as it accepts the distortions of the world. In my own view, accepting the distortions of the world brings us closer to a thinking of existence. Thought opens up to that which escapes its grasp. The poetic posture does not concern itself with defining, grasping, apprehending, but on the contrary reminds us of the extent to which the world refuses to be conceptualized and remains above all an enigma. The poetic posture, far from trying to exhaust the mystery of the world, marvels at how privileged it is to be its witness. Once again, this is not to imply that existential anthropology may be conflated with poetry, but rather to claim that it adopts a poetic posture in its epistemological outlook. Existential anthropology is less about considering human productions of worlds than considering human experience of the world—actual experience rather than representations—and all that eludes our grasp, including life itself. Hardships in life remind us of this fact. It is not without reason that these difficulties often provide inspiration for intellectual reflection. Michael Jackson's chapter on the life and death of a close Sierra Leonean friend (this volume) and Albert Piette's *Le Temps du Deuil* (2005), about the death of his own father, are two examples among many others. It follows that existential thinking makes possible the introduction of the life of the anthropologist into his own writing. If we take this posture seriously, this marveling before the simple fact of being, the conventional notion of fieldwork is somewhat shattered, as it is no longer a question of marveling within one highly localized field of investigation, or within one particular population; the whole of life becomes one's field, and not just certain situations marked out ethnographically. This is very clear in Piette's work, where phenomenography serves as a springboard for fundamental thinking about human existence, and also in Jackson's writing, where situations are not only reported from Sierra Leone or Australia, but from a variety of places and times that make up the mosaic of Jackson's own existential journey through life.

In existential anthropology, we are thus confronted with this central question of human existence. But this question is tackled very differently by Jackson and by Piette. While both writers come together in criticizing the abstraction of human experience through lofty notions of society and culture, their existential perspectives take quite dissimilar directions. This chapter has considered some of these variations. These dissimilar directions seem to stem from differences in the places the writers find their inspiration and focus their anthropological attentions. Jackson delves into phenomenology to define his existential anthropology, whereas Piette develops his thinking about ethnographical methodology (the notion of minor mode) so that existential anthropology can then serve for us to rediscover phenomenology. Inspired by Sartre, Jackson aims to conceive of human freedom in the face of fatality, while for Piette the central question is that of the "resting mental attitude" (*reposité*) concomitant with lucidity. In my own view, existential anthropology is less based on theoretical foundations than on an epistemological project and posture. Its project is to describe "moments of being," and anthropology itself constitutes a moment of being for the anthropologist. Its epistemological posture could be characterized by a withdrawal from the level of cultural representation in anthropological understandings of the relation of the human being to the world. This can be seen as a repudiation of the rationales that theories of action use in understanding human existence, and opening up a thinking of existence that is by its very nature seen as constantly evasive and fundamentally equivocal. It is a wholehearted acceptance of the irreducibility of human existence. The most fruitful thinking is not one that glosses over the limits of thought, but one that dares confront those limits.

Notes

Many thanks to Richard Crossley for his help with this chapter.

References

Heidegger, Martin. 1996. *Being and Time: A Translation of Sein und Zeit* (trans. Joan Stambaugh). Albany: State University of New York Press.
Jackson, Michael. 1998. *Minima Ethnographica: Intersubjectivity and the Anthropological Project*. Chicago and London: The University of Chicago Press.
———. 2005. *Existential Anthropology: Events, Exigencies and Effects*. New York and Oxford: Berghahn Books.
———. 2012. *Between One and One Another*. Berkeley: University of California Press.
———. 2013. *Lifeworlds: Essays in Existential Anthropology*. Chicago: University of Chicago Press.
Lévi-Strauss, Claude. 1963. *Totemism* (trans. Rodney Needham). Boston: Beacon Press.
Piette, Albert. 1992. *Le mode mineur de la réalité. Paradoxes et photographies en anthropologie*. Louvain: Peeters.
———. 2003. *Le fait religieux. Une théorie de la religion ordinaire*. Paris: Economica.
———. 2005. *Le temps du deuil*. Paris: Les éditions de l'Atelier.
———. 2009. *Anthropologie Existentiale*. Paris: Petra.
———. 2011. *Fondements à une anthropologie des hommes*. Paris: Hermann.
Woolf, Virginia. 1985. "A Sketch of the Past." In *Moments of Being*, Jeanne Schulkind (ed.). New York: Harcourt Brace and Company.

Contributors

Laurent Denizeau holds a PhD in social anthropology (Université de Lyon, 2007), and is a lecturer and researcher in the Interdisciplinary Center of Ethics at the Catholic University of Lyon. His research focuses on orthodox monastic life and the experience of belief in France (and in Greece), and the body in pain, suffering, and recovery from the perspective of an existential anthropology. He is concerned especially with forms of human presence to the world, modes of release from order and meaning, and meditative relations to different situations. He is the author of *Petite Ethnographie d'une Tradition Monastique* (Paris, 2010).

Michael Jackson is Distinguished Professor of World Religions at Harvard Divinity School. He has done fieldwork among the Kuranko of Sierra Leone, the Warlpiri of Central Australia, the Kuku-Yalanji of Cape York Peninsula, and with African migrants in Europe. He is the author of over thirty books of ethnography, poetry, and fiction. He writes: "Perhaps the most central question in my work has been how human beings everywhere seek, alone and in concert with others, to strike a balance between a sense of closure and openness, between acting and being acted on, between acquiescing in the given and shaping their own destinies. Most of my books explore the ways in which inherited customs, habits and dispositions both constrain activity and consciousness *and* are reconstructed, resisted and replenished in quotidian practices, rites, narratives, and unspoken experience. As I see it, one of the most urgent tasks of anthropology is to close the gap between theoretical and practical knowledge, and between the academy and the wider world, exploring the immediate, intersubjective underpinnings of abstract forms of understanding, disclosing the subject behind the act, and the vital activity that lies behind the fixed and seemingly final form of things. At the same time as one explores and discloses connections between worldviews and lifeworlds, one endeavors to test one's views—whether personal, theoretical, ethical or political—*in* the lived world, and in so doing critique and revise them. One's goal is never absolute knowledge, but rather a deepened pragmatic understanding of the possibilities of human coexistence in a pluralistic world."

Michael Lambek holds the Canada Research Chair in the Anthropology of Ethical Life at the University of Toronto Scarborough. He works in the anthropology of religion with special interests in the conceptualization of "religion," spirit possession, mythopraxis, and Islam in the Western Indian Ocean; medico-religious heterodoxy in Switzerland; and ordinary ethics. His books include *A Companion to the Anthropology of Religion* (edited with Janice Boddy, 2013); *Ordinary Ethics: Anthropology, Language, and Action* (ed., 2010); *A Reader in the Anthropology of Religion* (2nd ed., 2008); *Illness and Irony* (edited with Paul Antze, 2003); *The Weight of the Past: Living with History in Mahajanga, Madagascar* (2002); *Ecology and the Sacred* (edited with Ellen Messer, 2001); *Tense Past* (edited with Paul Antze, 1996); *Knowledge and Practice in Mayotte: Local Discourses of Islam, Sorcery and Spirit Possession* (1993); and *Human Spirits* (1981).

Hans Lucht is an anthropologist and senior researcher at the Danish Institute for International Studies,Denmark. He has done extensive fieldwork among sub-Saharan migrants in Ghana, Niger, Italy, Greece, and Denmark, and his book, *Darkness before Daybreak: African Migrants Living on the Margins in Southern Italy Today* (Berkeley, CA, 2011) documents the perilous journeys these migrants make, across the Sahara to Libya and from Libya to Europe, in search of better lives. He coined the term "existential reciprocity" in his first fieldwork among Ghanaian fishermen in the Guan fishing village of Senya Beraku, thirty miles west of Accra, Ghana. He shows how an ethic of reciprocity underlies Guan conceptions of what they owe the sea and the sea owes them, what they can expect from the Ghanaian State and from local authorities, and what is unfair about the industrialized fishing that has impacted their lives and livelihoods, obliging them to migrate. His fieldwork experience led him to explore the ontological and ethical assumptions that underpin migrant imaginaries. The migrant's struggle for ontological security is a struggle against stigma, against being diminished, degraded, or unfairly treated in his everyday dealings with locals, and of having to constantly justify to himself and others the sacrifice he has made in leaving kith and kin for an ostensibly better life abroad. And yet the migrant seldom doubts his *human* right to be given a chance, to vindicate his claim to a share of the bounty of the society he has entered. A logic of sacrifice informs the migrant imagination—the axiom that one must give up in order to gain, empty oneself in order to be filled, place one's hope in another, elsewhere, in order to achieve personal autonomy. The assumption of common humanity, and an implicit ethic of generalized reciprocity, transcends the worldview that worth is relative to birth. It implies a cosmopolitan sense that one inhabits not so much a world without borders as a world in which one is entitled to cross those borders in quest of a better life, to see it for oneself, whatever the risks and whatever the cost.

Albert Piette is professor of anthropology at Paris West University Nanterre and researcher at the Centre for Ethnology and Comparative Sociology (CNRS). In his fieldwork, he has observed carnivals and festivals in Belgium, and quotidian life in Catholic parishes of France. He is the author of over fifteen books in French. His books are about the epistemology and observation of details, religious phenomena, and rituals. He has also written an "autography" of mourning and the process of forgetting. In his most recent books, he deploys the notion of phenomenography in building an existential anthropology, focusing especially on the details of human presences in order to understand collective life and the differences between humans and other animals. He seeks to develop anthropology as an empirical and theoretical science, different from sociology and social anthropology. What does this mean? In his essay *On Repenting*, Michel de Montaigne writes, "I am not portraying being but becoming: not the passage from one age to another (or, as the folk put it, from one seven-year period to the next) but from day to day, from minute to minute." In a footnote to his *Essays*, Montaigne explains that he does not create a portrait, a static analysis of himself, but gives his observations from day to day—and observations on his variations. Using this perspective, Albert Piette thinks that it is important to observe the microcontinutiy of the individual, living various moments and situations according to changing modalities of presence-absence and passivity-activity. Existence, in this sense, is not reducible to the poolings of the social sciences, or the effects of relationships, and cannot be integrated into a logic of belonging.

Devaka Premawardhana recently received his PhD from Harvard University and is assistant professor in the Department of Religion at Colorado College. He has conducted ethnographic research in Brazil, Sri Lanka, and Mozambique. His work highlights how the varieties of Christianity increasingly located outside Europe and North America challenge prominent Euro-American assumptions about religion, epistemology, and subjectivity. To date, his most explicit engagement of existential and phenomenological thought was published in *Nova Religio* (2012) as "Transformational Tithing: Sacrifice and Reciprocity in a Neo-Pentecostal Church." In this essay he acknowledges that Pentecostal prosperity practices seem to exceed what is rational, sound, and financially sustainable. Yet from the perspectives of those most involved, these may be less exploitative than empowering: a way of changing if not the circumstances of one's life, then at least how one experiences those circumstances. Premawardhana is currently preparing a book manuscript based on field research among the semi-nomadic, Makhuwa-speaking people of northern Mozambique. It will explore how religious change is experienced by people for whom regional change has long been a livelihood strategy: a way of dealing with ever-changing yet ever-precarious environments, both natural and political.

Mattijs van de Port is the chair of Popular Religiosity at the Vrije Universiteit Amsterdam and program leader at the Amsterdam Institute for Social Science Research at the University of Amsterdam. An anthropologist by training, he has conducted research on war experiences and collective fantasies in Novi Sad, Serbia; *fado* in Lisbon, Portugal; contract killings in the Netherlands; and since 2001, Candomblé and baroque forms of world making in Bahia, Brazil. In addition to his books—*Gypsies, Wars and Other Instances of the Wild: Civilization and its Discontents in a Serbian Town* (Amsterdam, 1998), and *Ecstatic Encounters: Bahian Candomblé and the Quest for the Really Real* (Amsterdam, 2011)—van de Port has made recent and extensive contributions in numerous journals to the research on Candomblé, and is currently exploring the phenomenon of "permeable boundaries" in Bahia.

Sónia Silva is an associate professor of Anthropology at Skidmore College. She is the author of *Along an African Border: Angolan Refugees and Their Divination Baskets* (Philadelphia, PA, 2011), a groundbreaking study of divination and divining baskets (*lipele*) among Angolan refugees in Northwest Zambia. Her existential-phenomenological perspective involves a shift of focus from examining how the meanings of objects are socially constructed or represented to how objects are used in the course of people's quotidian struggle for existence in a world where scarcity and inequality imply that prestige, dignity, honor, pride, presence, trust, health, well-being, love, and recognition are always at risk. Though economic and political values may attach to *lipele*, Silva shows us that the values they actually generate are more consistently and profoundly associated with life itself—with the struggle to meet and cope with its vicissitudes, the effort to find ways of acting with confidence and hope, the desire for well-being.

If exchange is involved in people's interactions with *lipele* it is existential rather than economic—a matter of transforming their situations in ways that open up new possibilities of action. Anthropomorphism is thus a kind of retrospective respect a person pays an object that has brought him or her some benefit—a recognition that the threefold principle of reciprocity holds equally true of relations between persons and relations among persons, animals, and things. Silva continues to work on ritualization, fetishism, and objectification from an ontological and phenomenological perspective, focusing on situations of existential crisis, social suffering, and interpersonal violence.

Index

Abidjan, 108
Abrahamic traditions, 60, 77–78
Accra, 110
Actaeon complex, 105–6
actor-network, 93–94
Adorno, Theodor, 1, 3, 7, 20, 26n10
adulthood, 136, 142. *See also* life course
adventure, 133–37, 146–47
Africa, 133
Agadez, 111, 114–15
agalmatophilia, 106
aging, 135, 142–44, 148
Alpes, Maybritt Jill, 108
Alto-Zambeze, 151n5
amputees, 126, 128, 141, 143–45, 149–50
    and basket making, 130
    landmine amputees in Angola, 141, 144
    and nonproductivity, 144
Angola, 126, 141
    cease-fire, 139, 151n4
    civil war, 125, 127, 130, 132, 137, 138–39, 142, 149, 151nn4–5 (*see also* civil war in Angola)
    colonial war, 127, 129–30, 138, 148, 151n4 (*see also* colonialism in Angola)
    east Angola, 127, 138–39, 151n5
    independence, 125, 127, 130, 148
    liberation struggle, 125, 127, 130, 141, 148, 151n4
anthropography, 216, 228
anthropology of Christianity, 33, 35–36, 39–41, 47, 49–50. *See also* Robbins, Joel
Arendt, Hannah, 34, 49, 140. *See also* natality

Arlit, 109, 113
Armando, 132
Assemblies of God, African (AOGA), 37, 38, 50, 52n9
Augé, Marc, 147

Badiou, Alain, 6–7
Bahia (Brazil), 84, 86, 88, 94, 97
Bataille, George, 102n11
beekeeping, 129, 130, 141–43
believing, 191–203, 217, 222, 226, 229, 234
    origin of, 205–10
Bergmann, Sigurd, 148
Binswanger, Ludwig, 2, 26n8
body
    closing the body, 86, 91–93, 101
    opening the body, 86, 88–90
    porous bodies, 88–89
    the body of the reader, 97
border customs, 141, 148
boundary, 85, 88, 100
Bourdieu, Pierre, 15–17
boys initiation camp, 132
Burness, Dr., 143–44

Cameroon War (1914–1915), 163
Camus, Albert, 156, 175
Candomblé, 85, 87–93, 97, 102nn5–6, 102n12
Cape Verdeans, 126
category mistakes, 78
Catholicism, 36, 53n14, 192–203
Cavell, Stanley, 81n17
Certeau, Michel de, 5, 7, 98
Chavuma, 126–27, 129–30, 132, 133–34, 136–41, 144–45, 148–50, 151nn3–5

childhood, 127, 128, 145
Chinoya, 138
Chivundo, 138
choice and constraint, 131, 139, 140. *See also* necessity and freedom
Chokwe, 126–27, 145
civil war in Angola, 125, 127, 130, 132, 137–39, 142, 149, 151nn4–5
    and Cuba, 130
    and Neto and Savimbi, 130
Clifford, James, 147, 151n10
CMML mission, 133, 144
colonialism in Angola, 127, 130, 133, 138, 149
    colonial settlements, 137, 148, 150, 151n7
    colonial tax, 131
    colonial war, 127, 129
Comaroff, Jean, 40
conversion, 31–32, 34, 36, 39, 42, 47–48, 53n17, 53n18
Copperbelt, 136, 143
Couto, Mia, 149
Cresswell, Tim, 150
culture, 39–40, 41, 53n12

Dakar, 108
Dasein, 223–25, 229
da Vinci, Leonardo, 122–23
    Mona Lisa, 123
death, 193–96, 200, 203, 207, 210, 218–19, 222, 229–30, 233
Deleuze, Gilles, 148
Descola, Philippe, 22
detail, 180, 183–87, 191–92, 205
Devereux, George, 5
Dilthey, Wilhem, 5–6
disabled person, 142. *See also* immobility
dualism. *See* monism
Dumont, Louis, 64–65
Dunbar, Robin, 211n18
Durkheim, Emile, 14–15, 127
dwelling, 147–48

elephants, 137, 144
Ellenberger, Henri, 8
employment, 129, 131, 136, 138
England, 138, 143, 144, 151n8
epigenesis, 174, 177n8
essentialism, 59, 150. *See also* reification; stereotyping

ethics, 62, 77–79
ethnology, 219, 228
existential imperatives, 105, 122
existentialism, 228
existential mobility, 3
existential reciprocity, 120
existentials (Heidegger), 182
existential stance, 125, 146
existential themes, 131, 150–51
existential value, 140
experience, 64–65, 71

FAPLA, 141
farming, 128–30, 136–37, 143
fear, 129–30, 132, 136, 138–40
fechar o corpo. *See* closing the body
fieldwork, 67–70, 126
fishing, 129, 134, 136, 140, 143
fleeing, 129–30, 133–34, 139–40, 143, 145
forced displacement, 125, 127, 131–34, 139, 148
    as dispersal of people, 129, 130, 132
    and the idea of forcefulness, 132, 139–40, 149
    and the idea of uprootedness from original homeland, 132, 134
    from Angola to Zambia, 127, 132–34
    from villages to colonial settlements in Angola, 130, 137, 148, 150, 151n7
Fortes, Meyer, 66
Frankl, Victor, 3
freedom, 128, 139–40, 148, 151
fuzziness, 127

Galvin, Kathleen, 144–45, 151nn8–9
Garfinkel, Harold, 16
Geertz, Clifford, 60–61, 75, 80n4, 105
globalization, 149
    from below, 119
Goffman, Erving, 17–18
Gombrich, Ernest, 123
Graeber, David, 5
growing up. *See* life course
Guan, 109
Guattari, Félix, 148

habitus, 48
Hacking, Ian, 74
Hage, Ghassan, 119
Harman, Graham, 22–23

Heidegger, Martin, 1, 24–25, 63, 147, 151nn8–9, 179, 181, 210, 215, 223–25, 229–33
hiding, 129, 130, 132, 134
High Renaissance, and representation of reality, 122–23
Homo neanderthalis, 182, 205–10
Homo sapiens, 182, 205–6, 209–10
human condition, 74–75, 210, 216, 223–24
human existence, 126–27, 135, 148, 179–80, 210
Human Rights Watch, 144
hunting, 136, 140, 150
Husserl, 11

immobility, 140, 146
    and amputation, 142, 143–45, 149
    and basket making, 130, 144–46
    as being stuck, 140, 142
    as being trapped, 130, 139, 149–51, 152n11
    and boundaries, 148
    and digital technology, 143–44, 146
    forced, 140, 149–50
    and friction, 148
    and old age, 125, 136, 142–45, 148 (*see also* old age)
    physical, 143, 144–45, 148
    relative, 125, 146
    as residue of globalization, 147, 149
    as social death, 142–43
    as stillness, 138, 140, 143, 146, 148
    and storytelling, 145–46 (*see also* mobility)
incommensurability, 58–60, 75–76, 78–79
individuality, 217, 227
Ingold, Tim, 23–24, 127, 137, 145, 148
international border, 132–33, 135, 137, 139, 141, 149
intersubjectivity, 10, 216, 219, 225–27
Inuit, 126
irony, 59, 79, 80
Iser, Wolfgang, 96
Islam, 36
Israeli kibbutz, 67
Ivory Coast, 109

Jackson, Michael, 58–59, 62–64, 73–74, 78–79, 80nn5–6, 105, 121–22, 128, 131, 135, 140, 151
Jamaicans, 126

James, William, 6, 12, 20, 27n14
    on radical empiricism, 1
Jaspers, Karl, 7
Johannesburg, 138
Johnson, Paul, 63
journeys, 126–27, 131–36, 139, 145–47

Kabompo, 132, 139
Kaunda, Kenneth, 141
Keane, Webb, 21, 27n19
Kierkegaard, Søren, 2, 59, 62, 79, 80
Kleinman, Arthur, 105
Koroma, Sewa Magba, 156–57, 161, 171
Korzybski, Alfred, 20
Kuntz, E.F., 139
Kuranko (Sierra Leone), 155

landmines, 125, 130, 141–42, 144, 149–50
    and amputation, 141, 143
    civilian mine injury, 142
    and maiming and killing, 130
    in Moxico, 142
    as traps, 130
Latour, Bruno, 22–23, 84, 87, 88, 93–98, 101
    reading Bruno Latour, 97–98
Lear, Jonathan, 65
Leonardo da Vinci. *See* da Vinci, Leonardo
letting-be-ness, 145, 151n8
Léua, 129
Levi-Strauss, Claude, 6, 16, 23, 25, 26n9, 58
Levinas, Emmanuel, 157
Libya, 104, 107, 112, 113, 115, 119
lifeworld, 125, 128, 131
life course, 125, 135–36, 138, 142–43
life story, 126, 128, 131, 136, 139, 140, 145–46, 148, 150, 151n3
    in anthropology, 131
    as narrative of movement, 125, 128, 150
    against stereotyping, 150
Lisbon, 138
Literary, 214–15, 221, 223, 225
Lloyd, Geoffrey E.R., 20
lovemaking, 84, 87–89, 91–92
Lubkemann, Stephen, 149
Luchazi, 138
Luena, 127–29, 135–36, 145
Lumai, 128
Lumbala-Caquenge, 137
Lumbala N'guimbo, 134
Lusaka, 136

Luso, 128
Luvale, 125, 132, 138, 143, 146
Luvuei, 128–32, 134, 139

MacIntyre, Alasdair, 78
Madagascar, northwest, 60–61, 65, 66, 78
madness, 85, 87, 90, 95, 96, 98, 99
Mahistedt, Andrew, 149
Makhuwa, 42–43, 46–47, 50, 53n13, 53n15
Makonde, 53n15
Malkki, Liisa, 132, 150
Marah, Kaimah Bockarie, 155–76
Marah, Kulifa, 163
Marah, Michael Noah, 155–57, 160–62, 166, 175
Marah, Noah Bockarie, 155, 158, 159, 163
Marah, Sewa Bockarie (S.B.), 164, 169
Marah, Tina Kome Bockarie, 162–64, 176n2
Maria, 136, 137
Marinetti, Filippo, 148
Marshall, Ruth, 34, 49
Mattingly, Cheryl, 78
Mayotte, 58–61, 67–70, 80n1
means of transportation, 126, 135–37, 143, 146, 149
media, 126, 133
Mediterranean (sea), 105
Meheba Refugee Settlement, 130, 132, 139, 148–50, 152n11
Merleau-Ponty, Maurice, 1, 6, 11, 156, 176
Michelangelo, 122–23
migration, 31, 34, 36, 39, 42–43, 49, 125–27, 131, 133–34, 149
    and death, 117, 119
    and EU, 104, 116
    Ghanaian connection men, 104, 107, 115–16, 120
    studies, 131
    trans-Saharan Desert routes, 104, 119
    voluntary and forced, 131
Miller, Donald, 35
minimality, 182, 189–91, 205, 209, 229–31
minor mode of reality, 5, 13, 178, 182–86, 190–91, 208–10, 227, 229–30, 236
Mithen, Steven, 211n10
mobility, 30–32, 38, 42, 45, 48, 50–51, 52n10
    as an academic field, 150
    acting with one's feet, 146, 151
    against immobility, 125, 128, 138, 146, 151
    and anthropology, 148
    and development, 149
    as experientially dense, 133, 150
    as existential imperative, 127, 146
    globalized, 148–49
    of material goods, 149
    relative, 146
    and slow motion, 126, 148
    and speed, 126, 134–35, 148
    surveillance of, 149
    See also immobility; movement
modernity, 31–32, 39, 127, 148–50
moments of being, 11, 214, 222–23, 225–26, 233, 235
monism, 75–76
Morocco, 108
Mount Namuli, 43, 51
movement
    as experientially dense, 133
    as life, 142, 146
    as line tracing, 145, 148
    moving freely, 140
    physical, 132, 135, 146, 148
    population movements, 127, 146
    running in fear, 132–33, 140
    similarities between different types of, 133
    as walking, 129, 132–34, 136–37, 141, 143, 145–47, 150, 151n2
    as wayfaring, 137
    See also mobility; travel
Moxico, 127–29, 134, 142
Mozambique, 30–31, 34, 36–37, 43–44, 50–51
MPLA, 127, 129–30, 138, 141, 151n5
mysticism, 87, 94, 96, 98–99, 102n5, 102nn11–12

natality, 34, 49–50. *See also* Arendt, Hannah
necessity and freedom, 139, 140. *See also* choice and constraint
Niamey, 104–24
Niassa province (Mozambique), 34, 36, 38, 42–44, 46, 52n8, 53n13, 53n15
Nietzsche, Friedrich, 163
Niger, 104–24

Obama, Barack, 30–31
Oedipal complex, 121
old age, 125, 136, 138, 142–44
    and feeling of uselessness, 142
    and nonphysical mobility, 144–45
    See also life course
ontogeny and phylogeny, 135
ontology, 6, 19–25, 190

Index

Orsi, Robert, 26n13
Ovid, 106

paths, 133, 136, 141–42, 148
Pentecostalism, 30–37, 39–42, 47, 49–50, 52n12
    Pentecostal ministries, 165–67, 172
person, concepts of, 77–78
personhood, 126, 142
    and productivity, 144
phenomenography, 1, 16, 19, 180, 186, 189, 204, 210, 222, 227, 233, 235
phenomenology, 161, 222, 235
Piette, Albert, 58, 73, 75, 78–79, 81n14
Piot, Charles, 32–33, 39, 41
Plato, 48
poetry, 233–34
polyontologism, 46–47, 50
Porto, 138
Portugal, 134, 138
possession, 84–85, 87–90, 96–97
presence, 180, 183, 185–91, 193, 195, 197, 199, 202–3, 208, 216, 219–21, 223, 227–30, 232
    presence-absence, 178–79, 182, 205
progress, 126
Protestantism, 40, 52n12
psychoanalysis, 65–67

Rappaport, Roy, 77
reading, 84, 87–88, 94, 96–98, 101
refugees, 126, 128, 130–33, 139–40, 145, 148–50, 151n6
    influxes of Angolan refugees into Zambia, 133, 139
    return to Angola, 151n6
    See also Meheba Refugee Settlement; stereotyping
reification, 125, 128, 133–34, 150. *See also* essentialism; stereotyping
religion, 6, 12–13, 191, 193, 203, 205, 210
repose, 186–88, 190, 210
reposity, 183–85. *See also* repose
resettlement campaigns, 43–45
rhizome, 145
Ricoeur, Paul, 12, 26n12
Riddle of the Sphinx, 135
roads, 129, 133, 134, 136–37, 140, 145, 149, 151
    "hit the road," 140, 151
Robbins, Joel, 33, 38, 40, 49. *See also* anthropology of Christianity

Romania, 138
roots, 45–47, 49

Sacks, Oliver, 10
Sacrifice, 170–71
Salazar, Noel, 126, 131, 149
Sapasa, 136–37, 151n3
Sarró, Ramon, 134
Sartre, Jean-Paul, 2, 26n5, 64–65, 77, 106, 128, 162, 164
    on the singular universal, 2
    progressive-regressive method, 6–7
Savimbi, Jonas, 130
Schutz, Alfred, 60
Schwartz Wentzer, Thomas, 155, 175
Scott, James, 43, 45
Scottish Gypsy Travellers, 126
selfhood, 39–42, 47, 50
Senya Beraku, 112–13
sfumato technique, 123
sibling rivalry, 169, 172
similarities, 133–34, 145, 149, 150
Simmel, Georg, 58, 64, 75, 81n14, 147
Smart, Alan, 126, 131, 149
Smith, Jonathan Z., 13
sociology, 219, 226, 228
Socrates, 9
South Africa, 138
Sperber, Dan, 13
spirit possession, 61–64, 80n3
stereotyping, 125, 132–34, 139, 144, 150–51.
    See also essentialism; reification
Stiegler, Bernard, 26n6
storytelling, 219
study of religion, 50
subjectivity, 217
succession, 66

Tabaski, 112
Taves, Ann, 13
the-rest-of-what-is, 85–88, 93, 94, 98
Todres, Les, 144–45, 151nn8–9
trade, 126, 129, 133–37, 141, 143–44
    commodities, 129, 135, 137, 141, 143–44, 149
    money, 129, 130, 134–35
travel
    accounts, 135, 136
    dwelling experiences, 147–48
    encounters, 146–47
    exploration voyages, 137

and gender, 136, 137
literature, 137
Luvale proverbs, 125, 138, 144
resting camps, 146
routes, 139
as series of short journeys, 146
through inhabited and uninhabited territory, 136, 146
tourism, 137
transport, 137 (*see also* means of transportation)
work trips, 137 (*see also* movement and mobility)
twin study, 174

UNHCR, 132–33, 139, 150, 151n6
UNITA, 127, 129–30, 138–39, 141, 151n5
bush bases or camps, 129–30, 148
as bush-people, 129–30, 139
as insurgency, 127, 130, 141, 151nn5–7
and Jonas Savimbi, 130
soldiers, 129–30, 141
United States, 136, 142, 147
and lean-tos, 147
Universal Church of the Kingdom of God (UCKG), 34–35, 52n5

Upper Zambezi, 127, 135–36, 138, 143, 146–49
Urry, John, 150, 151n2, 151n10

Vasari, Girogio, 123
Vico, Giambattista, 74
Viveiros de Castro, Eduardo, 20
vulnerability, 224

war, as being trapped, 130, 139, 150. *See also* Angola; civil war; colonialism in Angola; forced displacement; refugees
Wariboko, Nimi, 49–50
Whitehead, Alfred N., 21
Willerslev, Rane, 69
Winneba, 113
witchcraft, 168–69, 171
Witztum, Eliezer, 67
Woolf, Virginia, 11, 215, 220–21, 223, 225–26

Yaqui Indians, 134

Zambezi, 132
Zambezi River, 132, 136, 139, 143
Zambia, 127, 132–33, 137, 141, 149, 152
northwest Zambia, 126–27, 133
Žižek, Slavoj, 86–87

www.ingramcontent.com/pod-product-compliance
Lightning Source LLC
Chambersburg PA
CBHW070918030426
42336CB00014BA/2459